The Orkney Story

Crossing on the St Ola, *with the majestic cliffs of Hoy in the background.*

The
Orkney Story

Liv Kjörsvik Schei

Photographs by Gunnie Moberg

HIPPOCRENE BOOKS
NEW YORK

Acknowledgement

Writing this book has been a voyage of discovery for me, and I would like to thank those who in various ways have helped me on the way:

- George Mackay Brown for a friendship that has meant a lot to my family and myself;

- Connie and Alan Grieve of Stromness, the Muir family of Garso, North Ronaldsay, and my other friends in Orkney for their warm hospitality;

- Gunnie Moberg for an inspiring co-operation;

- Donald Hall of Lillesand for linguistic advice;

- the staffs at the public libraries of Kirkwall and Kristiansand;

- my children Venill and Lars for being such good travelling companions;

- but first and last my husband Anders Schei for being able and willing to listen.

Liv Kjörsvik Schei

© Liv Kjörsvik Schei & Gunnie Moberg 1985
First published 1985
All rights reserved. No part of this publication
may be reproduced, in any form or by any means,
without permission from the Publisher

Published in the United States by
Hippocrene Books
171 Madison Avenue
New York, NY 10016
ISBN 0-87052-150-0

Printed in Great Britain

Contents

List of colour plates (between pp. 128–9)

Stack Skerry with gannets
Orphir
Silage cutting
Skara Brae
Rackwick, Hoy
Loch Stenness
Puffins, Suleskerry

Cows beside Loch of Swannay
Primula scotica
Kame of Hoy
Sanday
Kirkwall
Broch of Gurness

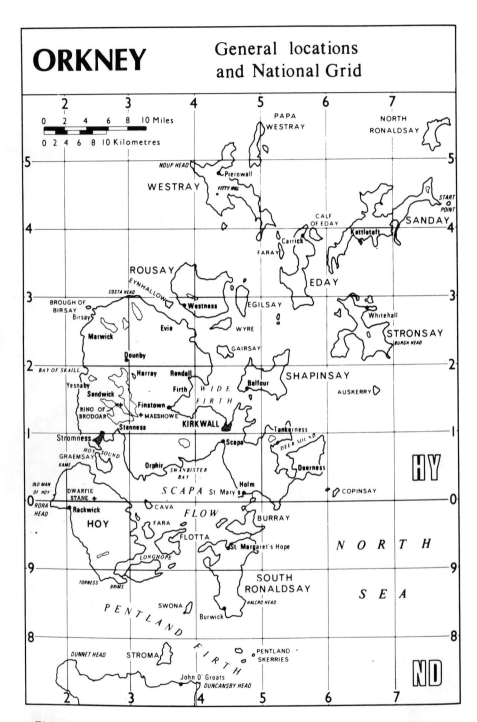

ORKNEY

General locations and National Grid

0 2 4 6 8 10 Miles

0 2 4 6 8 10 Kilometres

PAPA WESTRAY

NORTH RONALDSAY

NOUP HEAD

Pierowall

WESTRAY

FITTY HILL

START POINT

CALF OF EDAY

SANDAY

Kettletoft

Carrick

FARAY

ROUSAY

EDAY

EYNHALLOW

COSTA HEAD

BROUGH OF BIRSAY

Westness

EGILSAY

Birsay

WYRE

Whitehall

STRONSAY

Marwick

Evie

GAIRSAY

BURGH HEAD

Dounby

BAY OF SKAILL

Harray

Rendall

SHAPINSAY

Yesnaby

Firth

Balfour

AUSKERRY

Sandwick

WIDE FIRTH

Finstown

RING OF BRODGAR

MAESHOWE

KIRKWALL

Tankerness

Stenness

DEER SOUND

Stromness

Scapa

HOY SOUND

GRAEMSAY

Deerness

KAME

Orphir

SWANBISTER BAY

OLD MAN OF HOY

DWARFIE STANE

Holm

COPINSAY

RORA HEAD

SCAPA St Mary's

Rackwick

CAVA

HOY

FARA

FLOW

BURRAY

FLOTTA

LONGHOPE

St. Margaret's Hope

NORTH

SOUTH RONALDSAY

SEA

TORNESS

BRIMS

SWONA

HALCRO HEAD

Burwick

PENTLAND FIRTH

DUNNET HEAD

STROMA

PENTLAND SKERRIES

John O' Groats

DUNCANSBY HEAD

HY

ND

Fig. 1

1. Introduction

Beyond Britannia, where the endless ocean opens, lies Orkney.
Orosius, fifth century A.D.

Everywhere the sea is near.

Towards the west the great ocean – the Atlantic – beats against the island coast in a tireless rhythm. The spray cascades far inland from fast, angry waves which break more pieces off the western wall. But on rare summer days the ocean can also lie calm and translucent in a long shining line against an unbroken horizon.

Towards the east lies the North Sea, and at one time the distance was short between Norway and Orkney – perhaps two days' sailing in a fair wind. Many of the people living in the western part of Norway knew the islands 'west over sea' better than they knew other parts of their own country. For those who fished the North Sea this was true until Norway chose not to join the EEC.

For everyone else this old sea route has long been unknown and forgotten. Most people know vaguely that Orkney lies somewhere west in the North Sea, and that much of the rain hitting the Scandinavian countries comes from there.

People in Britain do not know much more about Orkney either. At the end of the last century the unnamed writer of a book called *Half Hours in the Far North* deplores this:

The islands of Orkney and Shetland are so little known that many persons, in other respects well informed, seem to look upon them as a collection of rocks either uninhabitable or inhabited by a race of men almost as untamed as the seals which play upon their shores, and with intellects little more developed; a race with whom the civilised world has no communion, living on fish, dressing in sealskin, gloriously ignorant of civilization, destitute of education.

During the Second World War, a prefabricated theatre, meant to be used to entertain the soldiers stationed in Stromness, was sent to Iceland, in the mistaken belief that no such place name could possibly be found in Britain. And even today it happens that parcels come from 'doon sooth' with customs declarations on them.

The oil business has helped place Orkney on the map, but it is perhaps the

Greenpeace action against the seal cull which has made the average Briton realize that Britain does not stop at Pentland Firth.

Today the sea route across the North Sea is not used anymore by the average traveller from Norway. Now the choice for people going to Orkney is between flying or going by the car ferry *St Ola* from Scrabster in the north of Scotland to Stromness. In the summer season there is also a passenger ferry from John O'Groats to Burwick in South Ronaldsay.

St Ola crosses the Pentland Firth – one of the most turbulent straits in the world. It is notorious for its tidal currents, eddies and dangerous whirlpools. The Pentland Firth is narrow enough to enable us to see the outline of Hoy from the Scottish mainland. In moderate weather the crossing takes two hours, though in a rough sea it may take twice as long, and it is undoubtedly the approach that gives the best first impression. Meeting the majestic sight of the cliffs of Hoy on the starboard side is overwhelming and not easily forgotten. When the ferry turns into Scapa Flow and Orkney opens up, green and fertile before us, we realize that it is first of all a farming community, in spite of the surrounding sea.

Today no one need take on the Pentland Firth to reach Orkney, for there are daily flights from the Scottish mainland to Grimsetter airport just outside Kirkwall. But the air-fares are very high. This is also true of the prices of many consumer goods, as the extra transport makes everything more expensive.

Anyone going to Orkney must realize that life on the islands is ruled by the weather. Grumblers complain that Orkney has nine months of winter and three months of bad weather. Although this is not necessarily true, it may work out like that, and one would be wise to come warmly dressed and be prepared for rainy weather. It is the cold and damp weather combined with wind which makes visitors sometimes feel cold to their very bones and believe they will never get warm again.

The wind is the real master – it rarely dies down completely. Mostly it blows from the west, bringing the rain in its wake. We can see the rainclouds building up far out in the Atlantic while we are still walking in sunshine. On the whole there is rarely one whole day without a shower or two – but the sun may shine brightly and warmly in between. If the weather is bad the Orcadians say with the Icelanders: 'wait a little!' But the wind is also an invigorating challenge. And when its fury has spent itself and is perhaps followed by calm, then the islands in the changing lights strike us with their supernatural beauty. A snowcapped and sungilded Ward Hill in Hoy, in the aftermath of a snowstorm, rises from the clouds like a fairy-tale palace.

What else is there besides natural beauty that makes people want to come back? Some even say that a summer without a trip to Orkney is a summer lost.

For anyone interested in history, Orkney has a greater density of ancient monuments than any other place in Northern Europe. And we find relics of all ages – from Stone Age houses to the ruins of the Second World War. The

The Standing Stones of Stenness. Orkney has a greater density of ancient monuments than any other place in Northern Europe.

latter are ugly scars in the landscape, for modern concrete does not age with dignity nor wear down in beauty. But perhaps even the concrete bunkers will some time bring joy to the heart of an archaeologist.

Others come to fish for brown trout or to dive in Scapa Flow. Still others are interested in birds and will venture anything to sight a rare species.

When so many travellers return year after year, there is also another reason: the people there and the openness and warmth they show visitors. We find in their lives something indefinable that has often been lost in the post-war way of life elsewhere. Maybe it is their serenity, harmony and feeling of continuity with the past. And the doors are always open – only the wind closes them.

There are many different bloods flowing in Orcadian veins. The islands have not always been thought of as an outpost, on the contrary they were at times in the mainstream of events, and wave after wave of settlers found their way to the north. Here they came, from unknown Stone Age peoples to the Picts, Celtic monks, Norsemen coming both as landgrabbers and as Vikings, Scots of all types from religious refugees to cattle thieves, shipwrecked Spaniards from the Great Armada, and today's settlers, who flee England's industrial cities to return to nature. Some stay, while others give up the fight with a new reality.

When people in the islands still emphasize the kinship with Norway and a common heritage, one of the reasons is that the Norse period, which gave them the St Magnus Cathedral and the memory of the jarls, was the Golden Age of the islands, when they played an important part in the northern world. Later they became a field of plunder, with slight influence on their own destiny.

In 1468, at a time when the whim of a monarch could change a people's destiny, Christian I of Denmark-Norway pledged the Norwegian royal estates in Orkney to the Scottish crown as security, with full redemptory rights. The King was heavily in debt and had to find some way of raising 50,000 florins of the Rhine to see his daughter Margrete married off to James III of Scotland. The Norwegian State Council was not consulted, and the pledging is therefore a sore point in Norwegian history.

On 1 April 1967 Britain sent a note to Norway inquiring why no reply had been received to their note of 10 October 1217 asking for peace and friendship. Norway's Minister of Foreign Affairs, John Lyng, sent a note back where he reminded the British that the question of sovereignty over Orkney and Shetland was still wide open, and that the debt could be paid off at any time.

This was an April Fool's joke, but perhaps with a serious undertone? The marriage contract, which is also the pledging document, states expressly the right of Norway's later kings to redeem the islands by paying back the debt, which is free of interest and remains unchanged at 463 lbs (210 kg) of gold or 5,093 lbs (2310 kg) of silver. For an oil-rich Norway looking for ways of investing her money abroad, this should be a promising possibility. But, of course, 500 years have passed, and a lot of waves have rolled in the North Sea since then.

The sea encircling the islands has also served as a bulwark against the outside world. We find a strong assertiveness and a separate identity. People are Orcadians first, then Scots or British; and like many others they want to think of themselves as descendants of the Vikings. 'I'm an Orkneyman, a good Scandinavian', said the distinguished poet Edwin Muir, who grew up on Wyre. But the Orcadians are also open to new ideas, so that we find a quite modern community, more vigorous than many other areas in Britain.

Orcadians went out to many countries in the new world. They were driven partly by overpopulation and partly by their sense of adventure. Many went to New Zealand and Australia, but the majority went to the 'nor'wast' in Canada – to the Hudson Bay area. There is a place called Orkney in Saskatchewan. The most famous settler of them all was Dr John Rae, who mapped large parts of the Canadian Arctic. But Rae is best known as being the first to find out what happened to John Franklin, who disappeared with his 129 men while attempting to find the Northwest Passage.

Kirkwall's 300-year-old library is the oldest public library in Scotland. It has its own 'Orkney Room' – a large room filled with books on Orkney and books written by Orcadians. The islands have given many the itch to write. There is hardly another place of comparable importance in the world which has been so thoroughly described.

When the story of the islands has been told so many times before, why then tell it again? Orkney is classical ground both to the archaeologist and to the Norse scholar, but new material is often uncovered so that fresh interpretations become necessary: the story is never told once and for all.

Beauty is in the eye of the beholder. To some the islands will seem the last place God made, to others an Eden, an enchanted place. This book attempts to show the islands as they are and as they were. It will probably not be without bias. But hopefully it will make you want to see for yourself.

2. Nature

Orkney is one of the three island counties around the northern coast of Scotland. Less than half of the 70 islands are inhabited and the number has been constantly decreasing, because of people moving from the smaller islands to the largest island, Mainland. Even the lighthouse keepers are moving because the lighthouses are becoming automatic. But at least it looks as if the drift from the islands to the Scottish mainland has stopped, as the population has increased in the last few years. The 1981 census showed a population of 18,862, an increase of ten per cent compared to the census ten years earlier.

Only some 8 nautical miles separate the islands from the Scottish mainland, and they are located between 58°41 and 59°24 north latitude, the same as Leningrad and the southern part of Greenland.

Geology
Geologically the islands have a simple structure, and are quite different from Shetland and the Scottish Highlands. A narrow strip of granite and gneiss goes from Graemsay along Brinkie's Brae above Stromness. Suleskerry, some 37 naut. miles out in the Atlantic, consists of Lewisian gneiss, the oldest rock in Europe. The rest is mostly red sandstone, along with limestone and with some volcanic rocks in between.

Being porous, sandstone is easily quarried and well suited as a building material. It cannot, of course, be polished, and it crumbles easily when exposed to wind and rain. This erosion shows plainly in the c.800-year-old St Magnus Cathedral, which is built mainly in red sandstone.

There are few profitable mineral deposits, and the finding of large deposits of uranium in the western part of Mainland was therefore quite unexpected.

The undulating Orkney landscape was formed in the last Ice Age when the covering ice wore down the brittle sandstone. In Sanday there is a boulder which the ice has probably brought along from Norway. Much fertile mud was also deposited, so that we rarely see outcrops of rock anywhere else than in Rousay and Hoy. It is these mud deposits that provide such good conditions for agriculture.

The total land area is 376 sq. miles (973 sq. km), and Mainland alone makes up more than half of this. From north to south the island group measures 53 miles (85 km), whereas the distance east to west is 33 miles (49 km).

Topology

Towards the east the islands are flat, but in the west they slope in low hills, which fall into the sea as steep perpendicular cliffs. These red sandstone cliffs are a magnificent sight from the sea. The cliff wall St John's Head in Hoy has a fall of 1099 ft (335 m), and is the highest perpendicular cliff in Britain. The west wind has rammed the long Atlantic waves thunderously against the sandstone cliffs and broken them down into fantastic and picturesque formations. There is no beach underneath to break the waves, so that piece by piece the coast loses out to the sea.

The cliffs along the coast are full of caves. When the upper part of a cave is battered down by the sea, a *gloup* is formed. A long narrow crevice ground into the cliff wall is called a *geo*. When much of the cliff wall between two caves disappears, natural stone arches can be formed. A pointed cliff may be left standing by itself like a needle. The best known needle, or stack, is The Old Man of Hoy, which has become a famous landmark and almost a symbol of Orkney.

Not only does the sea take, but it gives also. Shell sand rich in lime which is whirled up by the sea, reduces acidity in the Orkney soil. It also builds up the long low beaches so special to Sanday – known as *machair*. Here the Norse settlers found good pastures. And along the Churchill barriers from wartime around Scapa Flow there are now fine sandy beaches in the lee of the concrete blocks. In bays and estuaries the sand is blown up into bars. Such a bar is known in Orkney as an *ayre* (O.N. aurr), and is a natural habitat for many kinds of birds.

Sanday and North Ronaldsay are very low-lying and do not reach more than 49 ft (15 m) above sea level; they were therefore very dangerous to ships, who did not always see them until it was too late, and indeed the waters around them are full of old wrecks.

Hills and mountains cover much of Rousay and Hoy, but the mountains are not as high as they seem. The highest mountain is Ward Hill in Hoy at 1571 ft (479 m). A climb to the top gives a view of all the islands and far south into Scotland. The inner Hoy resembles the Scottish Highlands.

Seas and tides

The water between the islands is difficult to navigate. It is not deep, and the water would need to sink just 121 ft (37 m) to make the islands into one single land area.

Two strong tidal streams, one from the North Sea and the other from the Atlantic, meet in Orkney and make the system of ebb and flow extremely complicated. For example the high tide from the Atlantic arrives a couple of hours earlier than the North Sea high water wave. The tidal stream usually runs at 5 naut. miles per hour, but in Eynhallow Sound and in Hoy Sound the roosts are even faster. All use of boats is difficult and dangerous there, and it happens that even experienced sailors have their boats wrecked in Eynhallow Sound. In the old days the dangerous water gave protection against pirates. Today it keeps people from cruising in and out among the islands in small pleasure boats. It is not customary to visit the small uninhabited islands with coffee and picnic baskets, so holms and small islands offer undisturbed habitats for all kinds of bird life.

The great difference between ebb and flow is the reason why all piers have to be built far out in the sea. On the whole there are few good harbours, and not even Stromness or Kirkwall can berth ships of any size. The lack of shelter from the wind also makes all mooring difficult.

Climate

Orkney is protected by mountains only in the south, in Hoy. Otherwise the islands are open to the wind from all directions, and wind there is, at all times of the year. The climate is at its best during the months April, May and June, but an ordinary gale of 37 miles (60 km) per hour may occur at any time of the year. Some years there are hurricanes as strong as up to 160 miles (270 km) per hour. In Beaufort's wind scale, hurricane velocity begins at 74 miles (120 km) per hour!

The worst storm in living memory raged during the night of 15 January 1952. The Orcadians woke up to a chaotic morning of torn-off roofs and impassable roads. Seven thousand chicken-coops were gone, along with 86,000 hens! (Poultry-keeping never regained its importance after that.) This storm reached no higher than 120 miles (190 km) per hour in the wind scale, when the instrument broke.

Most storms usually come from the west or southwest, but it also happens that there are violent storms from the northeast. In the worst storm period – October–January – any thought of cleaning windows might as well be given up, since they will soon be encrusted with salt again after another gale.

Orkney has a typical ocean climate. The great low pressure activity in the Atlantic causes rain on half the days of the year. Still the average annual rainfall is not large by Norwegian standards. The air is in constant motion so that the rain clouds do not remain for long at any one time. Hoy has the highest annual rainfall with 59 in. (1500 mm), whereas the eastern Mainland has only 35 in. (900 mm). In comparison Flekkefjord in southwestern Norway has 70 in. (1800 mm) a year.

The average temperature for July is 13°C; really hot summer days are very rare. However, the mean January temperature is a mild 4°C. It is the Gulf Stream that makes the winter so much milder than the average for 59° north latitude. Frost does not last long, and the snow rarely stays longer than overnight; when it does, people are unprepared for it. The schools close and the children are sent home as soon as the snow gives any sign of settling, for only the main roads are cleared. Once 400 school children had to be put up in Stromness till the snow disappeared.

In the summer, the interaction between warm air and cold tides from the

January storms are frequent. This one in 1984 damaged many piers and boats on the Stromness sea front.

North Sea can cause a dense sea fog known as the *North Sea haar*. In the winter, the northern lights – aurora borealis – tremble across the sky on clear nights. The local name is *The Merry Dancers*. Salt crystals swirling in the air may be the reason why both the sunrise and the sunset sometimes seem to have a clearer, richer set of colours than anywhere else. It is as if a shimmer covers everything.

Woodlands

The salty air has also been blamed for the fact that the islands are without trees. But the large roots sometimes found in the peat hills show that the islands were not always treeless. It has also been a common belief that the Norse settlers cut down the woods, either to prevent the Picts from hiding there or because they needed the fuel. It is, however, more probable that climatic changes upset the growth so that the trees disappeared and peat spread like a dark carpet over what was once fertile fields. It may all have happened without human assistance.

The only natural wood left in the islands – the most northerly in Britain – is in Hoy. On the north side of Hoy we find most of the wild trees in Orkney: birch and rowan, willow and aspen. Hazel, which used to be common, is now dying out.

Many people have tried to plant trees around their houses. There are well-known tree plantations at Binscarth near Finstown and at Melsetter House in Longhope. Trees grow willingly where they find shelter from the wind, but it is the houses that protect the trees and not the other way round. As soon as the trees grow into the wind they become bent and misshapen. But the idea of using trees as protection for agriculture has become more and more accepted. It is the non-native sycamore tree that has proved best suited.

Flora
Because the islands are mostly without natural woodland, they also lack many woodland plants. Still the flora is surprisingly rich and varied, with some 650 species of flowering plants. As the time of growth is so short, the flowering season is intense. In June Brough of Birsay is covered by a thick carpet of thrift, or *Armeria maritima*, in every conceivable shade of pink. Wild lupins and daffodils grow as lavishly in other places. In contrast to the otherwise bare open landscape, the visual impact is overwhelming.

There are no water lilies, but there are as many as 21 species of wild orchids. The rare Oyster Plant (*Mertensia maritima*) grows by the water's edge, and in a few places the little red Primula Scotica clings to the cliff edge.

Daffodils, Stenness. These grow lavishly along the roadsides. The visual impact is overwhelming in contrast to the otherwise bare open landscape. The chambered tomb of Maeshowe is seen in the background.

It is a flower special to northern Scotland and where to find it is a well-kept secret.

We might perhaps expect to find cloudberries and cowberry, but crowberry and a few blueberries are the only kinds of wild berries to be found. On the other hand there are several species of wild heather, and bog cotton brightens the moors. The immediate impression given by the islands is of hills of heather and cultivated fields.

Birds

The rich soil yields good feeding habitats for many kinds of birds. The lack of trees makes the woodland birds stay away, but on the other hand there is a large spectrum of sea birds and waders. Bird life is overwhelming in number, if not in variety. Some 300 species are well authenticated; of these, 90 species breed regularly in the islands (in comparison the number is 43 in the Faeroe Islands). Large numbers of sea birds head for the coastal cliffs to nest. Orkney is on one of the world's main migration routes for birds, so that in both spring and autumn the islands serve as a resting place for birds going to or coming from the northern regions.

It is the vast number of sea birds which first of all dominate bird life. The porous sandstone cliffs are ideal for nesting. Altogether there are some 30 bird cliffs in Orkney, which is one of the most important breeding grounds in the eastern Atlantic, especially for the common and black guillemots, the great black-backed gull, the common gull, kittiwakes, the Arctic tern and the Arctic skua.

On Mainland most of the bird cliffs face west: Marwick Head with colonies of up to 20,000 of both guillemot and kittiwake; Brough of Birsay, Costa Head, Black Craig and Yesnaby. On the eastern side facing the North Sea lies Mull Head in Deerness. Otherwise Westray, Papa Westray and Copinsay have the largest number of birds.

With as many as 70 different species Westray is the place to go for a bird watcher. There we find the best balance between intense cultivation and fairly extensive moorland, and it therefore has a wide range of habitats suitable for many different species, such as oyster catcher and corncrake. In addition Westray has perpendicular cliff walls at The Noup, which is now a bird reserve. It is the biggest cliff nursery in Britain, especially for guillemots, kittiwakes and auks. For guillemots the number of breeding birds is as high as 70,000.

The neighbouring island, Papa Westray – or Papay, as the Orcadians call it – is especially known as a gathering place for the Arctic tern. The North Hill Bird Reserve is the largest ternery in Europe. As many as 10,000 pairs of Arctic terns have gathered there, but the number has decreased somewhat lately. Terns are notorious for changing their nesting areas for no apparent reason. Of the Arctic skua, whose number has increased and which now breed in many places in the islands, about 100 pairs breed in Papay. They live in a constant state of war with the terns. The skua is a skilled flyer which

Noup Head, Westray is the biggest cliff nursery in Britain, especially for guillemots, kittiwakes and auks.

stalks the tern until it lets go of its prey, which the skua catches in the air. Altogether some 50 species breed on Papay.

It was at Fool Craig in Papay that the last great auk (*Alca impennis*) in Britain was shot by a collector in 1813. The auk is a classic example of how a species is hunted to extinction. Only a few centuries ago it was a common sight in the islands of the North Atlantic. The bird was the size of a goose, and a marvellous swimmer. But it could not fly, and was therefore an easy prey and caught in large numbers. When the species was in danger of extinction, collectors offered high prices for birds and eggs and thus hastened the end even more. The two last known great auks were beaten to death in Eldey, off Iceland, in 1844.

In the western ocean lie the outskerries Suleskerry and Stack Skerry. Suleskerry has a lighthouse which was manned until quite recently, but Stack Skerry is an inhospitable bird cliff right out in the middle of the ocean, accessible only in moderate weather, and even then the heavy swells make it difficult to climb ashore. Suleskerry is the breeding ground for Britain's largest colony of puffin, or *tammie-norrie*, as they are called in Orkney. More than 50,000 of this distinctive bird, so easily recognizable because of its large colourful beak, breed at Suleskerry.

The rock of Stack Skerry is a refuge for the gannet, the only nesting place in Orkney for this elegant ocean flyer. It is known locally as *solan goose*, from O.N. súla. The skerry is quite overcrowded: some 6,000 pairs nest there. As early as 1633 Stack Skerry is described as the nesting place of the gannet. And in an Orkney description from 1770 we are told that a boat set out for Stack Skerry and 'returned with a great quantity of young Solans, the feathers of which were good: the birds were eaten but were very wild and fishy tasted, with a strong smell'. The custom of catching young gannets lasted till the 1930s. The gannet is now a protected species all over Britain, apart from the Hebridean island of Sula Sgeir which is exempt from the protective legislation. Two thousand young gannets are still being hunted for food there every year.

Fowling and egg gathering were of value to the islanders both for food and income up to the turn of the century. Not just the young gannet, but birds of various kinds were hunted. Climbing the bird cliffs with ropes was the major fowling method; the birds then often just let themselves be taken from the rock ledges, then they were thrown down to waiting boats. It was dangerous work, but accidents were not common.

The uninhabited Copinsay is also known for its bird cliffs with mostly guillemots and kittiwakes. The island is now a bird reserve.

Another reserve for sea birds is the island of Eynhallow, which was bought by Orkney Islands Council in 1980 for £60,000. It is a nesting place for the fulmar, or *malliemak*, as it is called in Orkney. This bird was unknown in the islands before 1900, but it is now one of the most numerous ones and the most commonly seen bird in wintertime. It is feared by the other birds, for as a way of defending itself it vomits, and this can destroy the protective grease cover of the feathers of the birds which get sprayed. At worst they die because they are unable to fly or because they freeze to death. The fulmar is no larger than a common gull, but surpasses even the gannet in flying skill.

Whereas the number of fulmar has steadily grown, the corncrake, which only a few years ago was thought of as a pest because of the noise it makes, is no longer among the regular summer visitors. It is now becoming a rare species. It is possible that the recent cultivation of hill and moorland has taken its habitat away.

Birds of prey are threatened species all over Britain, and a possible explanation of why they no longer breed as before is that pesticides used in farming make the shells of the eggs too brittle. (So far oil spills in Scapa Flow have not been larger than could be tolerated; and it is more serious when oil tankers on their way to Sullom Voe in Shetland empty their tanks off Orkney, so that many sea birds are killed in the oil spill.) Hoy now remains as one of the few breeding grounds. A few pairs of golden eagle nest there. Hoy is also the home of the peregrine falcon, which is threatened by the same fate as the great auk. Collectors offer as much as £1,000 for a peregrine chick, so the fewer who know of their nesting places the better. The hen harrier, which was close to becoming extinct as a British bird, has staged a recent comeback since finding a refuge in Hoy.

One of the reasons why the hen harrier thrives in Hoy may be that it finds the food it likes there, for the favourite food of the hen harrier is the little Orkney vole (*Microtus orcadensis*) – a sub-species to be found only in Orkney, and the only wild animal peculiar to the islands. Its principal enemy is, however, the short-eared owl, which is quite numerous in Orkney.

A proposal for another bird reserve to be established in the southern part of Eday was resisted by the islanders, who thought that people should come before birds and that the most seriously threatened species in Eday was *Homo sapiens* and not bird life. While the population has decreased so sharply in some islands that the quality of life is endangered for those left behind, many of the bird colonies are larger than ever.

Animals
The birds can nest undisturbed in the hills and heather because so many of the common predators, like fox and badger, are lacking. Nor do we find snakes and frogs, only toads. The hedgehog was brought in by soldiers during the last war and seems to thrive. Another, more regrettable, imported species is the brown rat, also known as Norwegian rat (*Rattus norvegicus*), which came to the islands early in the eighteenth century, probably on Norwegian ships.

A species of blue hare is found only in Hoy. It becomes almost completely white in winter and is therefore very conspicuous in a landscape almost always free of snow. Another species of hare, the brown hare, is very common in Mainland. It is so numerous there that it has become a nuisance and is a target of organized shoots.

Wild rabbits are to be found in large numbers in many of the islands, especially where there are sandy hills. In the eighteenth century, rabbit skins were an important export article; today the rabbits are considered merely a nuisance. Rousay is especially afflicted and one can hardly walk on a tuft of grass there without scaring up a rabbit. The estimated population of rabbits for Rousay alone is 100,000. Not only do the rabbits eat the farmers out of house and home, but they also ruin the grassland, since as they eat the clover and the root with it, the land fills up with weeds instead. The farmers of Rousay have declared war on the wild rabbit. They do not believe that they will ever eradicate them altogether, but they hope to keep the number under control. On Mainland the number of rabbits was severely reduced after the outbreak of mixamatosis in the 1950s.

Earlier the otter was common everywhere in Orkney, but it is now rarely seen, and, although rather late in the day, will probably become a protected species soon. The fate of the otter is noticed by only a few people, whereas the fate of the seal in Orkney waters has echoed all over Europe. Since 1962 a highly controversial culling of the population of the grey seal (*Halichoerus grypus*) has been carried out every year. Just as regularly the controversy flares up again every autumn, with emotional letters to the local paper *The Orcadian*. The controversy was at its most bitter stage in 1978.

The grey seal can be distinguished from other seals by its Roman nose. In September to October the grey seals assemble in large colonies at their breeding sites, and after an 11 month pregnancy the pups are born just above the high tide mark. For the first couple of weeks the pup is regularly suckled by the cow, then the mother returns to sea and the pup has to manage on its own. Known in Orkney as *the selkie*, the grey seal is fond of people and very curious. When the seals sing from the skerries we understand why they would become part of legends and folklore – their atonal singing is remote, beautiful and haunting.

The current world population of the grey seal is estimated at some 100,000 animals; about two-thirds of this population live around the shores of Britain, especially Scotland, and Orkney is one of their largest breeding grounds. Because the grey seal was earlier hunted so mercilessly (for the hide, oil and meat) that the number dropped dangerously, the Grey Seal Protection Act was passed as early as 1914. This act protected the seals from 1 October to 15 December – the time of the pupping, and this resulted in an increased seal population.

When the fishermen started complaining that the seals took too much of the fish around the Scottish coast, permits were issued to kill 750 of Orkney's grey seal pups each year, beginning in 1962. As from 1970 this quota was raised to 1,000 pups. In spite of this the number of pups had in 1975 risen 30 per cent compared to 1964. The Scottish authorities therefore found it necessary to cull the seal population, both for ecological reasons and

Grey seal pup. For the first couple of weeks of its life, the pup is regularly suckled by the cow but then the mother returns to the sea and the pup has to survive on its own.

to protect the fisheries. The plan was to kill 900 cows and 4,900 pups each year over a six year period. This was supposed to reduce the British population of seals by one fifth. A Bergen firm was contracted to carry out the cull of the seals.

The international conservation movement Greenpeace sent their ship the *Rainbow Warrior* to the islands. It followed the Norwegian sealer *Kvitungen* around wherever it went. The controversy made the Scottish authorities give up their plans, and *Kvitungen* returned to Norway without having fired a single shot.

The annual seal cull has gone on as before, with 2,000 pups as the maximum quota. A group calling themselves the Sea Shepherds have in the last few years tried to stop all hunting by spraying the pups with paint or forcibly trying to stop the hunters.

3.
Orkney in prehistoric times

And then the question arises: for what purpose were stone circles like these erected, requiring as they did such an unduly great amount of work. So far it has not been possible to answer this question satisfactorily.

P. A. Munch *Reminiscences of Orkney* 1849

Orkney is the richest archaeological area in Britain. Some of the prehistoric monuments are unique in Europe. To wander among them can give us a feeling of following the centuries back in time. We cannot help but wonder how people lived here through the ages, and what drove them to settle so far north.

The term prehistoric times is used about the history of man preceding written sources. It is customary to divide prehistoric times into the Stone, Bronze, and Iron Age. But the various stages in the development did not occur at the same time everywhere. Bronze and iron were adopted for general use in the various places at different times, and certain prehistoric cultures have lasted till our times. Nor does history differentiate a people's spiritual development clearly in terms of time.

Scientific interest in prehistory came late, when some of the monuments in Europe were more or less ruined. The monuments in Orkney have not been particularly threatened by urban and industrial development, although it has happened that conflicting interests between farmers and archaeologists have caused problems. It is the sea which poses the most serious threat to prehistoric remains. Many of the most important monuments, such as Skara Brae and Broch of Burrian in North Ronaldsay, are just at the edge of the ocean, and year by year the coastline is eroded by the sea.

New monuments are being found all the time, and Orcadians have become used to seeing patient archaeologists on their knees digging. The stone monuments are not only well preserved, but also extremely interesting, and Orkney is one of the best places to study some of the major questions about European prehistory.

It was the internationally known scholar Vere Gordon Childe who first realized how important the Orkney monuments are for the elucidation of the wider problems of European history. Childe's work has been carried on by Colin Renfrew, a professor of archaeology at the University of Cambridge. In 1972–74 Renfrew supervised the excavation of the Quanterness chambered cairn not far from Kirkwall. In addition he also examined the Ring of Brogar, the Maeshowe tomb, and the Rousay cairns. The results of this research were published in 1979 in his book *Investigations in Orkney*.

Today it is difficult to write correctly about prehistory. Renfrew's conclusions, radio-carbon analysis and other scientific dating methods now in use, as well as the mathematical calculations of astro-archaeology, have questioned the formerly accepted chronology, so that the entire prehistory of the Western world may have to be rewritten. Among other things, this provides a longer chronological framework for the Orkney monuments than was earlier thought possible, at the same time as it changes the time scale of Orkney monuments in relation to each other. Thus the Standing Stones of Stenness and probably also the Ring of Brogar turn out to be some 1000 years older than previously believed, from about 2,900 B.C. The round burial chamber at the farm of Bigland in Rousay probably dates back to about 3,700 B.C., and the dwelling house of the settlement at Knap of Howar in Papay is roughly from the same period. This makes it the oldest preserved dwelling in northern Europe.

The first people to leave their mark on Orkney used stone as a building material. Earlier it was believed that this megalithic culture (from Greek *megas* – large, and *lithos* – stone), or stone culture, sprang up in the eastern Mediterranean, and especially in Egypt. It was believed that technical innovations of this culture then spread outwards, first to the west and then northwards. Settlers were thought to have brought their building expertise to the far north. Now the new dating methods show that many of the archaeological monuments in Orkney are much older than the pyramids of Egypt. Technical knowledge and skill can of course have spread from one country or people to another also in the Stone Age, even if it is no longer clear who was the teacher and who was the pupil.

Recent pollen studies show that the climate around 3,000 B.C. was not so very different from that which the Orcadians complain about today. The vegetation has also remained surprisingly constant during the last 6,000 years, so that the Orkney landscape has not changed significantly. But in the peat hills we find remains of trees, especially birch and rowan, but also fir, oak and willow. This indicates that in a distant past the climate must have been warmer and drier than it is today. But later climate changes destroyed the conditions of growth, and the islands became almost treeless, as they are today. This did not frighten the first settlers, who perhaps wanted open land – as they did not have tools which were suitable for felling trees.

The economy of the Stone Age was not much different from the traditional economic pattern of the recent past: primitive agriculture, hunting and fishing.

In the middle of the last century, during one of the many Orkney storms, a Stone Age village suddenly emerged from the sand dunes at Skara Brae in Skaill Bay on western Mainland. An amateurish excavation at the time did more harm than good. It was not until 1930 that the village was scientifically

Stone dresser, Skara Brae. This Stone Age village is now the most popular sight in Orkney.

examined by Childe, who wrote about it in his book *Skara Brae*. This Stone Age village is now one of the most popular sights in Orkney. It was in use for several centuries, but was probably built around 3,200 B.C. The village was left in a hurry as if the people who lived there were surprised by something which forced them to flee. As in Pompeii, everything remained the way it was left. Outside hut No. 7 were the remains of a necklace which broke during the flight.

Many reasons have been suggested for this sudden flight – from natural disasters like sand storms or earthquakes, to attacks by hostile bands. For some unknown reason the people never returned. The houses were left exposed to the elements, and gradually they filled up with sand.

Ten huts lie close together, connected through covered passageways. We cannot help being touched by how homelike these huts appear – with dressers and boxbeds of stone, small shelves built into the wall and an open hearth in the middle. We must assume that there was an opening for light and smoke in the roof. In a way this interior is not so radically different from the later Norse style, though on a smaller scale.

At Links of Notland in Westray archaeologists are excavating yet another Stone Age settlement in the sand dunes, also on the edge of the sea.

Important to the Stone Age culture are the passage graves or chambered tombs, which were built using incredible effort and with primitive tools. We know that the main tool of Stone Age man was a polished flint axe. We also know that their pottery was highly developed, and that in addition to their simple farming they also kept domestic animals – sheep, cattle and small horses. In the Unston chambered tomb on Mainland pieces of pottery were found with the imprint of *bere* – a type of barley still grown in Orkney.

Obviously Stone Age people had their ideas of a life after death, and these thoughts of a kingdom of the dead drove them to build impressive stone chambers for their dead. In the Isbister tomb in South Ronaldsay skeletal remains of some 340 people were found. Nearly 100 of these are children past infancy. The dead were left unprotected before being placed in the communal grave – that is the corpses were exposed to wind and rain or temporarily buried somewhere else till they had decayed. After some time the bones were then put in the burial chamber.

The burial probably followed certain ritual ceremonies. Fourteen skeletons of a white-tailed species of eagle that died out a century ago were found in the Isbister tomb. In many graves there are traces of fire, as if a last meal had been prepared for the dead. In the Midhowe stalled cairn in Rousay – older than the Maeshowe type of chambered tomb – the goods left with the dead showed that their family did not want them to enter the kingdom of death empty-handed. There were pieces of pottery, a flint knife, a stone club and hammer, and bones of domestic animals, seabirds and fish, as well as shellfish.

The people who were buried at Isbister were not all that small; they had long heads, low brows and underhung jaws. Child mortality was high, and life expectancy so low that 25 would seem a good age. There was clear evidence of deficiency diseases, arthritis and painful wisdom teeth.

More than 50 passage graves survive in Orkney in spite of some of them having been roughly handled at times when farmers cleared the land and used the stones as building material. The graves vary in quality, but they have many common features. The entrance passage, which has given the name to these graves, is long and narrow and leads to a stone chamber where upright slabs sometimes form compartments along the walls. For every new layer of stone added, the walls slope gradually inwards until the opening in the roof can be covered by a large stone.

Such graves are scattered all over the islands. Professor Renfrew suggests in *Investigations in Orkney* that they correspond to the tribal areas of the early Stone Age. Probably the people who built these graves lived in communities like Skara Brae and used them over a long period of time. Renfrew believes that quite small communities, perhaps a kind of extended family, consisting of no more than 20 people, came together to build a burial chamber, which had both social and ritual significance.

Considerable work was invested in cutting and moving the stone for such a chambered tomb or cairn, but not more than could be expected from

Skull from Isbister tomb, South Ronaldsay. Skeletal remains of some 340 people were found in the tomb. Mr Ronald Simison, who discovered and excavated this remarkable site, shows a 5,000-year-old skull.

winter work for such a small community over a five-year period. The tomb served as the pivot of the small community. It was important both for the dead and the living, as it served both as a place of burial and as a territorial marker for a unit of agricultural land – this latter idea Colin Renfrew deduces from the way the tombs are placed.

In the early Stone Age we thus find a decentralized society which, to judge by burial practices, was also relatively egalitarian. But three of the ancient monuments in Orkney, namely Maeshowe and the two large stone circles, would require so much labour that it would be far beyond the capacity of a small tomb-community, and would have required the effort of a much larger social unit. It is not really surprising, therefore, that according to investigations these three are among the most recent of the Stone Age monuments – though older than the pyramids – with scientific dating placing them around 2,900 B.C. A development towards a centralized society may therefore have taken place in the later Stone Age.

Maeshowe is the finest and most interesting of the chambered tombs. The stone work in this tomb is of high quality – the stones are fitted together with a precision which seems incredible when we consider the tools Stone Age man had at his disposal. In some places it is not possible to get as much as a knife blade in between the stones – and those are stones weighing as much as three tons! In a grave like this, which was probably built for a chieftain and his family, we should have expected grave-goods of a similar quality. But Vikings waiting to go on a crusade broke into the tomb in the twelfth century and scribbled runes on the walls – one of the most interesting collections of runic inscriptions anywhere. Maybe it was these Vikings who carried away anything that might have been there. The inscriptions mention a treasure found in Maeshowe and carried off and buried elsewhere. Nevertheless it is difficult not to wonder what kind of Stone Age treasure could possibly have interested the Vikings.

The two stone circles known as the Standing Stones of Stenness and Ring of Brogar stand on the narrow strip of land between the Stenness and Harray lakes on Mainland. Here and there in the Orkney landscape we also find individual, isolated standing stones which to today's observer seem to have been placed completely haphazardly.

The Standing Stones of Stenness is probably the oldest of the stone circles. It is simple, with only 12 stones. Radio-carbon dating places it in 2,900. It was not possible to date the Ring of Brogar in the same way, as there were no organic remains that could be used for analysis. There are traces of 60 stones in the Ring of Brogar. They are placed on the circumference of a circle at intervals of almost exactly six degrees. The deviation is not more than one sixth of a degree. The ring is a perfect circle within a margin of error of one per cent. Around the Ring of Brogar is a deep ditch dug into the solid bedrock, which alone is an impressive work of engineering, considering that it was done with flint axes or other stone implements.

Ring of Brogar stands on a narrow strip of land between the Stenness and Harray lochs on Mainland.

There are many besides P. A. Munch who have wondered about the purpose of the stone circles and the effort necessary to erect them. Generally they have been accepted as evidence of a people's religious aspirations in the distant past. Through the ages the stones have stood in enigmatic circles and become part of myths and legends. The early Norse settlers often linked them to giants and supernatural powers.

During the last few years there has been a dramatic change in the understanding of the stone circles and their purpose. This is the result of combined research in many fields, such as biology and physics, climatology, statistics, astronomy and archaeology. If the results of this research are correct, then the Stone Age culture of northern Europe does not compare unfavourably to the old civilizations of Babylonia and Egypt. Not only were they capable of applying complex geometric concepts to erect stone circles, but they could also carry out highly sophisticated calculations about the movement of the sun and the moon. These astronomical observations were unequalled until the Renaissance some 4000 years later.

It was the Oxford professor Alexander Thom who did much of the background work for the new theories. He was struck by the fact that the stone circles had cost an enormous effort and therefore must have a purpose beyond the merely religious. By measuring the stones accurately and subjecting the findings to statistical processing, he concluded that the people who built the stone circles were familiar with very advanced mathematical concepts. They had also developed their own megalithic 'yard' of 2 ft 9 in. (83 cm). For some reason the important measurements in what they built were mostly a multiple of this unit. The megalithic yard was used at all Stone Age sites all over northwestern Europe. On the whole it appears that knowledge spread from one Stone Age settlement to another.

In Thom's opinion Stone Age people also constructed their own 16-month calendar. The stone circles were observatories of astronomical phenomena and could be used to determine the midsummer and the midwinter solstices. It would also be possible to predict lunar eclipses, and this may be another reason why the circles were built. Many of the isolated standing stones served as alignments. This work was based on observations over a long period of time and would have taken years of patient trial and error in positioning stones.

Those who challenge Thom's conclusions point out that he picks out whatever happens to support his case, and that sites are often no more than a few stones lined up to a point on the horizon. But Thom's ideas have been gaining acceptance and have also been amplified by others. Dr Euan Mackie of Glasgow University believes that early man worshipped the moon first, later changing his main allegiance to the sun. From this early cult of moon-worship developed a society led by an elite of astronomer-priests, whose knowledge of astronomy gave them a powerful status among the people. A stone circle like the Ring of Brogar served both as an observatory and as a ceremonial centre. This presupposes a highly organized society. As there is no trace of this social structure in the Bronze Age, the end of their civilization may have come very suddenly.

With the Bronze Age, which in Europe is reckoned from about 1800 B.C., a new culture seems to be gaining ground. It is mostly the pottery finds which tell us how people lived in the Bronze Age. Even if the finds in Orkney are not numerous or rich, there are traces of the so-called Beaker folk. The name arose because of the characteristic shape of the pottery they made and used: bell-shaped vases or beakers which were decorated with easily recognizable geometrical patterns. The Beaker people were familiar with the use of metal, and although they came originally from Spain, their search for metals took them to England in the transition period between the late Stone Age and the Bronze Age.

We do not know whether the Beaker people came as far north as Orkney and there mixed with the original population, or whether the people there adopted the Beaker culture from wandering traders and copper and bronze smiths, but new norms and values appear to have arrived with the Bronze Age. Burial customs changed; individual graves with the dead placed in a foetal position in small stone cists are characteristic of the Beaker culture. These cists are so common in Orkney that such finds are not always

Cist, Birsay. Individual graves like this, with the dead placed in a foetal position, are characteristic of the Beaker culture. Since tractors came into use, and with that deeper ploughing, large numbers have been found by farmers.

reported. When tractors came into use in the 1930s and deep ploughing began, whole graveyards were sometimes found. This large number of graves indicates that the Bronze Age inhabitants were quite numerous. Some of the grave-goods also indicate that they could navigate well enough to carry on a trade with other parts of Europe. In contrast to Stone Age man who does not seem to have had weapons, Bronze Age man had both bows and battle axes.

With the Iron Age, from around 100 B.C., the living conditions changed once again. 'With iron we plough the soil, plant trees, clear gardens, cut stone, build and do all other kinds of useful work,' says the Roman naturalist Pliny in the first century after Christ. But iron is also used to wage war, to kill and plunder.

The climate in Europe worsened somewhat towards the end of the Bronze Age, and the migration of tribes began all over Europe. Land-hungry flocks with iron weapons were a serious threat to those who already had land of their own. It became necessary to build defences for protection against marauders.

One day in the summer of 1929, the Orkney poet Robert Rendall was sketching the view of the Rousay Sound from the Knowe of Gurness. Suddenly one of the legs of the stool he was sitting on went down into a hole. He removed some stones around the hole and saw a narrow set of steps going into the mound. Thus the Broch of Gurness was found – one of the best preserved brochs in Orkney.

The characteristic towers which were built in Scotland in this transition period between prehistoric and historic times are called *brochs*. Probably the word broch is a distortion of the Norse *borg*, meaning castle. Evidently the Vikings at once assumed them to be defensive structures, for the best preserved broch of them all, Mousa in Shetland, is referred to in the saga as Moseyjarborg. The brochs are especially interesting as they are peculiar to northern Scotland with the Hebrides, Orkney and Shetland. If we look at their distribution, we find that Orkney has relatively more than any other place. Altogether there are traces of some 100 such brochs in Orkney, whereas the total number is about 500. This may mean that broch-building began and developed in Orkney and then spread from there. We do not find anything similar to this broch-building anywhere else in Europe. As all brochs are surprisingly uniform and they were built at practically the same time, we may perhaps perceive one man's work behind them.

A broch is a large beehive-shaped tower with walls which are from 10 to 16 ft (3 to 5 m) thick. The idea behind them is not unlike that of the mediaeval castles. The brochs vary in size and height; the Mousa broch in Shetland is almost 49 ft (15 m) high. The brochs have only a low entrance and no windows; the door could be barricaded against intruders, and interior galleries circled the walls. A circular staircase led to the central opening in the roof, which had two functions – to let in the light and air, and to enable the defenders of the broch to strike at the enemy. As a rule a well was dug inside the broch. It could, therefore, probably withstand a siege.

The brochs are usually strategically placed close to farm land. It is possible that the broch usually housed the chieftain and his family. Round the brochs we often find the remains of huts where people lived in peacetime. Finds round the brochs show that people have tilled the soil, spun yarn and woven cloth. If danger came they probably all sought refuge in the broch. We cannot help being struck by the similarity to the early feudal settlements which later often became European towns.

It seems natural to ask – who were the broch-builders? We are now approaching historic times, but the information is still limited and confusing. Locally the brochs were till recently called Pict towers. All the same there is little or nothing to connect the Picts with the brochs. It is also strange that we do not find brochs in all of the Pictish territory which, judging by the place names and the engraved stone symbols they left behind, extended as far as the southeastern coast of Scotland, around Aberdeen.

The broch period lasts from 100 B.C. until A.D. 100. Many theories as to the origins of the broch-builders have been put forward, but it is not possible to be conclusive, and it is just as difficult to be certain about whom the broch-builders wanted to defend themselves against. We know that as early as A.D. 84 the Romans sailed with quite a large fleet around the north of Scotland, but we cannot conclude from this that the Roman expansion was the direct cause of the brochs being built. Nor did the Roman invasion of England come until A.D. 43, after the brochs had probably already been built.

A society of tribes could have lived in constant warfare against each other and have built the brochs in mutual defence. It is also possible that the Picts were the attackers and that a conquest actually took place. The most probable conclusion, however, is that we are dealing with one and the same people through most of prehistoric times, but that their beliefs, customs and way of life altered with changing conditions and influences.

4.
The Picts and the first Christian church

From the beginning the Peti and the Papae inhabited these islands. Of these, the one people, the Peti were hardly taller than pygmies. They worked marvels in building towns in the morning and at night; but in the middle of the day they lost their strength entirely and hid in terror in little underground houses. But at that time the islands were not called Orkney but Petland, and that is why the sea dividing the islands from Scotland is still called the Petland Sea by the people there. It is the most terrifying sea abyss; its current on an ebb tide swallows up the strongest ships and on a flood tide spits out the pieces of them. Where this people came from we know nothing about. But the Papae are named for the white robes they wore like clerics, just as all clerics are called Papen in German. The island of Papey is still named after them.

*Historia Norvegiae, c.*1170

This is an extract from an old manuscript in Latin, found in Scotland by P. A. Munch in 1849 and published by him as 'Breve chronicon Norvegiae'. The text is unique because it is the only Scandinavian source mentioning a pre-Norse settlement in Orkney. As we can see, the story seems as elusive as a fairy-tale but, studied together with other historical sources, its essence is surprisingly true.

Péttar or *pétar* was the Norse name for the Picts, whom the Norsemen knew from the eighth century. It was the Romans who called them *picti* – the painted ones. It is possible that the Picts were in the habit of using warpaint; it is also possible that by using this name the Romans wanted to brand their northern enemy as wild and primitive tribal warriors. For the fact is that right up to the Roman withdrawal from the province of Britannia in A.D. 411 they had to maintain a constant line of defence along the northern border against the attacks of the Picts. The Romans first built Hadrian's Wall and later the Antonine Wall, crossing Scotland at its narrowest, from Firth of Clyde to Firth of Forth, to keep the northern tribes out of Britannia. The Romans knew them first as four different tribes, but from the end of the third century A.D. they began referring to them collectively as the Picts.

At the height of its power the kingdom of the Picts extended all over northern Scotland. It was a highly organized society, but it was surrounded by enemies and was often at war. One of the enemies was the Scots, who originally came from the north of Ireland, but had established a small kingdom in Argyll which they called Dalriada. We can reckon the history of

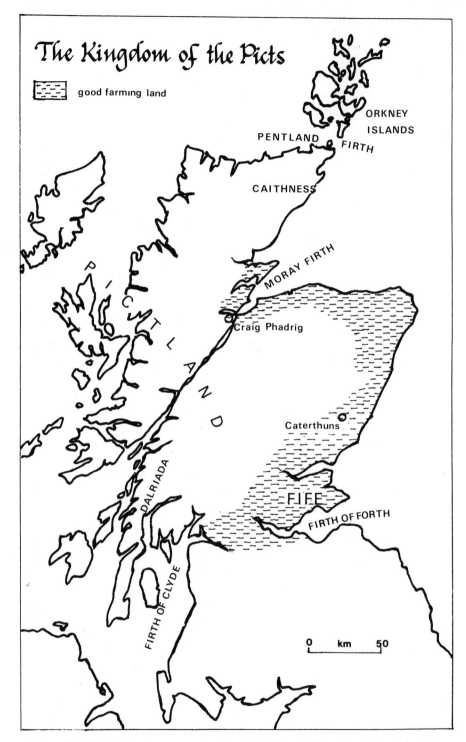

Fig. 2 *The Pictish kingdom, c.300–843 from* The Way it Was: The Kingdom of the Picts *by Anna Ritchie (Chambers)*

the Pictish state from about A.D. 300 until 843, when the Picts united with the Scots of Dalriada under the Scottish King Kenneth McAlpin, and after that ceased to function as a sovereign nation. The Norse expansion probably upset the balance of power and forced such a union, as together they might hope to withstand the Viking pressure.

There is no reason to doubt that Orkney was part of the kingdom of the Picts, but probably the islands had a certain amount of self-rule, perhaps with an under-king. The Welsh historian Nennius maintains in his *Historia Britonum* from the middle of the ninth century, that the Picts lived in Orkney and harried from there. He also tells that in the year A.D. 449 the Saxons harried in Orkney from 40 ships, and even then the Picts were living there.

Who, then, were the Picts? Historical research gives no clear answer, and many of the conclusions are highly controversial. The closest we can get to an answer seems to be that the name Picts is used about the various tribes who from ancient times lived in the area. One of the reasons why so little is known is that the Picts left no written decipherable records. The so-called 'Pictish Chronicle', the only surviving manuscript, is only a list of kings.

The finding of the Pictish symbol stones in Orkney is the first indisputable proof that the Picts lived there. The stones are recognized as Pictish because of the characteristic pictures which are carved into them – characteristic of the Pictish area and not found anywhere else. The pictures have been cut with both skill and imagination, and show people in battle scenes and on hunting trips. But it is the enigmatic, abstract symbols which first and foremost appeal to the imagination. Nobody knows what they mean.

A half-moon with a V-shaped rod is a recurrent symbol. There are several stones with this symbol, and one of them was found in St Peter's Church in South Ronaldsay. Most of the symbol stones probably date from the sixth and seventh centuries. Gradually the style changed, and we find stones with crosses or biblical motifs. The designs are intricate and reminiscent of the illuminated manuscripts made in monasteries. A simple, beautiful, incised cross was found in the Broch of Burrian in North Ronaldsay.

Nobody knows what function these stones filled. Were they perhaps territorial markers? They may have been burial stones for the dead, even if they do not seem to have been placed over the actual graves. The same symbols are carved into jewellery, but so far they have not been found on house walls.

Besides the symbol stones the Picts left inscriptions, which so far have not been deciphered. The Picts used a form of writing called *ogam*, which originated in Ireland in the fourth century A.D. Perhaps the Picts learned ogam from the Scots of Dalriada. Memorial stones with ogam inscriptions have been found scattered around the Pictish kingdom. Three ogam inscriptions have been found in Orkney, and they were probably made as late as in the eighth or ninth century.

Fig. 3 Pictish symbols, on stone from St Peter's Church, South Ronaldsay

In its simplest form, ogam has 20 letters: five vowels and 15 consonants, with another five being added later. The letters are made up of lines which vary in number from one to five. This makes it possible to imagine that the letters were originally made as a finger alphabet. The five fingers held in different positions could make letters, in more or less the same way that a modern alphabet for the deaf might be used. The key to the ogam writing was never lost – it is only the Pictish inscriptions that do not lend themselves to translation. The reason for this is that they were written in an unknown language which was not even of Indo-European origin. There were probably two languages in use, an original language and a Celtic dialect which had developed through immigration from outside and through frequent contact across fluctuating boundaries.

The Picts were probably the descendants of the broch-builders. For them the broch can no longer have been a necessary defence structure, as they started using the stones of the brochs as building materials. Both around the Midhowe broch in Rousay and around the Gurness broch in Evie we find small villages built close to the broch walls. In the village at the Broch of Gurness there are two traceable periods of building; around A.D. 200 a number of small houses with one or two rooms were built, and then, around A.D. 600, the demands made on the quality of housing seem to have risen, for the houses then built on top of the old walls had four small rooms branching out from a central hall with a hearth.

From the excavations made at the Buckquoy farmstead at the Point of Buckquoy, the northwestern tip of Mainland, we learn more of everyday life in Pictish times. The farm was in use over a long period of time. There are three housing layers – people just built another house on top of the old one when they needed more space or grew tired of the old one. The people on the farm lived simply, but had everything they needed within reach. They fished and kept domestic animals, but it is not known whether they grew grain. The Picts left the Buckquoy farm around 750. There are traces of a Norse farm building on top of the Pictish walls.

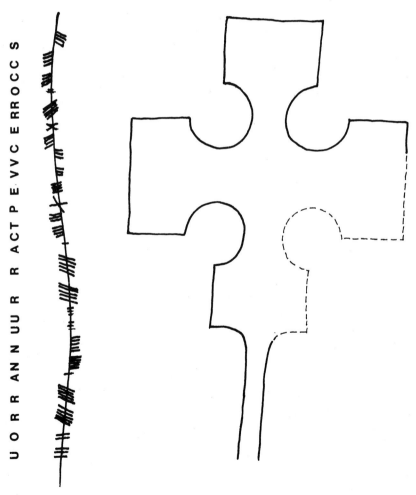

Fig. 4 Ogam inscription and cross stone from the Broch of Burrian, North Ronaldsay

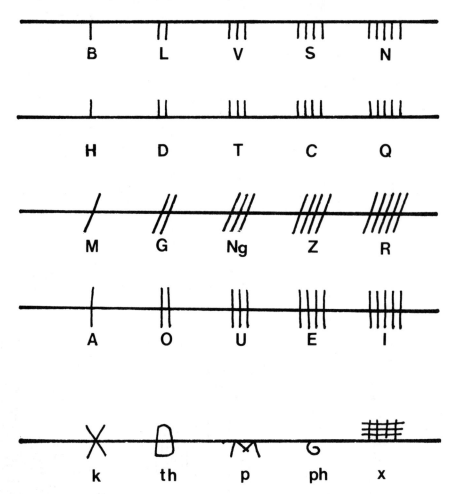

Fig. 5 Ogam alphabet, as it first appeared. The five letters below were added on later.

A skeleton found at Buckquoy shows a man about 25 years old, who must have been around 5 ft 7 in (1.70 m) tall. If this is the corpse of a Pict, as seems probable, then the statement in the *Historia Norvegiae* that the Picts were the size of pygmies is a figment of the imagination, inspired perhaps by the so-called Pict houses. These are small underground rooms which are often reached through a long sloping passage. The Picts probably used them as store rooms for food.

There are conflicting theories as to how the Picts were Christianized. It was the Briton St Ninian who, from his monastic school Candida Casa in the region now known as Galloway, began the mission to the Picts. This was towards the end of the Roman period. Some believe that it was St Ninian himself who brought Christianity to Orkney, whereas others consider it doubtful that he ever came so far north.

Midhowe broch and cairn, Rousay. The Picts were probably the descendants of the broch builders and started using the stones of the brochs as building materials for small villages close to the broch walls. The cairn is covered with a 'hangar'.

The best known figure in the early Christian period is, however, St Columba, who is often described as the apostle of the northern Picts. Originally he came from Donegal in Ireland, but with 12 followers he settled on the island of Iona in the inner Hebrides in the year 563. Here he built a church and a monastery which became the pivot of his missionary work. According to legend, St Columba visited Bridei, King of the Picts, at his court in the Inverness area. The King of Orkney was then staying at the Pictish court, and it was apparent that he took orders from Bridei. St Columba appealed to Bridei on behalf of the monk Cormac and his companions, who wanted to settle in Orkney.

Some of our people have already set sail, desiring to find a hermitage in the untravelled ocean; if they, by chance, should come after a long journey to the islands of Orkney, commend them earnestly to this sub-king, whose hostages are in your power, so that no harm may befall them at his hands.

Adamnan: *Life of St Columba*

The two old church bells that have been found, in Birsay and North Ronaldsay, are shaped and decorated in a style peculiar to the early Celtic Church. We read in the extract from *Historia Norvegiae* that the papae also lived in Orkney in pre-Norse times. The Irish called their priests by the Latin word *papa*, which means father. And in *Íslendingabók* we are told by Ari Frodi that there were Irish Christians called *papi* living in Iceland before the Norsemen came.

The Celtic Church was different from the Roman Church – it was more old-fashioned and closer to the original Church. It was also more loosely organized and was not divided into parishes or bishoprics. It was first of all a missionary Church which sprang from monastic communities, and it was the abbots in charge of the monasteries who were the leaders of the Celtic Church. The monks were called culdees, a name which is derived from the Irish *céle de* and means a friend of God. They modelled their ways on the gospels and preached a simple faith. Originally the monks were hermits, who joined together to worship God. Their community did not have the firm structure or the strict rules which had developed in Roman Catholic monasteries. Nor was there any organized cooperation between the various communities.

Most monasteries were small, with 10 or 12 monks. They grew the food they needed. In their search for solitude and tranquillity they sought out remote holms and promontories, where the feeling of being alone with nature can sometimes be overwhelming. In the Brough of Deerness, which today is almost inaccessible but may not always have been so, are ruins of monastic cells from the early Christian period. Another such site is the Brough of Birsay. The monks did find their 'hermitage in the untravelled ocean'.

Perhaps Cormac represented the vanguard of Christianity in Orkney, but it is impossible to say how far the influence of the Celtic Church went. It

The Brough of Deerness, which is almost inaccessible today, has ruins of monastic cells from the early Christian period.

may be that Christian influence at a later stage came as much from the mainstream Roman Church. In the latter half of the seventh century, the Picts in the south were overrun by the Northumbrians and ruled by them for some 30 years. During this time the position of the Roman Church in Pictland became strong enough to take over eventually from the Celtic Church. A well-organized mission was sent to Orkney, and its influence there can be found in all the churches in Pictish settlements dedicated to St Peter.

It is not the story in *Historia Norvegiae* alone that shows that the Norsemen knew the Picts and the Christian monks or priests; the place names tell the same story. The Pentland Firth was in Norse times known as Pettalandsfjǫrðr; the *n* has been erroneously included in recent times and is often unpronounced locally. The name was applied to the sea dividing the Norse area from Pettaland – the land of the Picts. We also find farm names such as Pittaquoy. And names like Papa Westray and Papa Stronsay, in the sagas called Papey meiri and Papey minni, Paplay in South Ronaldsay and Papdale outside Kirkwall, tell us where the monks lived.

In the end we are left with the most difficult and controversial question of them all: what happened to the Picts? What became of them? In *Historia Norvegiae* we find this explanation:

In the days of Harald Fairhair, the Norse king, some vikings from the family of Rognvald the Strong sailed with a large fleet across the Sulend Sea, robbed these people of their ancient homes, drove them away and conquered the islands.

Another possibility suggested by the historian A. W. Brögger, is that the Picts had become so weakened that the Norsemen found an almost empty land, a museum. The fact that the Picts are not mentioned in the sagas may be taken as support of such a view. Apart from a vague story of Picts defending their land in Rousay, there is no tradition of battles between Picts and Norsemen, and so far no archaeological finds indicate war and destruction.

That the sagas do not mention the Picts may of course mean that they were not there, but may also mean that they were so obvious that they were not worth mentioning. We must just accept that there is no clear answer. Probably some of the Picts fled to the mainland, whereas others lived a shadowy existence for a generation or two, perhaps even a century, before they became part of the new population. Some of the ogam inscriptions and the cross slabs were made deep into Norse times, which indicates a period of co-existence.

5. The early Norse period

Only some 250 miles (400 km) separate the southwestern coast of Norway from the fertile Orkney soil. What could be more natural than for people farming their few acres between mountain and fjord to leave for something far better?

The Viking Age in the west began in 793 with the attack on the monastery at Lindisfarne on the east coast of England. The chronicle writer describes with horror how suddenly it happened. It was the light, fast ships which made such a foray possible – indeed the ships forged the Norse expansion. An early technical development within shipbuilding and navigation formed the basis for the landtaking which, during the ninth century, turned the North Sea into a Norse sea.

The Vikings were in their own time described by those they hit the hardest: the monks in the monasteries. The courage required of the settlers and their families found no place in the chronicles. Within a century a migration of people took place from Norway to new settlements in remote places in the west: Orkney, Shetland, the Faeroes and Iceland. All these areas were similar to those they left so that the environment could be utilized in the same way, and they could carry on life more or less as they knew it before. This movement has much in common with emigration to North America from the rural districts in Norway during the nineteenth century. In both cases the population in Norway probably grew faster than the economy could deal with. A few went first and showed the way, then rumours of rich land spread, and the stream of emigrants began.

It was natural that Orkney and Shetland were colonized first, as they were closest and the voyage there was the least dangerous. The exodus probably began as landtaking. The dream of plunder only came when it became apparent that the riches were theirs for the taking – the monasteries with their wealth were open and unprotected. Maybe the Viking raids were an extra source of income for people who normally were settlers, or maybe we can speak of two different ways of life with sometimes even conflicting interests. In any case Orkney became a base both for Viking expeditions further west to Ireland and Man, and for new landtaking in the Faeroes and Iceland. Thus it is even possible that the attack on the monastery at Lindisfarne came from Orkney.

Place names and archaeological finds can give answers to some of the questions about when and how the Norse settlement in Orkney took place. The place names fall into a different, older pattern than the one to be found in Iceland (see Chapter 13).

Much information is probably still to come from archaeology, for surprisingly few systematic excavations have been made on Norse sites. Perhaps the Norse relics have seemed too recent compared to everything else that history has left behind in Orkney.

Burials are the chief source of archaeological information about the early Norse period. At Pierowall in Westray – the old Hǫfn, a main port of call for ships going between Norway, Orkney and Ireland – a Norse graveyard was found. The oldest of the graves go back to around 800. In a woman's grave an oval brooch was found; such brooches were used in pairs as part of the ordinary women's dress. An identical brooch has been found on Unst in Shetland. Identical brooches have been found in Norway too, most of them in Rogaland. Were they made by the same metal worker? At any rate these finds show that southwestern Norway and Orkney must have communicated closely in the early ninth century.

The grave finds are mostly of good quality but cannot be described as rich. The finds indicate that those who settled were not chieftains or Vikings, but ordinary farmers. They became influenced by Christian burial customs quite early, and it was probably only the first settlers who fitted out their dead with grave-goods.

Excavations at the Buckquoy farm in Birsay, which Norse farmers took over from the Picts, show that the settlers, in addition to taking along their own equipment, also used many of the ordinary Pictish utensils and tools. This supports the view that encounters between Norsemen and Picts were mainly of a peaceful nature.

In 1858 a boy who was out hunting rabbits found a hoard of some 90 silver objects in the Bay of Skaill on Mainland: armrings, brooches, even a fish-hook of silver! There were also English and Arabian coins, and these show that the hoard, which weighed 16 lbs (7.3 kg), must have been buried between 950 and 1000. This is the largest silver hoard ever found within the area of the old Norse empire. It is not known whether the hoard was Viking booty or whether it was the result of peaceful trade expeditions.

Scottish written sources are silent about the Norse settlement. Through the Icelandic Orkneyinga saga we learn about the political history of the islands from the time the earldom was established some time in the ninth century. The saga goes on to describe the earldom under the great earls Thorfinn the Mighty and Rognvald Kali Kolsson, and ends with the death of Harald Maddadarson in 1206. The saga is a mixture of history and literature and it is not always easy to distinguish the one from the other. But probably at least the last part of it is historically correct.

The Orkneying saga is also called the *Earls' Saga*. This is a more appropriate name for it, for the ordinary Orkney man and woman are not mentioned very often in the saga. It is a sequence of historical pageants where the light falls on the Earl and the circle closest to him. In this way the Orkneyinga saga conforms with the pattern of Icelandic history-writing, although perhaps in many ways it is closer to the family sagas than the sagas of the kings. It is a story full of dramatic incidents, full of the lust for power in stubborn minds.

Sigurd Eysteinsson from Giske, the brother of Rognvald, Earl of Möre, is known as the first Earl of Orkney. He started the expansion southwards on the Scottish mainland that came to characterize the earldom, and which ironically in time led to its downfall as a Norse dominion. Sigurd conquered Caithness, Sutherland, Ross and parts of what is now Moray. The reason why one of the most northerly counties in Scotland is called Sutherland – the land suðr or to the south – is that it was named from the north, from Orkney.

Sigurd was followed by his brother's son, Einar Rognvaldsson, a half-brother of Hrolf the Walker, who became Duke of Normandy and the direct ancestor of William the Conqueror. According to tradition Earl Einar taught the islanders to use peat for fuel and thus he became known to posterity as Turf-Einar. He was a good earl – at least he was one of the few who died in bed. He had three sons. The two older ones fell with Eirik Blood-Axe in the Battle of Stanesmoor in England in 950, and so the youngest son, Thorfinn the Skull-Splitter, inherited the earldom from his father.

Thorfinn the Skull-Splitter left five sons when he died in 963. Odal law with its equal shares for all heirs also applied to the earldom, and this led time and time again to disastrous family feuds with brother against brother. Three of Thorfinn's sons let themselves be charmed by Ragnhild Eirik's daughter. Evidently she had been taught well by her parents Gunnhild and Eirik Blood-Axe in the ways of intrigue. Ragnhild married all three in turn, and managed to kill off two of them. In the end, Hlodvir Thorfinnsson was the sole surviving brother. He was a great chieftain, says the saga. Hlodvir married Eithne Kjarval's daughter, an Irish princess. It was said that she had 'the sight'. The Celts were often believed to have this gift. Their son was Sigurd Hlodvisson, who was also called Sigurd the Stout.

Sigurd is one of the great earls in the Orkneyinga saga. He inherited the earldom from his father in 980. Sigurd fought constantly against the Scots, who were pressing Caithness from the south. A Scottish earl called Finnleik challenged Sigurd to fight him; since Sigurd would be the weaker of the two he asked his mother's advice. Eithne gave her son a raven banner she had made and told him:

Had I thought you might live for ever, I'd have reared you in my wool-basket. But lifetimes are shaped by what will be, not by where you are. Now, take this banner. I've made it for you with all the skill I have, and my belief is this: that it will bring victory to the man it's carried before, but death to the one who carries it.

Orkneyinga Saga

Sigurd did not much like what his mother said, but she was proved right. Three standard bearers fell, but the battle was won.

In Gunnlaug's saga we hear of how the arrogant young Icelander Gunnlaug Illugason starts on a journey to visit kings and earls. 'At that time Earl Sigurd Hlodvisson ruled in Orkney, and he always received Icelanders well', the saga tells us. Gunnlaug visited Earl Sigurd in 1002, and recited a poem he had made in Sigurd's honour. Unfortunately this poem is lost. To show his appreciation the earl gave him a broad axe with a handle inlaid in silver. Later Gunnlaug spent a winter and summer with Sigurd in Orkney and 'they harried that summer far and wide in the Hebrides and in Scotland and fought many battles'.

Sigurd was a powerful earl and a troublesome neighbour. He married the daughter of Malcolm, King of Scots, and they had a son, Thorfinn. This child was fostered by King Malcolm, his maternal grandfather. According to the custom of the day the fostering of a child was a token of respect and friendship, but such a foster-child was at the same time often a hostage, a pledge in a pact of non-aggression.

Earl Sigurd joined King Sigtrygg Silk-Beard, a Norse king in Ireland, in a campaign against Brian Borumha, King of the Irish. The so-called Battle of Brian was fought at Clontarf outside Dublin on Good Friday 1014. Both Brian and Sigurd fell in the battle, which was won by the Irish, and the Norse colonization of Ireland received a blow from which it never recovered. The saga explains Sigurd's death by the fact that he himself carried the raven banner because nobody else would do so.

The battle is described in the Saga of Burnt Njál; it must have resounded throughout the Norse world. The strange Song of Darrað – Darraðarljoð – tells us how Odin's maidens, the valkyries, are weaving the fate of the men fighting in the Battle of Brian. Men's heads were used in place of weights, and human entrails in place of the warp and woof; a sword served as the treadle and an arrow as the batten. While working their loom they recited their dark, fateful song.

When Sigurd died, his son Thorfinn was only five years old and still with his grandfather in Scotland. But Sigurd had three older sons from an earlier marriage: Sumarlidi, Brusi and Einar Wry-Mouth. These three divided the islands among themselves after their father's death. Whereas Sumarlidi and Brusi were peaceable men, Einar was difficult and obstinate, as his nickname suggests.

On a tall stone outside the twelfth-century Oddernes church in Kristiansand, a runic inscription tells us: 'Eyvind, godson of King Olaf the Holy, built this church on his land'. This was the chieftain Eyvind Urarhorn who in the summer of 1019 sailed from Ireland to Norway. He waited for better weather at Osmondwall in Hoy, and there he was captured by Earl Einar, and killed.

Snorri Sturluson, the historian, tells us that Einar had been defeated in a battle against the Irish, and he had grown tired of seeing Eyvind playing into enemy hands in Ireland. But the killing of Eyvind started one of the endless chains of misdeeds and revenge we hear so much about in the sagas, for Eyvind's men went home and told King Olaf Haraldsson of what had happened. And, says the Orkneyinga saga:

The King hadn't much to say about it, though it was plain he thought Eyvind's death a great loss and took the whole episode as a personal affront. As a rule the King said little about the more serious offences against him.

Sumarlidi died, and Einar died in an underhanded attack by Thorfinn's friends. King Olaf used to his own advantage the ensuing struggle for power in the islands between the two remaining brothers Brusi and Thorfinn. He quickly appropriated the islands and gave the half-brothers a share each in fee, making them swear an oath of fealty to him. Brusi and Thorfinn strongly disliked this state of affairs, but became reconciled and shared the earldom between themselves. But Thorfinn had the greater authority all the time, as he had the support of the King of the Scots behind him.

'But to make sure I can rely on you I want your son Rognvald here with me.' This is what King Olaf tells Brusi, who had to let his ten-year-old son remain in Norway with the King. Rognvald Brusason grew up with King Olaf and went with him when he fled to Russia in 1028. Only 19 years old, Rognvald led a wing of the King's army in the Battle of Stiklestad, where Olaf was killed. He rescued the badly wounded Harald Sigurdsson from the battlefield and carried him across the border into Sweden. This was King Olaf's young half-brother, later known as King Harald Hardrada, who was killed at Stamford Bridge in 1066, trying to invade England. Together with other survivors from the Battle of Stiklestad Rognvald and Harald made it back to King Yaroslav in Russia. When it became known that Earl Brusi was dead, Rognvald was installed as earl of two thirds of Orkney by King Magnus the Good in 1035. Thorfinn ruled the other third, but had also won large parts of Scotland in addition to those areas he had inherited from his grandfather.

For ten years Rognvald and Thorfinn ruled Orkney together, in peace and friendship. Rognvald often went along on raiding expeditions in the south to safeguard Thorfinn's land. The saga explains the breach between them by Thorfinn demanding for himself a larger share of the earldom. The conflict between them came to a final end when Rognvald was killed in Papa Stronsay where he had gone to get malt for the Christmas ale.

The Icelander Arnor Thordarson describes the long struggle for power between close friends and kinsmen in his poems: 'I saw both my benefactors battering the other's men – fierce was my grief'. Arnor was called *jarlaskáld* – the earls' poet – because both earls were his friends and he had married into their family. He felt as if the bitter conflict were tearing him apart:

> awkward our choice
> when Earls are eager
> to fight – friendship
> is far from easy.

About Rognvald Brusason the saga says that 'of all the Earls of Orkney he was the most popular and gifted, and his death was mourned by many'. It was probably Rognvald who built St Olaf's church in Kirkjuvágr – Kirkwall – that the town may be named for. Today only a doorway remains.

When Rognvald died there was nobody left to challenge Thorfinn's complete control of Orkney, but for a long time he does not seem to have been there much. 'Thorfinn spent most of the time in Caithness and Scotland, leaving his stewards to look after the islands . . .'. For Thorfinn's territory was large: nine earldoms in Scotland, apart from the Sudreys and parts of Ireland. But about Thorfinn's life in Scotland the saga does not have much to tell.

Thorfinn married Ingibjorg, the daughter of the Norwegian chieftain Finn Arnason, and thus became part of one of Norway's most influential families, the Arnmödlings. But it was also a controversial family; it was Finn's brother Kalf Arnason who led the peasant army against King Olaf in the Battle of Stiklestad.

Our knowledge of Scottish history in the first half of the eleventh century is very uncertain. Thorfinn's grandfather Malcolm II had no sons, but his daughter's son Duncan I ruled until he was killed in battle by the unknown Macbeth in 1040. Macbeth seems to have been a good king who ruled for 17 years until he fell in battle against Duncan's son, who became King Malcolm III. Malcolm, who was nicknamed Canmore (Big-Head) in Gaelic, married Thorfinn's widow, Ingibjorg Finn's daughter, also called Earls' Mother. Their son Duncan became King of the Scots after his father.

A theory which was recently put forward suggests that Macbeth and Thorfinn are one and the same person – the Norse Earl of Orkney in the north and Macbeth, 'son of life', in Gaelic Scotland, where the name Thorfinn would sound pagan. Such a double identity can explain much that seems contradictory in the sagas, but it also raises many new questions; and it can hardly be proved. But in any case it is quite a coincidence that both Macbeth and Thorfinn went on a pilgrimage to Rome around 1050, and that one source mentions a visit by 'Malbeatha, King of Orkney'. It is also strange that the young King Malcolm would marry the much older Ingibjorg, for dynastic marriages were usually entered into for the very definite purpose of securing succession. But the marriage makes more sense if Ingibjorg was the widow of a King of Scots, instead of an earl in distant Orkney.

King Harald Hardrada stayed for a while in Orkney to recruit an army before he began his campaign against England. Thorfinn was then dead, and it was his sons Paul and Erlend who joined King Harald. Would the outcome of the Battle of Stamford Bridge perhaps have been different and would England's history have changed its course if Thorfinn had fought for the king?

Thorfinn had his main seat in Birsay. There he also built a minster called Christ Church, and this became the seat of the first Bishop of Orkney.

The doorway of St Olaf's Church, Kirkwall, is all that remains today of the church which was probably built by Earl Rognvald Brusason.

Brough of Birsay. We know from the Orkneyinga Saga that Earl Thorfinn had his main seat in Birsay. Until recently the brough has been the accepted site, but this is now disputed by some archaeologists.

Under Thorfinn the earldom was at its greatest in size and power.

Like Norway and Iceland, the earldom of Orkney was ruled by an aristocratic class of chieftains, but it staked out its own course very early. Especially during the early period all power was concentrated in the earl's hands. Thorfinn appointed *göðings* (a kind of chieftain) who formed a political élite. Even though we find traces of the assembly, the Thing – Tingwall (O. N. þingvǫllr) in Evie and Dingieshowe (O. N. þingshaugr) in Deerness – it seems to have been of less importance than in Norway and Iceland. The Orkneyinga saga does not describe the Thing as a political and legal meeting place.

The earls themselves owned large farms – such a farm was known as a *bu*. Thorfinn made the göðings run these farms and collect the taxes from the farmers. Odallers who owned their land were probably the largest group in the early days of the earldom. They paid taxes to the earl, mostly in goods. Only cultivated land was taxed; the tax rates were fixed towards the end of the tenth century. The land was divided into *eyrisland* according to its yield, so that every eyrisland paid the same amount in tax. An eyrir was about an ounce of pure silver. As an example, Sanday had 36.5 eyrisland, whereas Eday had only two, because the soil was poorer there.

In Pictish times cultivated land was fenced off by stone dykes. The Norse settlers seem to have taken over the same land division, which they called *tun*, and which later was known as township. Every tun represented one whole or one half a taxable eyrisland.

The Norse period made Orkney part of a North Sea empire. The islands were strategically placed on the sea route between Norway and the lands in the west, as well as for further expansion southwards, and thus the islands became divided in their interests. The earls had to achieve a difficult balance between two kingdoms, of which Norway had to be reckoned with first. Even if the King of Norway was further away, his strong fleet could easily bring him to the islands. Norse power was strongly centralized with great freedom of action for the King. Scotland was mostly torn by inner conflict and too hard pressed by England in the south to be able to worry about the islands in the north.

6.
Magnus Erlendsson – the saint

Comitis generosi, militis gloriosi
Martyris certamina concinat Orchadica
Gens plaudens; nam caelica terit Magnus limina.
    Mediaeval sequence in festo Magni Ducis Mart.

During restoration work on St Magnus Cathedral in 1919, a wooden casket containing skeletal remains was found. It had been walled up in a pillar of the choir. The skull showed the mark of a frontal attack with an axe. The body of St Magnus was not lost after all – for perhaps a foresighted priest had hidden it at the time of the Reformation, and then the knowledge of it had been lost. Some bones are missing, having been given according to Catholic custom to a sister church in the Faeroes, the St Magnus Church at Kirkjuböur which was consecrated but never completed. An anatomical examination showed that Earl Magnus must have been of average height and physically weak.

What is it that through the ages has made some people saints? Is it not often a coincidence of character and circumstance – very often against a background that is political in the widest sense? It may seem as if this is especially true of Magnus Erlendsson, for there is not much that is remarkable in what the saga tells us about him.

The novelist Sigrid Undset also thinks along these lines in her essay 'St Magnus, Earl of Orkney':

St Magnus is no eccentric saint. Nothing that the sagas say about him is especially remarkable. When his character nevertheless is so striking, it is because it contrasts so sharply with the whole world he lived in. He is the man who moves against the tide. That is what a descendant of the Orkney earls would have to be, if he seriously chose Christ as his lord and master – contrary to his friends' idea of what makes life meaningful and of what is man's dignity and honour.

Norske helgener, 1937

Thus Sigrid Undset does not measure Magnus by absolute standards, but sees him in relation to his times – when the old faith and the old Viking warrior ideals clashed with Christian principles.

The otherwise sober Orkneyinga saga sings his praise:

St Magnus, Earl of Orkney, was a man of extraordinary distinction, tall, with a fine, intelligent look about him. He was a man of strict virtue, successful in war, wise, eloquent, generous and magnanimous, openhanded with money and sound with advice, and altogether the most popular of men. He was gentle and agreeable when talking to men of wisdom and goodwill, but severe and uncompromising towards thieves and vikings, putting to death most of the men who plundered the farms and other parts of the earldom ... He lived according to God's commandments, mortifying the flesh throughout an exemplary life in many ways which, though revealed to God, remained hidden from the sight of men.

His intentions were clear when he asked for the hand of a girl from the noblest family there in Scotland, celebrating their wedding and afterwards living with her for ten years without allowing either to suffer by way of their lusts, and so remaining chaste, without stain of lechery. Whenever the urge of temptation came upon him, he would plunge into cold water and pray to God for aid.

If the remains in the St Magnus Cathedral really are St Magnus', as seems certain, then we know that the Orkneyinga saga was mistaken in describing him as tall. It may be that the saga writer wants to glorify him further by not only giving him the qualities of a saint but by showing him also as the traditional Viking chieftain.

After Thorfinn the Mighty died *c*.1065, his two sons Paul and Erlend shared the rule of Orkney. Both of them went with Harald Hardrada on his final military campaign to England, and survived the Battle of Stamford Bridge. They governed well and got along with each other. It was not until their sons grew up that there was friction between them. Paul's son Hakon and Erlend's elder son Erling were both quick-tempered and proud. Magnus, Erlend's younger son, was more peaceful by nature, says the saga. Things became so bad that prominent men had to try to reconcile the earls, and power was divided between them. This worked for a while, but the arrogant and stubborn Hakon urged his father to take more than his share of the power, and the conflict flared up again. The chieftains then asked Hakon Paulsson to stay away from the islands, and he left – for Norway. It must have been obvious to everybody that it was Hakon who caused the conflict.

Magnus Erlendsson was born around 1075. The sagas tell us that he was popular and well-liked. The longer Magnus saga says that 'many men leaned towards the sons of Erlend and would not let them bear a lower lot there in the islands, for they were better friends of the people and more beloved of men'. But 'Hakon harboured many a grudge for this all his day'.

Magnus Erlendsson lived at a time when Christianity had begun to establish itself as a religion and philosophy. But to desist from violence was not necessarily looked upon as a Christian virtue. Indeed the faith had often been introduced through violence in the north. All the same, for some, life gained a new dimension which the old ideal of the Viking warrior did not fill. The available sources do not tell us whether this was true of Magnus, but it does not seem very likely. As an earl's son he did perhaps for some time receive instruction from monks, possibly in the monastery at Eynhallow. Nevertheless, the Magnus saga tells us that Magnus in his youth took part in Viking raids, and 'he seemed for some winters like wicked men'.

The Orkneyinga saga follows Hakon Paulsson on his Scandinavian wanderings. He came to Norway towards the end of the rule of Olaf Haraldsson the Peaceful and soon went on to Sweden, where he stayed for some time. A soothsayer told him his destiny:

... your life will be a source of stirring events. My feeling is that you will end up as a sole ruler of Orkney, though you'll most likely think you've waited long enough for it. I think your offspring will rule there as well, and as for the journey you're about to make west to Orkney, momentous events will result from it, matters of great consequence. During your life you'll be the cause of a crime for which you'll barely be able to atone – perhaps never – to that god you believe in.

The prophecy, a commonly used device in the sagas, here serves to explain or perhaps justify Hakon's later actions which are now viewed as part of his destiny.

Hakon learned that people in Orkney would prefer him to stay away, and his claim was not likely to win popular support there. Therefore he persuaded the new King of Norway, Magnus Bare-Legs, to make a western expedition. Hakon whispered in his ear that if he conquered the Nordreys and the Sudreys – Orkney and the Hebrides – he could raid Ireland and Scotland from there. Probably he counted on gaining support from the King for his claim to power in the islands. If so, he had reckoned without his host, for Magnus Bare-Legs was second to none in lusting for power, and he could manage very well without Hakon Paulsson.

Magnus Bare-Legs set out on his western expedition in 1098. He took Orkney without a fight, removed the two earls and sent them as prisoners to Norway. As the new overlord of the islands he installed his eight-year-old son, Sigurd. He took the earls' sons along on his further expedition to the Sudreys. Hakon must have been full of bitter gall that his betrayal hit himself as hard as the others.

Magnus Erlendsson was made the King's cup-bearer and 'used to serve at the King's table'. This was considered an honourable task. Why was Magnus singled out in this way? Hakon's mother was of royal birth, and one would expect him to precede his cousin in rank. Was it perhaps because Magnus Bare-Legs knew that Magnus Erlendsson was more highly esteemed at home in Orkney?

After having raided the Sudreys and subdued them, Magnus Bare-Legs went further southwards. Off the coast of Wales, in the Menai Strait, he fought a hard battle against two local earls, Hugh the Stout and Hugh the Proud. This is how the Orkneyinga saga describes what happened as the battle began:

When the troops were getting their weapons ready for battle, Magnus Erlendsson settled down in the main cabin and refused to arm himself. The King asked him why he was sitting around and his answer was that he had no quarrel with anyone there. 'That's why I've no intention of fighting', he said. 'If you haven't the guts to fight', said the King, 'and in my opinion this has nothing to do with your Faith, get below. Don't lie there under everybody's feet.

And the saga states briefly that Magnus took a psalter and sang as long as the battle lasted.

The saga narrator wishes to tell us something about Magnus' character through this incident. Defiance like this is unique in the sagas, but what is it directed against? Does the saga want to make Magnus Erlendsson into a Christian pacifist? That he sits down right in the shower of arrows seems to point to such a view. It is a deliberate action which requires courage. He must also have known that it was dangerous to provoke Magnus Bare-Legs. The saga writer may have chosen this way of telling us that Magnus Erlendsson's whole personality has changed. But the saga also suggests another motive when it lets the King remark drily that he does not think that Magnus' behaviour has anything to do with his faith. Such an act of defiance could also have been a political protest – Magnus does not want to fight for the Norse King who holds his father hostage. It is easy to read too much into an incident like this, which after all is mentioned only briefly in the saga, but it seems a likely possibility that Magnus uses his faith as a shield against the King. Magnus Bare-Legs sees through it, which may have been the intention. If so, we perceive a complex mind behind the simple saga narrative.

It is perhaps not surprising that Magnus fell out of grace with the King after this battle. Magnus must also have felt that he was playing with fire, for one night when they were anchored off the coast of Scotland he escaped from the King's ship. He made his way to the King of Scotland and stayed with him for a while. He travelled from one place to another, but he never went back to Orkney while Magnus Bare-Legs was King.

Magnus Bare-Legs fell in Ulster in 1103. His sons Sigurd, Olaf and Eystein became kings after him. The Orkney earls Paul and Erlend died in exile in Norway, and Erling Erlendsson fell in Ulster with Magnus Bare-Legs. It was the two cousins Hakon Paulsson and Magnus Erlendsson, therefore, who could claim the power. They went in turn to Norway and were well received by the kings, who probably considered it to be desirable to have the power shared by two earls – according to the well-known divide and conquer principle. Hakon at first refused to share the power with his cousin and went to such a length as to raise an army against him. But friends intervened and made him see reason. And the saga says that 'there was peace and goodwill in Orkney as long as their friendship lasted'.

Nevertheless, the breach between Hakon Paulsson and Magnus Erlendsson would probably have had to come sooner or later. The original difference between them in temper and character had been further deepened by the lives they had led – Hakon on military campaigns in the west with Magnus Bare-Legs, last of the Viking kings, and Magnus in Church circles and at the Scottish court of the young King Edgar, the son of King Malcolm Canmore and his pious second wife, Margaret. Perhaps there was friction between the cousins, perhaps life in the islands was more primitive than he could stand, for the longer Magnus saga states that

Magnus went to England and spent one year at the court of King Henry I. Hakon seized this opportunity to strengthen his position in the islands. Then one day Magnus was back, with five well-equipped warships, to demand his share of the power once again. After a period of shaky co-operation, the breach became unavoidable. At an open meeting of the Thing, it was decided that the earls had to reach a final solution. The two kinsmen were to meet on the small green island of Egilsay for peace and goodwill in Easter Week of 1117.

Hakon and Magnus were each going to bring two warships to Egilsay and come with the same number of men. Magnus came first, and when he saw Hakon approach with eight ships, he realized what Håkon had in mind. But he did not want to flee nor let his men fight for him:

I don't want to risk your lives saving my own, and if there's not to be peace between me and my kinsman, then things must go according to God's will.

Orkneyinga saga

He spent the night in the church at Egilsay.

Hakon's men found him the next morning down by the shore. What the two earls said to each other was repeated by Holdbodi, a farmer from the Sudreys, who was one of the two men who stayed with Magnus till the end. Magnus offered Hakon three choices:

First, that I should go on a pilgrimage to Rome, or even as far as the Holy Land, to visit sacred places. I'd take two ships with me to carry all we need, do penance for both our souls, and swear never to return to Orkney.

St Magnus Church, Egilsay, is probably not the original church in which St Magnus spent his last night but was built later in the twelfth century.

This offer was rejected at once. Nor was the second, exile in Scotland, accepted. To the third choice, for Magnus to let himself be mutilated and blinded, Hakon said, 'I'll accept these terms, and make no further conditions'. But the chieftains present demanded the death of one of them, for they would no longer have the two earls rule jointly. Then Hakon said, 'Better kill him then, I don't want an early death; I much prefer ruling over people and places.'

Hakon wanted his standard bearer to kill Magnus, but he refused. Hakon then ordered his cook, Lifolf, to kill Magnus, but he started to cry. Magnus comforted him. After having prayed and received the sacrament, Magnus said to Lifolf:

Stand in front of me and strike me hard on the head, it's not fitting for a chieftain to be beheaded like a thief. Take heart, poor fellow, I've prayed that God grant you his mercy.

And the saga goes on to say that then 'he crossed himself and stooped to receive the blow'.

At first Hakon would not allow Magnus' body to be taken to church. But Thora, Earl Magnus' mother, had prepared a feast for peace and goodwill at her home in Paplay after the meeting of the earls. Instead Hakon came alone. The Orkney writer George Mackay Brown describes this poignantly in his story 'The Feast at Paplay'. Thora herself waited on her son's executioner. And there is much pathos in her plea to Hakon:

I was expecting the two of you, but now only you have come. Will you do something to please me in the eyes of God and men? Be a son to me and I shall be a mother to you. I'm sorely in need of your mercy, so let me have my son taken to church. Hear my prayers now, just as you yourself hope to be heard by God on the Day of Judgment.

Hakon was moved by Thora's plea and agreed to let Magnus be buried in consecrated ground. Magnus was buried at Christ Church – the church Thorfinn had built.

It can be said about Magnus that in death he was great. His death as described in the saga was simple and dignified and easily interpreted as the death of a true martyr. It also showed the courage demanded by Viking tradition. Even before the end of the year people started to go on a pilgrimage to his grave, and the sick and ailing would go home cured.

Christ Church, where Magnus was buried, was at that time the seat of the Bishop of Orkney. For a long time Bishop William seemed to doubt the tales of miracles at the grave; nor was anything else politically possible. Hakon ruled Orkney alone, and he ruled well and was much liked. When he died in 1123, there was peace and prosperity in the islands.

Underlying the simple and dramatic saga story is a power struggle between Church and state, and it is the Anglo-Scottish and the Norse elements which clash. We saw that Hakon and Magnus had different political backgrounds: Magnus moved in English and Scottish court circles,

Statue of St Magnus, from the altar of Luröy Church, Nordland, Norway. Devotion to St Magnus spread quickly after his death throughout the Norse areas. This little church lies close to the Arctic circle. (Photo: University of Bergen)

whereas Hakon followed the Norse King. Being a grandson on his mother's side of King Magnus the Good of Norway, it probably seemed quite natural for Hakon to identify himself with Norse royal power. The Anglo-Scottish and the Norse Churches were also struggling to gain a foothold in the islands. For a long time the Bishop of Orkney was chosen from York in England. But Hakon got William, who was the candidate preferred by the Norse Church, appointed Bishop of Orkney. The Pope would not accept William and twice wrote sharply to Norway and demanded that the English bishop candidate should be installed instead.

It was not in the interest of the Norse Church to have a saint in Orkney who indirectly enhanced the status of the Anglo-Scottish Church. Perhaps William, who knew Magnus, was not struck by his saintliness? Nor was it possible for Earl Hakon or his son to accept canonization of Magnus – for political as well as personal reasons. As it transpired, it was to be the young Rognvald Kali Kolsson from Agder who adroitly used this conflict to his own advantage.

Magnus' body was tried in consecrated fire in 1135. The reverence for Magnus was now accepted and spread quickly throughout the Norse areas. One of the stained glass windows in the Nidaros Cathedral at Trondheim represents St Magnus together with St Olaf, St Sunniva and St Hallvard. Close to the Arctic circle, in the little church at Luröy, Nordland, there was a statue of St Magnus on the altar. He became the patron saint of Orkney. His life story was written by Master Robert 'when twenty winters had passed from his martyrdom'.

The Reformation meant the end of reverence for the saints, but today interest in St Magnus has been reawakened. It is perhaps George Mackay Brown who more than anyone else has inspired this interest. Whereas Sigrid Undset in her essay on St Magnus gives a one-sided and simplified portrait of a saint, Brown, who like her has converted to Catholicism, tries to see him in a wider perspective. In his novel *Magnus* he contrasts Hakon and Magnus in a conflict where Magnus represents the spiritual dimension and Hakon the man of decisive action. It is an unhappy combination which leads to strife and discord in Orkney and only serves the Norse King who does not want a strong earl. Magnus' dramatic death in Egilsay is a ritual sacrifice, but also a catharsis in a dramatic conflict – it is a purification, a cleansing which makes peace possible. George Mackay Brown's Magnus character is perhaps no more historically correct than Sigrid Undset's saint is, but it is more interesting. In 'The Feast at Paplay', Brown in a few lines draws a portrait of Ingerth, Magnus' untouched wife, as a silent bitter shadow.

From mediaeval times a beautiful polyphonic hymn to St Magnus has been preserved. The Orkney-based composer Peter Maxwell Davies has used this mediaeval hymn in one of his compositions. He has also composed an opera *The Martyrdom of St Magnus* where the libretto is built on Brown's novel *Magnus*. In June every year there is a St Magnus Festival in Orkney. The opera about St Magnus was composed for the first of these.

The Martyrdom of St Magnus. *This opera by Peter Maxwell Davies opened the first St Magnus Festival in 1977 and was performed in the saint's own cathedral in Kirkwall.*

7. The time of greatness

I want you to make a vow to him, that should he grant you your family inheritance and his own legacy, and should you come to power, then you'll build a stone minster at Kirkwall more magnificent than any in Orkney, that you'll have it dedicated to your uncle the holy Earl Magnus and provide it with all the funds it will need to flourish.

Orkneyinga saga

The man who says this is Kol Kalason from Bringsverd in Agder, an important man in southern Norway. He married Gunnhild Erlend's daughter, the sister of Magnus Erlendsson, the saint. At a meeting at Tunsberg in 1129, King Sigurd Magnusson the Pilgrim – as a boy of eight he was given charge of Orkney by his father Magnus Bare-Legs – gave their young son Kali half of Orkney, the part his kinsman St Magnus had had. The King 'gave Kali the name Rognvald because Kali's mother Gunnhild claimed Earl Rognvald Brusason to have been the most able of all the Earls of Orkney, and people saw this as a sign of good luck'.

Political flair and psychological insight were necessary to be able to make use of the growing Magnus cult and the popularity of the first Earl Rognvald to bring forward the young Kali as an heir to the earldom. Earl Hakon's son Paul ruled Orkney alone. He was calm and steady and a good earl. He was not willing to give away any part of the earldom:

I understand this claim, and that there's a lot of craftiness gone into the making of it. They've got the help of the Kings of Norway to take the earldom from me ... I'll defend Orkney with the aid of my kinsmen and friends for as long as God lets me live.

The story of Kali Kolsson's way to power is a colourful part of Orkneyinga saga. The chieftain Svein Asleifarson of Gairsay outwitted Earl Paul, and in 1136 the way was open for Kali to become Earl Rognvald of all of Orkney.

The saga describes Earl Rognvald as being of average height, well-proportioned and strong-limbed, and an examination of his skeletal remains, which were found in the St Magnus Cathedral, corroborates the saga in this. He must have been between 40 and 50 years old when he died in 1158. The saga writer endows him with the versatility and courteous manners of a knight as well as with the Viking's love of adventure. He is described as the most popular of the Orkney earls, along with his namesake

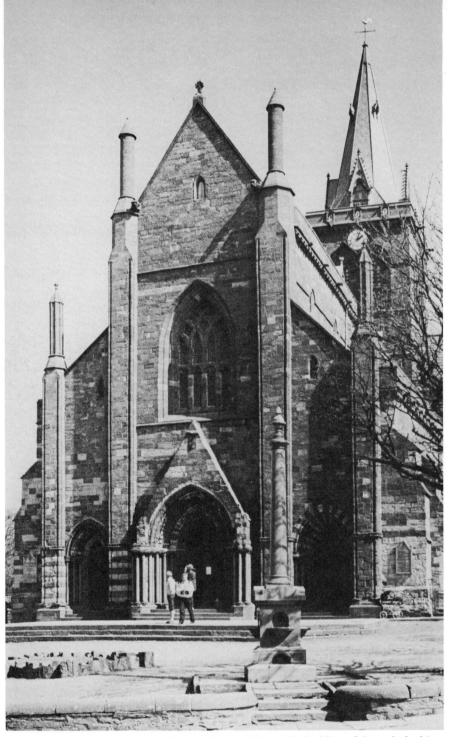

St Magnus Cathedral, Kirkwall. Earl Rognvald began the building of the cathedral in the twelfth century.

Rognvald Brusason. But he did not hide his light under a bushel:

> At nine skills I challenge –
> a champion at chess:
> runes I rarely spoil,
> I read books and write:
> I'm skilled at skiing
> and shooting and sculling
> and more! – I've mastered
> music and verse.

There is a lightheartedness and joy of life in the story of Rognvald which we do not usually find in the Orkneyinga saga.

Rognvald was a man of his word, for he at once began building a stone minster at Kirkwall. His father, Kol, supervised the work. In order to obtain the necessary means to build the church, Rognvald let the farmers buy the *oðal* – absolute property right – to their farms for ever. This was agreed upon at an assembly meeting. On the whole it seems that the assembly – the Thing – gained in importance in the twelfth century, and this may have been due to Rognvald's influence.

In 1150, Rognvald went on a visit to King Ingi Haraldsson in Bergen. It was partly a political visit and partly because Rognvald wanted to meet the King whose father, Harald Gilli, was one of his closest friends in younger days. On this trip he brought along the young Harald Maddadarson, the nephew of Earl Paul Hakonarson and the heir to his part of the earldom.

Crusades were in fashion, and during his visit to Bergen, Rognvald was inspired by the thought of the Holy War. Together with many of the leading Norwegian chieftains he set out from Orkney in 1152. Among those who were with him was Erling Wry-Neck, one of the men closest to King Ingi.

It was when the crusaders were storming a dromond – a swift ship of war – in the Mediterranean that Erling got the wound in his neck which made him carry his head to one side for the rest of his life, and thus earned him the nickname Wry-Neck. The Orkneyinga saga gives a detailed description of the crusade which does not seem to have been essentially different from the earlier Viking expeditions. Earl Rognvald was a good poet who gave a lively description of everything they saw and did on the way.

Maybe it was unwise of Rognvald to stay away from the earldom so long. The last five years of his life were spent unravelling the tangles which had been made while he was away on the crusade. In 1158 he was killed in Caithness. The saga speaks very highly of him:

Earl Rognvald was deeply mourned, for he had been much loved in the isles and in many other places too. He had been a good friend to a great many people, lavish with money, moderate, loyal to his friends, a many-sided man and a fine poet.

But it may have been his father's advice and strength which helped him to power. The saga writer does not count Rognvald among the three most powerful earls; the ones he chooses are Sigurd Eysteinsson, Thorfinn Sigurdarson and Harald Maddadarson.

When an archdiocese was established at Trondheim in 1153, Orkney became one of the ten bishoprics of this Church province. Kirkwall became the bishop's seat some time earlier, and Bishop William probably moved there from Egilsay. It is possible that he began the building of the Bishop's Palace. William was succeeded in office by Bjarni Kolbeinsson, the son of the chieftain Kolbein Hruga in Wyre. Probably it was Bishop Bjarni who founded the Church school at Kirkwall – the present Kirkwall Grammar School – which is one of the oldest schools in Scotland.

Earl Rognvald was canonized in 1192 and became enshrined in the cathedral. It had taken many years. Even though legends have arisen around Rognvald, he does not seem to have been worshipped much outside Orkney. Whereas the worshipping of Magnus came as an irresistible force from the people, almost against the wishes of the Church, it seems as if it is the Church authorities themselves who want to reward the cathedral builder and crusader Rognvald Kolsson by making him a saint.

Rognvald Kolsson was the last of the really Norse earls. It is true that his successor Harald Maddadarson was fostered by Rognvald from the age of five, but both by family and through marriage he was more Scottish than Norse. The saga considers him one of the three great earls, but gives no reason for saying so. Earl Harald was in a position of dependence on the King of Norway for Orkney and Shetland and to the Scottish King who considered Caithness part of Scotland. He fell out with both of them.

Norway was being torn to pieces by inner strife over royal power, and Earl Harald let himself be drawn into this conflict. The continuous war waged by King Sverre Sigurdsson was costly, and he probably claimed taxes from the islands. Nominally Orkney was a tributary country under Norway, but earlier this right in principle to levy taxes had never been strictly enforced.

Many of the leading chieftains in the islands gathered a strong army and went against King Sverre. Erling Wry-Neck was a well-known name to them after he had accompanied Earl Rognvald on the crusade. Erling was killed in battle against Sverre. The men of Orkney and Shetland chose Erling Wry-Neck's grandson Sigurd Magnusson as King. They seized Viken – the area around the Oslofjord – seemingly without difficulty, and had Sigurd proclaimed King at the assembly of Haugar, near Tunsberg. The *Eyjaskeggjar* – Island Beardies – or *Gullbeinar* – Golden Legs – as they were called, held the country as far north as Stad, and spent the winter of 1194 in Bergen.

The Island Beardies were one of the most serious challenges Sverre faced in his time as King, until he came on them unexpectedly and triumphed over them in a naval battle at Florevåg outside Bergen, on 3 April 1194, The islanders were strong both in numbers and daring – there seem to have been some 2,000 men fighting on either side – but they lost in the end to Sverre's military skill. The leaders of the Island Beardies were killed in the battle, and their young pretender while trying to swim ashore. One of Erling Wry-Neck's sons survived the battle and during his flight he stopped long enough to make a long and carefully dated runic inscription on the church door at Vinje in Telemark, a bitter indictment against Sverre killing his kinsmen.

King Sverre held Earl Harald Maddadarson responsible for the uprising, but gave him peace on hard conditions: the estates of those taking part in the uprising would fall to the crown of Norway unless their kinsmen redeemed them within three years; Shetland was to be governed direct from Norway and no longer be a part of the earldom (the two island groups were not reunited until 1379), and the King claimed half of all tax and tribute levied in Orkney and was also going to have his own sysselman, or district royal governor, there to look after his interests.

The last one of these terms must have seemed especially humiliating, for the first thing Earl Harald did when word came in 1202 that Sverre was dead, was to kill the sysselman Arni Lörja. At the same time he had to buy himself a costly peace from the King of Scots because he had blinded and cut off the tongue of the Bishop of Caithness.

Harald Maddadarson was succeeded by his two sons, David and Jon. That was the last time the earldom was shared between two earls. David died in 1214. Like his father, Jon also fell out with the King of Scots because of his attitude to the Church.

In 1224, Earl Jon was called to Bergen to see King Hakon Hakonsson. It is possible that the King wanted to make sure of Jon's support in his conflict with Skuli Bardason. It is the conflict described in Henrik Ibsen's *The Pretenders*, and Ibsen makes a letter to Earl Jon in Orkney the pivot of the play. Jon had to let his only son Harald remain in Bergen as a hostage. Later the boy drowned on his way back to Orkney. Jon himself died without honour, and ironically it was the Norwegian sysselman who was behind the assault on him.

The death of Earl Jon was a turning point in the history of the earldom. With him the line of Norse earls died out after having ruled in Orkney continuously since the earldom was established.

Both Harald and Jon felt close to Scotland, but they lived in the islands. They accepted Norwegian sovereignty and placed the earldom of Orkney before their Scottish feu in Caithness. But geography is destiny. The feudal Scotland grew constantly stronger, and a Norway at war with herself only now and then managed a show of strength. The balance of both trade and political power in Norway shifted from Bergen to Oslo during the thirteenth century. And the steady traffic across the North Sea diminished accordingly – it was no longer so natural for Norwegians to go west over sea.

The Orkneyinga saga ends with the death of Earl Harald in 1206, and the later sources do not focus in the same way on the earldom. Its time of greatness was over. The islands disappeared out of history – as the Orkney writer Eric Linklater puts it – 'as a ship going down below the horizon'.

8.   Into darkness

The time after the death of Earl Jon has been called The Dark Period, because for some 150 years the historical records are few and sparse, and we glimpse only now and then what was happening in the islands. Coming to this time from the twelfth century is 'like the plunge of a train into a tunnel' says the Orkney historian J. Storer Clouston.

Nevertheless, it is particularly important to understand this period, because it is then that the power shifts from the Norsemen to the Scots. The earls' difficult double position, owing allegiance to the monarchs of two countries, had begun with Harald Maddadarson and lasted till the islands were pledged.

After the killing of Earl Jon in 1231, many of the leading Orkney chieftains were summoned to a hearing in Bergen. This is related in the saga of Hakon Hakonsson:

That same autumn the Orkneymen fared west and all went in one ship, the best men of the isles. That ship was lost and all who were in her. And many men have had to atone for this afterwards.

The saga writer seems to suggest that perhaps all hope of Norse succession was killed in this shipwreck.

It is not known how the earldom of Orkney came to be transferred to the Scottish noble family of Angus. Six earls of Angus follow each other up through the thirteenth century, and they are all blurred, shadowy persons. Still it is evident that they considered their status as vassals of the Scottish King in Caithness more important than their northern earldom.

During the thirteenth century, Scotland grew so strong that King Alexander II built fortifications around the coast, and he also began to covet the Norse islands around the coast. This pressure to the west and the north was kept up by later kings. Around 1240, Alexander sent a note to King Hakon Hakonsson and asked Norway to cede to him the Sudreys (the Hebrides) and the Isle of Man, but this was rejected by Hakon. Alexander III went on as his father had begun, and in 1261 sent Scottish emissaries to Hakon in Bergen to negotiate a purchase of the islands. When this did not succeed, Alexander permitted a brutal raid on the Isle of Skye.

'When this news reached King Hakon, he became very sad,' the saga narrates. King Hakon called out *the leidang* – the fleet of conscripted warships – 'as much as he thought the country could stand. He summoned all of this armed fleet to meet him early in the summer in Bergen'. The leidang fleet sailed from Herdlevær outside Bergen on 5 July 1263, and it was probably the largest war fleet ever assembled in Norway, comprising around 150 ships and 15,000 men. Earl Magnus of Orkney sailed with the fleet from Bergen to Orkney, but left it there. His divided loyalty to the two kings placed him in an impossible situation.

Hakon recruited both crews and pilots in Orkney and did not sail from there until 10 August. The old Vikings would have known better than to delay so long into the autumn. As it turned out the weather became his main opponent, as the fleet ran into terrible storms. The final confrontation between Scots and Norsemen at Largs in Argyllshire, 3 October 1263, was more like a skirmish than a battle, but it was decisive. The fight was lost for Hakon, and he turned back, to die in Kirkwall.

Hakon Hakonsson was one of Norway's greatest kings, but he was probably more of a politician than an army commander and strategist. Through negotiations he had in 1261–62 brought Greenland and Iceland under the Norwegian crown, in return for services, it is true, that later would prove to be very difficult for Norway to give.

This western campaign revealed the weakness of the Norse empire: it was scattered over a large sea area. It was built on and depended on Norway's strength, her ships, but communication between the various areas was possible only in the summer months. This did not matter at all in the Faeroes, Greenland and Iceland where no external enemy threatened, but the islands around the Scottish coast were torn between two kingdoms, and the North Sea offered no advantage to Norway.

King Magnus IV Hakonsson was a peace-loving king and a pragmatic politician. In the Treaty of Perth in 1266 he ceded the Norwegian islands south and west of 'the great ocean' to Scotland. In return the Scots were to make a one time payment of 4,000 mark sterling and promise to pay 100 mark sterling annually to Norway. The payment was to take place 'for all time on the eighth day after Midsummer Day in Orkney, the king of Norway's land, in St Magnus' Church . . .'

For Magnus, it was essential to secure the constitutional status of Orkney and Shetland, as there was every indication that the Scottish King considered the Sudreys and Man as only the first step in his policy of expansion. It is, therefore, expressly stated in the treaty that Orkney and Shetland belonged under Norwegian sovereignty.

Earl Magnus and the King soon reconciled their differences and ten years later, in 1276, the earl's son, Magnus Magnusson, was installed as the new earl of Orkney at a meeting in Tunsberg.

King Magnus continued the law reform work which had been begun by his father, and in 1276 his great *Landslov* – national law – was completed. The purpose of this law was to have *one* common law for all of Norway and the Norse areas. It was recognized as law in the Faeroes, Shetland, Orkney and probably Greenland, whereas Iceland wrote its own book of laws. Since Orkney to a great extent was self-governed, the landslov was probably adjusted to local conditions, but if so, it is not known how this was done.

The legal relationship of the Orkney earl to Norwegian royal power was established in an agreement in 1267. And from 1308 his position was enhanced even more, because in an attempt to curtail the power of the nobility in Norway, the rank of earl became expressly restricted to the earl of Orkney and the king's own sons.

In 1280 King Magnus died and twelve-year-old Eirik Magnusson became King. The annual payment – 'the annuale of Norwaye' – had been paid only a few times. A marriage contract was therefore negotiated for the 19-year-old princess Margaret of Scotland and the child-king Eirik Magnusson. A continuous power struggle over Orkney and Shetland was probably an underlying reason for this marriage – the Norwegians wanted to safeguard their right of ownership, and the Scots wanted to gain a foothold in the islands.

The marriage contract, which was signed in Roxburgh, must surely be the strangest of its kind. If Eirik, on becoming fourteen years old, did not consummate the marriage 'the whole land of Orkney, with all rights due to Norway's king' was to be ceded to Scotland. If, on the other hand, it was Margaret who was unwilling to consummate the marriage, the King of Scotland was to 'cede to king Eirik the whole island of Man with all royal rights, and the king of Norway's letter ceding this island is to be rendered null and void'. The Scottish original of this contract has been kept in the Tower of London since the seventeenth century. It is signed by Peter, Bishop of Orkney, who was present and accepted it.

Margaret, who saw to it that her young husband was taught court manners, won all hearts at the court in Bergen. And there was no need to consider further the terms of the marriage contract, for by the time Eirik was fifteen years old he was the father of a daughter, Margrete. He had also become a widower, for Margaret died in childbirth, and she was much grieved in Norway. Eirik later married Isabella Bruce, a sister of the Scottish King Robert the Bruce.

Little Margrete became Queen of Scotland when she was three years old, for Alexander III died childless in 1286. The Scots demanded that she must come to Scotland before 1 November 1290. They negotiated a marriage contract between Margrete and the future Edward II of England. But the negotiations were just as much about a union between England and Scotland, and Margrete and her father, King Eirik, were only pawns in this power game. In the Treaty of Brigham of 18 July 1290 it is said that 'the rights, laws, liberties and customs of the kingdom of Scotland' were to be 'wholly and inviolably preserved for all time', but it is difficult to see how this could have been possible.

According to the agreement, Margrete and her companions were to meet the Scottish and English ambassadors in Kirkwall, on Norwegian territory.

However, the voyage had been delayed too long and the autumn season was so far advanced that Margrete became ill during a terrible crossing and died in the arms of Bishop Narfi of Bergen – according to popular tradition at St Margaret's Hope in South Ronaldsay. One source gives the day of her death as 16 November 1290, but it was probably before that. All ambitious political plans had to be dropped.

Margrete's fate fired the popular imagination. King Eirik met a lot of criticism for sending his little daughter off into the unknown. This is from an old ballad:

> Gud fyrilati Eiriki kongi,
> hvat hann mundi gera:
> sendi sitt barn i ókunn lond,
> moykongur at vera.

> God forgive king Eirik,
> for what he did:
> sending his child to unknown land,
> to become queen.

Many people would not accept that Margrete was dead, and a woman who later claimed to be Margrete was believed by the common people of Bergen. She said that the Lady Ingebjörg Erlingsdatter, who accompanied Margrete on the voyage, had been bribed by Scots who wanted the princess out of the way. But 'the false Margrete' had her claim rejected and was burned at the stake at Nordnes in Bergen.

In 1320 we find Earl Magnus Jonsson among those who signed the Declaration of Arbroath, a document affirming the independence of Scotland from England. Magnus was the last of the Angus earls. Through intermarriage the earldom passed to Malise of Stratherne, an even more obscure family.

So little is known about this period that it is not even possible to tell whether two earls called Malise followed each other or whether it is one and the same person all the time. Most probably father and son had the same name. Succeeding the second Malise was his son-in-law Erngisl Sunesson, a Swedish nobleman. But he fell out with the Norwegian King Hakon VI Magnusson because he had become involved in a Swedish intrigue against the King. He was therefore stripped of his title, and it does not seem to have have been more than a title to him, since there is nothing to indicate that he ever set foot in Orkney.

For some years Orkney was without an earl, but in 1379 Henry Sinclair, the son of Malise's daughter, was appointed by King Hakon. He also got Shetland back as part of the earldom, after the two island groups had been separated since 1195. King Hakon must evidently have thought highly of Henry's qualities as a future earl and faithful vassal to be willing to risk this. The Sinclair, or St Clair, family came originally from Normandy, but their roots in Scotland went back to the eleventh century.

Henry Sinclair broke the series of shadowy earls. He seems to have tried actively to fulfil the strict conditions King Hakon made for him. But Hakon died in 1380 and, as time passed, Henry came to rule almost like a king himself, and perhaps went too far. One of the conditions was that he should not fortify the islands unless the King agreed to it. Nevertheless he built a strong castle in Kirkwall, and it is not known whether this was done with the King's consent.

Henry Sinclair also won renown as an adventurer and explorer. He is supposed to have conquered the Faeroe Islands in 1380; since the Faeroes were Norwegian territory, he would in that case have won them from his feudal overlord, the Norwegian king. According to an Italian account from 1558 he is also supposed to have made a trip to Iceland and have rediscovered Greenland together with the Venetian knights Nicolo and Antonio Zeno, but this tale has turned out to be a fabrication.

Henry Sinclair's successor bore the same name, but seems to have spent little time in the islands. Just before he died in 1420 he appointed his brother-in-law, David Menzies, as his representative in the islands. The Bishop of Orkney, a Scotsman called Thomas Tulloch, and Menzies were both appointed administrators by King Erik, while the young Earl William Sinclair was a minor.

Menzies especially must have been hated for his misrule, for as early as 1424 the people of Orkney sent a long list of complaints to King Erik, where Menzies is accused, among other things, of having brought in a lot of foreigners who 'were a veritable pest to the people and did much harm and great injury in the country'. He took the seal of the country from the Lawman and used it as he pleased, and when a 'goodman of the country called Criste Ælingeklæt said that then he could write under that whatever he pleased', then this goodman was fined. A later descendant of this Ælingeklæt is the well-known Orkney writer Eric Linklater.

Earl William was installed as earl in 1434, and gradually he became drawn into the sphere of interest of the King of Scotland, and came to play a considerable role at the Stuart court. He became Chancellor of Scotland in 1454, and the year after he was also appointed Earl of Caithness. He must have known and understood what the goal of all Scottish policy was in the north and have tacitly accepted it.

Once more, a Princess Margrete played a part in the history of Orkney. King Christian I of Denmark-Norway and King James II of Scotland negotiated a marriage for their minor children. The Scots put forward hard claims: Scotland was forever to be free of the annual payment for the Sudreys and Man. Since it had hardly ever been paid, the payment with interest amounted to all of 343,000 marks, and this debt was to be cancelled. In addition, Margrete was to have Orkney and Shetland as a dowry, and after her death the islands were to pass to her children.

But James II died in 1460 when his son was only nine years old, and the matter was not further pursued for some years. The marriage contract was

The marriage contract between Margrete, daughter of Christian I of Denmark-Norway, and James III of Scotland, signed in 1468. (Photo: Tage Ludvigsen, Rigsarkivet, Copenhagen)

then signed on 8 September 1468, when all financial claims on Scotland were given up. Margrete was to get a dowry of 60,000 florins of the Rhine. Of this sum 10,000 was to be paid in cash, and for the balance Christian pledged the royal Norwegian estates in Orkney. He retained full redemptory rights, without a time limit.

In this matter the Scottish motives are clear; the marriage contract was for them a means of realizing an old dream of bringing the islands around the coast under Scottish rule – a wish which is not difficult to understand. But why should Norway agree to this arrangement, without gaining anything? The answer to this is not hard to find either – everything indicates that the Norwegian *riksråd* (state council) was not consulted.

But why did Christian I accept these terms? There is no clear answer to that, but perhaps he wanted a political alliance in the west so that he could concentrate undisturbed on securing the union with Sweden. Besides, he naturally wanted a good marriage for his daughter, and it seems that the bridegroom always profited in royal matches. Probably the pledging was forced on him because he could not raise the money in any other way.

For dynastic reasons, Norway and Denmark had drifted into a union which was to last till 1814. Norway recovered very slowly from the Black Death which in 1350 had wiped out half of a population believed to have been 300,000. The majority of priests and bishops died too; therefore it is not strange that from this time onwards Orkney filled up with Scottish clerics. Norway had been weakened in so many ways, both politically and economically, and from 1450, when Christian I was crowned as King of Norway in the cathedral at Trondheim, Norway's fate as part of Denmark was sealed.

Christian I was a disaster for Norway. He was constantly short of money, and was unable to pay the 10,000 florins of the Rhine in cash. At the last moment he therefore pledged Shetland as well, as an unexpected bonus for Scotland. Thus he simply gave away a large part of Norwegian territory. It is true that the pledging of land was not unusual at that time, and on his behalf it must be said that he probably did not consider the arrangement as final.

The original contract of 28 May 1469 for the pledging of Shetland was found in the British Museum in 1968 by Dr Barbara Crawford of the University of St Andrews, after it had been missing for 200 years. It is of the same tenor as the contract for Orkney; only the King of Norway's estates are pledged – the question of sovereignty is not mentioned. Therefore the right of redemption belongs to the Norwegian crown: '... per nos heredes nostros vel successores, Norwegie reges – through our heirs and successors, the kings of Norway'.

In February 1471 Scotland annexed both island groups, after having first forced Earl William Sinclair to exchange his earldom estates for landed property in Scotland. We do not know whether Christian protested against this unilateral transaction, but he did not at any rate approve of it. All later Danish-Norwegian kings were bound by their coronation charter to redeem the islands, and some inept attempts were made, most probably to appease the Norwegian state council, but as there was no force behind the words, all attempts proved futile. The last time the question of the islands was discussed was during the peace negotiations at Breda in 1667, after a war between England on the one side and the Netherlands, France and Denmark-Norway on the other. Denmark-Norway then made a final attempt to get Orkney and Shetland back.

When Norway left the union with Denmark in 1814, Denmark, under the terms of the Treaty of Kiel, kept the originally Norwegian dominions of the Faeroe Islands, Iceland and Greenland, but Orkney and Shetland were not mentioned. *De jure* the islands must therefore still be considered as Norwegian, but *de facto* they are part of Britain, because common law here wins over the written law.

For a long time the question of sovereignty was unknown and forgotten, and it caused both surprise and amusement in the House of Commons when the question was raised by a Scottish member in 1907. But even today, says the French historian Delavaud, the pledging throws 'une ombre de souveraineté norvégienne sur deux archipels de la Grande-Bretagne – a shadow of Norwegian sovereignty over two island groups in Great Britain'.

9. *Orkney in Scotland*

When by an Act of the Scottish Parliament the Earldom of Orkney and Lordship of Shetland were annexed to the Scottish Crown in 1471, it was expressly stipulated that the islands were 'to be given away in time to cum to na persain or persains excep alenarily to ane of ye Kingis sonis of lauchful bed'. King Christian himself had stipulated that native laws and customs should be maintained. Twice, first in 1503 and again in 1567, the Scottish Parliament clearly recognized their obligation to maintain Norse law. But reality proved to be otherwise. There were simply too many factors working against a status quo.

For King James to take over from Earl Henry Sinclair the lands and privileges of the Orkney earls and make them Crown property was a stroke of genius which ensured that the islands could in actual fact never be redeemed. From then on the Scottish monarchs treated the *skatt*, the old Norse tax, as their own private income to do with as they liked. In addition the islands were made liable to Scottish taxation. Many of the judges and ministers knew nothing and cared less about odal law, as Norse law was called in Orkney.

It is likely that the king also had a hand in transferring the Bishopric of Orkney in 1472 from the Norwegian Church province to the new Archbishopric of St Andrews. In that way also the clerical ties between Orkney and Norway were severed. It seems to have come as a complete surprise to the Archbishop at Trondheim. Indeed, it seems to have been almost unknown to the Pope himself, for in 1520 we find Pope Leo X instructing Bishop Donald of Orkney to send his gift for the building of St Peter's Church in Rome to the Archbishop at Trondheim, who would then send it on to Rome. The Archbishop had the question of the Bishopric of Orkney included in the agenda of the last meeting of the Norwegian State Council ever held, at Bud in Romsdal in 1533.

Norway got her Lutheran Reformation as early as 1536, whereas the Calvinistic Reformation of Scotland did not come until 1560. King James V recommended Robert Reid, the last Catholic Bishop of Orkney, to the Roman Church in a very interesting letter where he deplored that the people in Orkney, which lies 'almost under the Pole', are very backward in religious matters 'owing to their close relationship to Norway, Denmark and Germany' – all reformed countries.

The King did not take on the earl's duties himself, nor did he give the earldom to his lawful son, as stipulated by the Scottish Parliament. In fact none of the kings did. Instead the islands were given to tacksmen who paid rent to the King. The first two tacksmen were both Bishops of Orkney. In 1489 the tack was given to Lord Henry Sinclair, Earl William's grandson, who seemed to rule Orkney wisely, until he fell in the Battle of Flodden in 1513, along with King James IV. Affairs were left in the hands of the Sinclair family, and for some time Orkney was governed much as it had been. But the islands became flooded with adventurers and carpet baggers who had come for the pickings.

The numerous Sinclair family fell out among themselves. William Sinclair was helped by the Earl of Caithness who, with some 500 men, landed in Orphir intending to march on Kirkwall. But James and Edward Sinclair of Warsetter, who had popular support in the islands, met them with a local army at Summerdale, in the moors of Stenness, past the Loch of Kirbister.

The Battle of Summerdale is enveloped in myth and legend – both a witch and St Magnus are involved. Perhaps that is why the Orkneymen won such a resounding victory – the earl and a large number of Caithnessmen were killed. According to legend only one Orkneyman fell, and his own mother killed him by mistake. He returned from the battle in the uniform of a fallen Caithnessman. His mother believed he was an enemy soldier and hit him on the head with one of his own stockings filled with stones. This was the last battle known to have been fought in Orkney.

There seems to have been some fear in Scotland that, unless handled with care, the Orcadians might turn to Denmark for support, for James Sinclair was rewarded instead of punished for his part in what had indirectly been a revolt against the King's authority. But in 1540 King James V made a state visit to Orkney, staying in the Bishop's Palace. He probably wanted to see for himself how things stood, and as he came with 12 ships he perhaps wanted to make a show of strength as well.

For at least a century after the pledging, relations between Orkney and Bergen seem to have gone on much as before. Ships from Orkney could come and go in Bergen without paying customs until the end of the sixteenth century; and for a long time there was a steady immigration of islanders to Bergen. Thus an Orcadian called Little Jon was one of the first mayors of Bergen, around the time of the Reformation in 1536. In a contemporary description of Norway he was described as 'god-fearing, pious and just'. Quite a few of the immigrants were coopers and weavers. As they did not use family names, only patronymics, it is impossible to trace their descendants. An exception is Axel Mowat, who came from an Orkney branch of a Scottish noble family. He married Else Rustung, whose sister Anna insisted that she was married to Bothwell, the third husband of Mary Queen of Scots. It was a son-in-law of Axel Mowat who founded Norway's only barony, Rosendal in Hardanger.

Bishop's Palace, Kirkwall. King James V stayed here during his state visit to Orkney in 1540.

But the islanders who settled in Bergen were not all paragons of virtue. In a complaint from 1584 it is stated that 'citizenship should not be given to every runaway Scot, Dutchman, Englishman, Orcadian or Færoese without proof of identity', because they 'in truth are of no use to this country, but even of the greatest harm'.

When James V of Scotland died in 1542, his French wife ruled as a regent while their daughter Mary was a minor. She installed a Frenchman, Bonot, as her tacksman in Orkney. By this time the Church had become an all-powerful landowner in Scotland, with annual revenues ten times those of the Crown. This was not so strange considering that land was the accepted fine for offences against the Church. Church lands were feued to laymen who also were given abbeys as benefices.

France had helped the Scots against the English but were demanding their pound of flesh in return, so that when Mary, Queen of Scots, married the Dauphin in 1558, anti-French feeling ran high. It combined with resentment against the Catholic Church to fire a national revolt. Despite the religious fervour of John Knox, who was also a social reformer, the main issues of the Scottish Reformation were really political and military. By the Treaty of Edinburgh of 1560 France and England agreed to withdraw their troops.

In Orkney the Reformation came to be more a question of land than anything else. As there existed at that time a very real language barrier between the Orkney people and the Scottish ministers, the Reformation will hardly have had much spiritual meaning. On the other hand, it probably helped speed up the process of cultural and linguistic change, as happened in Norway.

The transition to the Reformed Church was quiet – indeed the last Catholic bishop, Adam Bothwell, also became the first Protestant one. As he stood in apostolic succession from Catholic to Protestant, in 1568 he crowned Queen Mary's infant son James VI.

Bishop Bothwell's cousin was James Hepburn, Earl of Bothwell, who became Queen Mary's third husband. She made him Duke of Orkney, a new title. When the Scottish aristocracy forced her to give him up, he fled to Orkney to seek refuge there, but he was turned away by Robert Stewart, who was then Sheriff of Orkney. Instead Bothwell ended up in Bergen where he had to face the fury of his first wife, Anna Rustung, who had him thrown in jail. He ended his days as a prisoner at Dragsholm Castle in Denmark, hoping till the end that his title of Duke of Orkney would give him his freedom back. He promised King Fredrik II of Denmark-Norway that he would transfer the islands to him, and this is the reason why the King refused to give him up to the Scots, in spite of their insistence.

Robert Stewart was one of the numerous illegitimate sons of King James V. His half-sister, Queen Mary, in 1564 granted him the Sheriffship of Orkney and Shetland together with all the Crown rights and estates there. As a young boy he had been given the right to the revenues from the Abbey of Holyrood by his father, and this he now exchanged with Bishop Bothwell for the bishopric land in Orkney. Thus he became more powerful than the ancient earls ever were. In 1581 he was made Earl of Orkney.

In 1567, perhaps as a safeguard against Lord Robert, the Scottish Parliament decided that Orkney and Shetland 'aught to be subject their awne lawis'. This did not work out to the advantage of the islands, as the local courts and all forms of legal procedure were simply used by those in power for their own private ends. By an Act of the 'Lordis of Secret Council' of 1611, all Norse laws in use in Orkney were therefore abolished, and all magistrates then had to use 'only the proper laws of this kingdom'. Still a modified home rule did seem to exist for some time.

Lord Robert, and later his son Patrick, called Black Pate, who succeeded him as earl in 1592, have been notorious in the islands to this day. They have been accused of every crime in the book, from tampering with the old Norse weights and measures – to make the farmers pay more in rent and skatt – to high treason. Robert Stewart's crimes were listed in 'The Complaints of the Inhabitants of Orkney and Zetland in the Year 1575'. Charges were also brought against him for conspiring with the Danish King.

It is difficult today to separate fact from fiction as, like the Vikings before them, the Stewart earls had their history written by their worst enemies. Of course, they had the possibility to rule as petty kings, and probably they used it to the full, but the often repeated charges against them were never proved. Owing to the interference of the Church, Patrick Stewart was summoned to Edinburgh in 1609 and placed under arrest. He was executed in 1615, only a month after his young son Robert had been put to death for starting a rebellion in Orkney. The fact that he was able to muster a following for this in Orkney does perhaps show that the Stewarts were not as black as they were painted. On the other hand there may have been local loyalty behind their support, as young Robert's mother is said to have come from west Mainland, and most of the rebels also came from there.

The downfall of the Stewarts was more likely to be because the power they represented was felt as a threat by King James VI than because of the wrongs they did to the Orcadians. The Stewart period was the last time Orkney played an independent role politically.

In 1643 the earldom lands and rights were granted by the Crown to the Earl of Morton. The Mortons controlled the earldom estates until 1766 when they were sold to Sir Lawrence Dundas of Kerse, later Earl of Zetland. In 1696 King William III made a Lowland soldier, Lord George Hamilton, Earl of Orkney. His descendants hold the ancient title which is now completely without ties with Orkney.

In 1650 the Marquis of Montrose landed in Orkney. He had won spectacular victories for King Charles during the Civil War 1642–51 between the King and parliament. Montrose was on his way to invade Scotland and recruited most of his army among Orkney youths who saw life as a soldier as a way out of poverty. He was finally defeated at Carbisdale in

Sutherland and betrayed to the anti-royalists by one of his old officers, Neil MacLeod of Assynt, from whom he had sought protection. Montrose was hanged in Edinburgh, but some of his officers are said to have entrenched themselves at Notland Castle in Westray.

Montrose's connection with Orkney is probably the reason why Oliver Cromwell maintained a garrison at Kirkwall during the period of the Commonwealth. The islanders are said to have got along splendidly with the Ironsides, who taught them new gardening methods and useful crafts. Still, one of Cromwell's soldiers (J. Emerson) wrote some ironic verses criticizing life in Orkney as he found it

> Their schooles of learning are in every house,
> And their first lesson is to hunt the louse.
> *Poetical Description of Orkney*, 1652. MS Faculty of Advocates, Edinburgh

On the whole, life for the common people seems to have been very hard throughout the sixteenth and seventeenth centuries. In the sixteenth century the landowning system began to change completely. After the Reformation in 1560 the process of creating large private estates out of Crown and Church land gathered momentum, most of them going to immigrant Scots. The feudalisation was even more marked under the Stewart Earls and after the abolition of the old Norse law in 1611. In 1619 'the King's removeable tenants' complain of their heavy burdens and that there is 'too heavy a taxation for the complainers to pay, and they would be constrained to leave the country and seek an abode in Norway or elsewhere'. By the end of the seventeenth century the percentage of people owning.the land they farmed had fallen to only three per cent, which means that the bulk of the population were tenants.

Before the kelp industry came, the farming cannot have been wholly primitive, for Orkney exported grain and malt to both Iceland and Norway. Chief imports from Norway were timber and tar for the making of boats. The number of ships which sailed from Bergen to Orkney and Shetland varied between six and nineteen. This trade was stopped for two reasons: there was fear of the forests in West Norway becoming exhausted, and to assist Canadian exports a heavy duty was imposed on timber from elsewhere.

Orkney seems to have been at its lowest ebb in the seventeenth century. Apart from the grammar school in Kirkwall, there was hardly a school anywhere in the islands. It happened sometimes that recalcitrant ministers were disciplined by being sent to Orkney. And Church discipline was severe: a person found guilty of 'blasphemie and dangerous boasting' had to stand barefoot before the pulpit at every Church service till he showed signs of repentance.

The religious strife that tore Scotland apart does not seem to have affected Orkney much. Murdoch Mackenzie, who was at one time a master at Kirkwall Grammar School, observed that

Scapa Flow. A naval base in the two world wars and then the site of a terminal for North Sea oil.

The religion is presbyterian as established in Scotland, without bigotry, enthusiasm or zeal; and without any dissenters except a very few of the episcopal persuasion. The mirth, diversions and reciprocal entertainments of the Christmas and other holy-days are still continued, tho' the devotion of them is quite forgot.

Orcades, or a geographical and hydrographic survey of Orkney and Lewis, 1750

Apart from a few of the leading landowning families, Orkney does not seem to have been involved in the '45, the Jacobite rebellion to bring the Stuarts back on the throne. The reason for this may have been that the Stuart cause was committed to Catholicism. Still the reason may not simply be a religious one, there may also have been a general unwillingness to become involved in Scottish affairs. At the Union of Parliaments in 1707, Orkney became part of Britain, and about this event the Orkney historian J. Storer Clouston writes that 'the first advantage Orkney ever gained from becoming part of Scotland was the privilege of eventually becoming part of Great Britain' (*A History of Orkney*, 1932).

Around the middle of the nineteenth century the agricultural revolution began, and life in Orkney acquired a new rhythm. It went hand in hand with a cultural awakening, a new consciousness.

Our own century has brought Orkney back into the mainstream of events, mainly through the focusing of interest on Scapa Flow, first as a naval base in the two world wars and then as the site of a terminal for North Sea oil.

10.
Scapa Flow in two world wars

But that was yesterday,
for now they come no more.
Lonely Scapa Flow by A. Windwich © Emerald Music Ltd

Today only the flames from the flare-off tower at Flotta break the peace and tranquillity around Scapa. If we look more closely, we become aware of the ghost town at Lyness, where the naval base was. A buoy bobs in the sea and reminds us of where the men of the *Royal Oak* found their grave. It is difficult now to imagine Scapa as it was in wartime, but the story of Scapa is a modern saga full of violence, horror and courage.

In both world wars Scapa Flow was the main base for the British Home Fleet. As many as 20,000 men were stationed there at times, actors in a drama where the Orcadians themselves mostly had to be content with being spectators, even if they had a ringside view! Through two world wars, Scapa Flow was in the centre of events, and the name is well known in modern war history.

As early as the time of the Napoleonic Wars, Scapa Flow was suggested as a wartime naval base, but it took a century for the plans to be realized. When war was imminent in the summer of 1914, the British Home Fleet was assembled in Scapa Flow under the command of First Sea Lord, Sir John Jellicoe. The fleet was reinforced and renamed the Grand Fleet. It was the largest fleet ever assembled by the British. Its enemy was the German Hochseeflotte. The German fleet had fewer ships than the British, but it had technical advantages in its favour, and was not at all the inferior opponent the British believed it to be.

The purpose of the Grand Fleet was not just to protect Britain's coasts against the enemy; its important duty was to keep the Germans away from the Atlantic by an effective blockade. The large anchorage at Scapa, with the North Sea on the one side and the Atlantic on the other, was geographically well suited for the purpose. But that was the only factor in favour of Scapa, for there were no defences, and the channels lay unprotected and wide open to attack in the west, south and east. Admiral Jellicoe wrote in his diary: 'I wonder I can ever sleep at all. Thank goodness the Germans imagine we have proper defences. At least so I imagine – otherwise there would be no Grand Fleet left now'. Winston Churchill, who was First Lord of the

Admiralty, reacted quickly, and gradually Scapa Flow developed the necessary defences and became a safe anchorage.

During the First World War, air warfare was still in its infancy, and it was mines and submarines that were the enemy's most feared weapons. To be constantly on guard against German submarines was essential, but it put great pressure on the crews of the fleet, as did the harsh monotonous life at Scapa – many months might pass between every time the men were ashore. A major confrontation with the enemy became a psychological necessity – for the Germans as well. It came, in the bitter Battle of Jutland, on 31 May 1916.

This is considered to be the largest battle ever fought at sea, both because as many as 250 ships took part in it and because some 8,000 men were killed. The British were sure of victory beforehand, but the accuracy of the German artillery proved superior, and the outcome of the battle was no clear-cut victory for the British. At any rate it was a Pyrrhic victory for them, for they lost the most ships and the most men – 6,097 dead. Thus it was not a triumphant Grand Fleet which returned to bury their dead in the naval cemetery at Hoy.

The crews were still clearing up and repairing the damage after the Battle of Jutland when the next disaster struck, on 5 June 1916. The British War Minister, Lord Kitchener, arrived at Scapa that day to embark for Archangel in Russia. The Russian war effort had deteriorated badly, and the plan was for Lord Kitchener to offer advice to the Russians on their methods of warfare on the East Front. The cruiser *Hampshire* was chosen for the voyage; it had escaped the Battle of Jutland without a scratch.

In spite of the storm that was raging, Lord Kitchener would not listen to any talk of putting off the departure. As the weather was worst on the eastern side of Orkney and the risk of running into a submarine was also greater there, Admiral Jellicoe decided that the *Hampshire* was to follow a route on the western side of Mainland, in the lee of the cliffs along the coast. Two destroyers were sent along as escort, but they returned soon after, because they maintained far less speed than the *Hampshire* and could therefore be of no use.

While the ship was between Marwick Head and Brough of Birsay, about 1 mile (2 km) from land, the ship was shaken by an explosion. Everything indicates that the *Hampshire* struck a mine; in fact a German submarine had shortly before mined the western side. The *Hampshire* sank within 15 minutes, and no boats were lowered. Lord Kitchener was never found. Only 12 of the crew managed to survive the hardships – first on overcrowded floats and then the climb up the perpendicular, 200 ft (60 m) high cliffs in rough seas and a raging storm.

People on shore saw the *Hampshire* sink. It happened at around eight o'clock at night, but in the confusion that followed, the messages were somehow misunderstood at naval headquarters, and it was past midnight before vessels arrived to look for survivors. The Orcadians wanted to take part in the rescue work, but were not allowed to do so. The lifeboat in Stromness was not permitted to go out. It was with great bitterness that people in Marwick and Birsay remembered this afterwards – they thought that local people who knew the area could have saved at least another 50–60 men from being beaten to death against the cliffs.

Many aspects of the sinking of the *Hampshire* have never been satisfactorily explained, and it is not, therefore, strange that for a long time there were the wildest rumours of spies and sabotage. Lord Kitchener was a famous and respected man. Not only was he the victorious leader of the campaign in the Sudan, where the borders of the Empire were extended once again, but he was also more than anyone else the symbol of the national will to win the war, for his face met the British from numerous conscription posters. His death came as a great blow.

Money was collected from the whole nation for a memorial to Lord Kitchener and the others who died when the *Hampshire* sank. This memorial is outlined against the horizon at Marwick Head.

Still another disaster is remembered with grief by people in Orkney. Just before midnight on 9 July 1917, HMS *Vanguard* blew up while at anchor in Scapa Flow. More than 700 men were killed. The probable cause of the explosion was the spontaneous combustion of cordite (it was difficult to store cordite safely in those days). Once again there were rumours of sabotage, and no one contradicted them, for it was better for the crews to believe that the Germans were responsible than to admit that they were staying on board possible death traps.

Germany capitulated on 11 November 1918. Under the terms of the Armistice, the German Fleet was to be disarmed at once. Until a final solution could be found, it was decided to intern 72 German warships at Scapa. The fleet remained there the whole winter of 1919 and was a strange sight. It was a hard winter to get through for the few Germans who were left on each ship. Their homeland was defeated and near starvation, and their own fate was not easy either. They were not permitted to visit each other or go ashore.

Vice-Admiral von Reuter was in command of the German fleet. He himself was an officer of the old school, but he had revolutionary elements among his men who wanted to set up sailors' councils like those formed in Russia. He received no other information from the British than what he could read in the newspapers. When war broke out in 1914 the fleet received standing orders from the German Kaiser that no ship put out of action must ever fall into enemy hands, and von Reuter felt himself bound by this order. He therefore prepared for the scuttling of the fleet. Every higher officer was ordered to sink his ship if the British tried to seize it or if he received a pre-arranged signal from von Reuter.

The peace terms for Germany were hard. The Armistice expired on 21 June 1919 without word of the Germans having accepted the terms. Admiral von Reuter was convinced that war would break out anew and that

Kitchener's Memorial, Marwick Head. The memorial commemorates the sinking of the Hampshire in which Lord Kitchener was drowned. Only 12 of the crew survived.

The German battleship Bayern. *The crew who had been picked up out of the water cheered loudly and waved their caps as she took her final plunge. (Photo: C. W. Burrows)*

the British would then seize his fleet at once. He therefore gave the pre-arranged signal to scuttle: at 12.16 p.m. on 21 June the first ship sank, and then most of the others followed in the next few hours. It was a fantastic sight and the people who saw it hardly believed their own eyes. The story of the painter who stood on shore and saw his motif disappear is a well-known one. The school-children from Stromness were on an excursion that day to see the German ships at close quarters and saw more than they had ever dreamed of. The smaller children thought it was a show put on specially for them!

There was some firing from British ships, and nine Germans were killed. When the Germans left their ships, they had not been ashore at all for 230 days.

In the years between the two world wars, the more or less submerged German ships filled Scapa. It was an ugly sight, but for a long time it was uncertain what could be done about them. In 1924 the work of clearing them away began, but when the Second World War came, they still had not all been removed.

History repeated itself. After war broke out in 1939, Scapa Flow became a naval base again, and Winston Churchill became First Lord of the Admiralty. He found the defences at Scapa to be extremely inadequate. The eastern openings had during the First World War been blocked by wrecked ships, but the wind and the current had moved the derelicts around so they no longer blocked the entrances. A naval report mentioned Kirk Sound as a place where a submarine might be able to get through. Churchill ordered new nets and blockings at Scapa. But time had run out.

Pictures taken by German reconnaissance planes showed Scapa full of ships and also the inadequacy of the eastern defences. In the evening of 12 October, Commander-in-Chief Admiral Forbes took the Home Fleet out because he feared an air attack. In the northeastern corner of Scapa he left behind the *Royal Oak*, a veteran from the Battle of Jutland. This was the ship which returned Queen Maud's body to Norway after her death in England. The *Royal Oak* was full of anti-aircraft and was to defend Kirkwall.

Commodore von Dönitz, Commander-in-Chief of the German U-boat force, now saw a chance of realizing the old German dream of entering Scapa Flow itself. He chose Kapitänleutnant Günther Prien of U-47 for the task, which required courage and skill.

What happened after that is still not quite clear, even after more than 40 years. Eye-witness accounts are contradictory, and Günther Prien went down with the U-47 in March of 1941, when it was torpedoed off Iceland. The log-book of the submarine shows that Günther Prien, in the evening of 13 October, navigated through Kirk Sound into Scapa Flow, believing that most of the British Home Fleet would be there. At 1 o'clock in the morning of 14 October torpedoes were fired at the *Royal Oak*, which sank within minutes. No witnesses on shore saw what happened and, as when the

The H.M.S. Royal Oak *buoy, Scapa Flow. At 1 o'clock in the morning of 14 October 1939, torpedoes were fired by the German submarine U-47 at the* Royal Oak, *which sank within minutes. 833 men died.*

Hampshire sank, men were fighting for their lives while those who could have helped them slept peacefully close by. 833 men died.

The general opinion was that this must be another *Vanguard* disaster, but there was also talk of sabotage. Many of the survivors have always refused to believe that the ship was torpedoed. But the propellor of a German torpedo has since been found near the wreck by a diver from Kirkwall, and no serious historian now doubts that the *Royal Oak* was indeed torpedoed by the U-47 after it had breached the defences of the Flow. The wreck of the *Royal Oak* lies at a depth of around 30 metres (98 feet) and can be seen from the air when the sea is calm. The ship has now been declared an official war grave, and is marked by a big green buoy.

Günther Prien and the crew of U-47 were received by Hitler and given the Iron Cross and all possible honours. The film of their homecoming was shown at all the cinemas to the tune of 'Wir fahren gegen England'; Prien's autobiography *Mein Weg Nach Scapa Flow* sold 750,000 copies.

To make it impossible that anything like the *Royal Oak* disaster could ever happen again, the eastern entrances were blocked off completely. The problem was how to build barriers that could withstand the tidal current and the ramming power of the waves. It was Churchill who thought that only concrete would do the trick, and big blocks of concrete were strewn helter-skelter. The work on the so-called Churchill barriers took four years and was a difficult and rather dangerous job which cost ten lives. Most of the work was done by Italian prisoners-of-war.

Today there is an excellent road across the Churchill barriers. It connects Burray and South Ronaldsay with Mainland, and is thus important to the people there. The chapel which the Italian prisoners made out of two Nissen huts is located on Lamb Holm close to the road. It is still being kept up by those who built it and used it in wartime, and has become one of the sights of Orkney.

In March 1940 the air attacks began. The first civilian war casualty in Britain was a man who was killed when some houses by the bridge of Waithe, between Loch Stenness and Scapa, were hit. An air defence became essential, and the R.A.F. and Navy built as many as four stations. Kirkwall got Britain's first effective radar system. Heavy anti-aircraft artillery, strong search-lights and balloons gradually made the Orkney barrage so deadly that no enemy plane dared approach Scapa, even though the nearest German airfield in Norway was only some 250 miles (400 km) away.

In April 1940 both Britain and Germany had plans for a landing in Norway. Germany won the race and invaded Norway just ahead of the Allies: plan 'Weserübung' succeeded instead of plan 'Wilfred'. The British Home Fleet had sailed from Scapa Flow at 7.30 p.m. on 7 April but was for various reasons unable to intercept the German naval forces at sea, and the German campaign in Norway therefore began as planned at 5.15 a.m. on 9 April.

The Italian chapel built from two Nissen huts.

The landings at Namsos and Åndalsnes and the assault on the German ships at Narvik were later operated from Scapa. But by then the Germans were virtually in control of Norway, and there was little the navy could do. The decisive factor against the Home Fleet was the Luftwaffe – more than 1000 German planes took part in the Norwegian campaign and the Allies were helpless against them. The cruiser *Suffolk*, trying to bombard Sola airport near Stavanger, was under air attack for nearly seven hours and barely made it back to Scapa.

One of the worst tasks of the naval war was taken care of from Scapa for three and a half years. It was the escorting of convoys from Iceland to Murmansk – also called the suicide run. The route along the northern coast of Norway was the shortest way to the Soviet Union, but it was also the most dangerous one. Not only did the escort ships have to take up the fight against German planes, U-boats and warships, they also had to fight intensely against nature. Icing was one of the serious hazards. *St Sunniva*, the sister ship of the Pentland Firth ferry *St Ola*, was sent on the Murmansk run as a rescue ship but turned top-heavy with ice and sank with no survivors.

The worst year for the convoys was 1942, and the most unfortunate convoy of them all was PQ 17 in June 1942. Of the 34 ships in the convoy, 23 were sunk. Churchill called this one of the most tragic naval episodes of the war. The fact that the Russians did not seem to appreciate the sacrifices demanded of the convoy crews, but gave them a rather cold welcome, did not make the trips any easier.

In Scapa people were used to seeing the ships put out to sea, all spick and span, only to limp back weather-beaten and worn down, with exhausted crews on board. Then peace came, and Scapa's importance was once again over. The base was finally closed down in 1957.

The relationship between Orkney and the thousands of servicemen who were stationed there was not always a happy one. This had its natural causes:

> The bloody roads are bloody bad
> The bloody folks are bloody mad
> They make the brightest bloody sad
>   In bloody Orkney.
>
> Best bloody place is bloody bed
> With bloody ice on bloody head
> You might as well be bloody dead
>   In bloody Orkney.
>
>   Captain Hamish Blair

As this very controversial soldier verse expresses, many of the soldiers found the life at Scapa harsh and monotonous, and they probably did not realize how their complaints about the climate and lack of amenities hurt the Orcadians. But gradually a mutual trust grew up, and many of the ex-servicemen remember the warmth and hospitality shown them by the islanders as the only positive aspect of their time at Scapa.

For those who experienced Scapa Flow in wartime, it will always be full of ghosts. For the rest of us it is a strangely beautiful world where only the weather creates drama in its sudden changes between storm and calm.

11.   The folklore heritage

The Orkney I was born into was a place where there was no great difference between the ordinary and the fabulous; the lives of living men turned into legend.

Edwin Muir *An Autobiography* (Hogarth Press, 1954)

A culture which lives through oral tradition will disintegrate when the language dies. But through that which has been preserved of Orkney folklore, we glimpse a time past where beliefs and values coincided with the laws of behaviour and the way of life to form a consistent pattern. The course of life – from the cradle to the grave – was defined through established and accepted rites. The work on land and at sea as well as the changing seasons were associated with customs which changed but little from one generation to the next. The belief in a world where rocks and oceans, plants and animals were endowed with life as man himself, and the belief that people were surrounded by good and evil forces with which they had to learn to co-exist, survived side by side with the teachings of the Church into this century. Man used both steel and the cross to protect himself against evil forces.

There is one man who more than anyone else should be thanked for keeping the entire Orkney folklore heritage from disappearing without being recorded. This is Walter Traill Dennison, a farmer from Sanday, who towards the end of the nineteenth century wrote down stories he heard. '. . . he saved from extinction, single-handed, a whole corpus of myth, legend, and historical tradition which the educated Orcadians of his time ignored, even deplored.' This is said by Ernest W. Marwick, who was Dennison's successor, in *Orkney Folklore and Tradition* (Kirkwall, 1961). These two are the important names in the collection and study of Orkney folklore.

The difficulty Dennison met with in his work was that the stories were told to him in the Sanday dialect, an expressive mixture of Norse and Scots, and far from standard English. To write these stories down in English would mean robbing them of most of their distinctive character. Dennison therefore tried to find a way of writing which reproduced the language in which they were told, at the same time aiming to make this understandable for others; but he was criticized for having a coarse and vulgar language. The fact that he did not give in to this criticism, but remained true to his artistic vision, is even more remarkable when we consider that he was very religious, and that the Scottish Church looked askance at the old customs and the beliefs that often followed them.

Dennison's work came in the nick of time as the sources were already drying out. Others took up the work after him, and today all available material has probably been recorded. Ernest W. Marwick gives a general survey of all this material in his book *The Folklore of Orkney and Shetland*. There he also compares what he finds of popular beliefs, such as the belief in trolls and hogboon, with similar beliefs in Norway. Much of what follows here is based on Marwick's conclusions.

Customs, tales and popular beliefs in Orkney originate in Norway, but everything has been adapted to the life in the islands, and Lowland-Scottish elements have also been absorbed. Local stories of the Spanish Armada, the pressgangs, and the many shipwrecks were woven into the old material and gave to everything a distinctive Orkney character. This continued until quite recently – until the modern development in communication and media seems to have suppressed all oral tradition in Orkney too, as in so many other places.

The folklore which has survived reflects a practical, down-to-earth people of fishermen and farmers, who did believe in certain norms and values, but who first and foremost distinguished themselves by their ability to meet life as it is without heroics or big words, but perhaps with a pithy remark. We find the fantastic, but little of the mystical.

The Norsemen brought with them their belief in the giant (jotun), the trow (troll), the hogboon (nisse), the dwarf (dverg) and the huldrefolk. Norway's majestic nature had formed these creatures, who did not all fit equally well into the far softer Orkney scenery. According to Norse belief the giants lived in the mountains, possibly with several heads, and had eyes deep and dark as mountain tarns. They were nocturnal beings who burst and turned into stone in the sun. When the giants quarrelled, they threw boulders at each other, but they rarely hit anything, or anybody. Because they did not like to get their feet wet, they built bridges, which were called jutul-bridges. The giants were a product of the eeriness and horror one may feel in the Norwegian mountains at night, when all the surroundings take on monstrous shapes.

There are traces of the giants in Orkney too, but it must have been very difficult to believe in them there, and probably the belief in them died fairly soon. But there are some places named after them: a tarn in Papay is called Ettan's Pow – the jotun's pool. All the Stone Age monuments could of course be associated with giants who had been surprised by the sun. Such a stone monument in Rousay is known as Yetna-steen – the jotun stone, People say it goes to the loch close by for a drink just after midnight every New Year morning, as does the Quoybune-stone in Birsay. When the clock strikes midnight on New Year's Eve, the stone moves quietly down to the Loch of Boardhouse, dips its head into the water and goes back. One ought not to watch this, for those who have been so daring have been found dead or

Cubbie Roo's Castle, Wyre. The Norse chieftain Kolbein Hruga became the giant Cubbie Roo in Orkney folklore.

senseless beside the stone the next morning.

In Copinsay there is a large boulder which is known as the Giant Stone. According to tradition it was flung there by a giant from the farm of Stembister in Deerness on Mainland. Stembister is derived from *stein-bolstaðr*, which means stone-farm.

In the popular imagination many of the giant stories have become associated with the Norse chieftain Kolbein Hruga, who lived at Wyre. He became the giant Cubbie Roo, who was so big that when he walked, one step carried him from one island to another. When he became angry, he too threw stones, and around the islands there are many boulders for which he is responsible. Beside the Sourin shore in Rousay is the Finger-steen, which according to legend shows Cubbie Roo's finger marks. Cubbie Roo meant to throw this stone at the giant in Kiepfea Hill, but of course he missed. He tried his hand at bridge-building too, but lost all the stones, and that is why the Stone Age cairn at Wyre is called Cubbie Roo's Burden, because it was those stones he lost.

We also find traces of the female giant, the *gyger*. Some outcrops of rock in Swandale in Rousay are known as the gyro-stones. And at the bottom of the Pentland Firth, the gygers Fenia and Menia are grinding salt on the quern Grotti, just as they do in the Icelandic Edda. They are also to be blamed for the Pentland Firth being so turbulent.

It is especially Rousay and Hoy that are the haunts of the jotun. This is, of course, because these islands have most in common with Norway and were therefore natural homes for them. The same is true of the trolls, who also in Norwegian popular tradition have so many characteristics in common with the jotun that it can be difficult to tell them apart.

In Orkney the trolls have shrunk in size until they are often no larger than human beings, and they are also sometimes mistaken as such. But they have kept many of the distinctive characteristics of the Norwegian trolls: they are ugly, they can move quickly from one place to another and they spirit young girls off into the mountain where they make them weave and spin all day and stroke their heads at night. As the troll children are sickly, the trolls are forever trying to take human children and put their own in their place. The time element is also different – one who has stayed with the trolls loses all sense of time. This is described in the story of the bridegroom from Sandwick, who was taken by the trolls and put ashore on Suleskerry, west in the Atlantic. He thought he had been there only a few hours, but when he returned, he found he had been away for seven years and his bride was married to another.

To protect themselves against the power of the trolls, people might place steel above the door. A page from the Bible tied around the horn of a cow would safeguard it against anything the trolls could do. Of course the trolls did not like to hear the word *troll* so it might suffice to say it aloud. What the troll feared most of all was thunder. That is why thunder was till quite recently called 'Geud's weather', and the God referred to was Thor, the Norse god of thunder, who was believed to be on man's side against the giants and trolls.

The troll name was eventually changed into *trow*. Sickly people were spoken of as *trowy*. We find place names like Trolla Vatn in North Ronaldsay and the fishing grounds Ooter and Inner Troola in Birsay. The place names with trow, like Trowie Glen in Hoy, are often combined with Scottish elements, so the change from troll to trow may have come comparatively recently.

In Norse mythology, Thor's hammer Mjöllnir was forged by dwarfs, who were known as excellent smiths. They lived in boulders or mountain sides. They were very talkative, so the echo from a mountain side was in Norway called *dvergmál* – dwarf speech. In Evie on Mainland a hillside is called Dwarmo, and they say the echo is very good there! In Hoy we find the Dwarfie Hammers. That the Norse settlers called the stone monument there Dvergasteinn, now the Dwarfie Stane, agreed completely with their beliefs. The stone is the only one of its kind in Orkney, and it is natural that the popular imagination would connect it with supernatural powers of various kinds. In his novel *The Pirate*, Sir Walter Scott described a visit to the troll who lived in the stone. In Jo Ben's description of Orkney in the sixteenth century the Dwarfie Stane was seen as the home of giants.

As the trow did not live in mountains, but in hills or earth mounds, the distinctions between them and other hill-dwelling creatures grew rather blurred. This was especially true of the hogboy, or hogboon, a relative of the Norwegian *nisse*, and originally a direct descendant of the Norse *haugbui* or *haugbonde* – hill-dweller or hill-farmer. In pre-Christian times the farmer

The Dwarfie Stane, interior. The living quarters of a troll in Sir Walter Scott's novel The Pirate.

was buried in a mound on his own farm. People believed that his spirit would then stay on the family farm – this was especially true of the farmer who first cleared the land. The haugbonde-tradition had a certain importance for the odal-right to a farm – a farmer claiming odal-right could refer to his ancestors' graves and spirits. The haugbonde would go on caring for the farm and would see to it that everything was done the way it should be. He used to come out at Christmas, and thus he somehow turned into the nisse in Norway. In Orkney he went through a similar change.

It is not so long since every mound in Orkney had its hogboy or hogboon. This was also true of Maeshowe itself. James Farrar, who excavated Maeshowe in 1862, wrote: 'The country people state that the building was formerly inhabited by a person named Hogboy, possessing great strength'. The fear of getting on the wrong side of the hogboon kept people from opening the many Stone Age graves. Even into the nineteenth century milk and flour were poured through a hole in the mound at the Skelwick farm in Westray.

The hogboon was ill-humoured and full of tricks, but like the nisse in Norway it could also become attached to the people on the farm. There is a story that on the farm of Hellihowe in Sanday there was a new mistress of the house, who gave the hogboon neither milk nor beer, and who scraped the

The hogboon of Hellihowe. Drawing by Ian MacInnes.

pots before she put them away. In return the hogboon plagued the farm
people in all possible ways. In the end they grew so tired of his tricks that
they decided to move. One fine morning they went off with all their worldly
goods, and as they approached the new farm the farmer became happier and
happier because he was getting away from his tormentor. But then the

99

hogboon set his head up out of a kirn and said: 'We're gettan a fine day tae flit on, guidman'. This story is identical to the Norwegian tale 'Mannen ville fra nissen flytte'.

The elves or fairies were often called just 'the peerie folk'. To a certain extent they are confused with Scots-English legendary creatures, but the northern elves and fairies were malevolent. They especially attacked the cows, and were therefore greatly feared by the farmers. They might shoot the cows with elf-arrows, which left lumps or blisters. Cows that had just calved were especially at risk. In the end people believed that every sick cow had been attacked by the peerie folk, and wise women, called spaewives, did a good business trying to cure them. They all had their own methods and cures. As late as 1884 the story is told that a man had tried all possible ways of saving his cow, but in the end he had to give up 'for her heart was riddled with fairy shot'.

Sometimes at night one could see the fairies dancing round a fire, and the next morning there would be a dark ring in the grass. Ernest W. Marwick says that he had such fairy rings pointed out to him when he was a child.

The famous lighthouse engineer Robert Stevenson once lost a 100 ft (30 m) measuring line when he visited the Ring of Brogar together with Sir Walter Scott in 1814. The woman who found and kept it believed it was the fairies who had put it there!

It is not really so surprising that much of the belief in good and evil forces was bound up with the sea. The sea is the untamed, dramatic element in Orkney. It gives rich gifts, but it also represents the dangerous, unexpected element – for it is the highway of the enemy.

Among the oldest stories from the sea we find the tale of the Stoor Worm – the big worm – the Miðgarðsormr which in Norse mythology encircled the earth. It was the largest and most terrifying of all living things on earth, one of the nine curses of mankind. Just the tongue of the monster alone was hundreds of miles long. When it was in a rage it could sweep everything that got in its way out into the sea. But Assipattle – the Ashlad (Askeladden) of Norwegian folk tales – sailed his boat into the mouth of the Stoor Worm and down through its throat and set the liver alight with burning peat, before he returned safely home again. The Stoor Worm threw himself around till the earth shook. His teeth fell out and turned into Orkney, Shetland and the Faeroe Islands. Then he rolled himself up and died, and his big body became Iceland. But his liver is still burning, and sometimes the flames from the fire can blaze over the mountains of Iceland.

The myth of the Mither of the Sea has probably arisen to explain life in the sea and the inter-change between storm and calm. She is a benign being who stills the storm and makes the sea warmer. She is life-giving and guards all life in the sea. Her enemy was Teran, which in the Orkney dialect means raging fury. Each spring the Mither of the Sea returned to the sea. Then there was a terrible struggle between her and Teran, and this could last for days and weeks. Therefore the spring storms were called 'the Vore tullye' –

The sea trows and the fishermen. Drawing by Ian MacInnes.

the spring struggle. This came more or less around the vernal equinox.

Teran loses the struggle and is tied up and put on the bottom of the sea. There he attempts all the time to free himself, and this can cause rough weather in the summertime as well. But the work of watching Teran, quieting storms, and looking after all the life in the sea, makes the Mither of the Sea more and more weary as the autumnal equinox approaches. Therefore Teran manages to free himself, and in the following terrible struggle for mastery of the sea – 'the Gore vellye', the autumn struggle – the Mither of the Sea is defeated. She flees the sea to gather strength for another summer, and Teran has the sea to himself all winter.

Another terrifying sea creature was Nuckelavee. He was evil through and through and also monstrous to look at. He rode a horse as ugly as himself, and he tried by all possible means to lure people to the sea and drown them. Only the Mither of the Sea and his own fear of fresh water could deter him. Animals which fell in the sea were said to be enticed by Nuckelavee. He was also blamed for bad years and droughts.

In the myth of Nuckelavee it is possible to recognize the Norwegian *nökk*, both in the name itself and in a certain similarity otherwise. In Norwegian tradition the nökk used to assume the shape of a horse to lure people to him, and then he would gallop with the rider into the sea. In Iceland the nökk was called *vatnhestr* – waterhorse. But in Norway there was a nökk in every tarn, and it was the draug that lived in the sea. In Orkney the nökk and the draug have become one terrifying creature whose haunt is the sea.

The sea was also full of sea trows. They were ordinary trows who for some reason had been chased into the sea by the others. Apart from being full of shells they were no different from the land trows. They were stupid, as most trows are. They were also too lazy to fish themselves, so they would steal the fish from the fishermen, or even the bait from their lines when the fish were scarce. The sea trows wanted very much to come ashore, but they dared go no further than the beach, as they feared the land trows.

The sea was not only peopled with fantastic fable creatures. It was also the home of the Fin Folk, who did have supernatural powers, but who were otherwise hardly distinguishable from people on land. The Fin Folk appealed very strongly to the popular imagination. The Fin man and the Fin woman were very different from one another: the young Fin woman was the mermaid. The Fin man was well-formed and strong, with a dark and gloomy face. He had magical powers and fins like a fish, but to the human eye they looked like part of his clothing. He could live both in the sea and on land, but he preferred the sea. He was a good rower – seven strokes took him from Orkney to Norway. His permanent home was called Finfolkaheem and lay at the bottom of the sea. In the summer his home was in Hildaland.

The relationship between the Fin man and people ashore was not always so friendly. One reason for the quarrels was that the fishermen often fished on the Fin man's fishing grounds, and then the Fin Folk might take revenge by holding on to the fishing line until it broke. Sometimes they would even take the anchor stone away too. But there was a way of avoiding that. The fishermen could scratch a cross in the sinker and perhaps also the boat – then the Fin Folk could do nothing, for they dreaded the sign of the cross.

The Fin women lost their mermaid beauty as soon as they married – and what is more, they even grew quite ugly. The Fin woman was then often sent ashore to get silver money, which the Fin Folk were very fond of; she would pretend that she had just moved to Orkney from Caithness or Shetland and that she earned a living spinning and knitting. She had great magical powers and could cure all kinds of diseases both in people and beasts.

The daughters of the Fin Folk were the enchanting mermaids. Their shining golden hair reached to the waist. They had a tail when they were in the sea, but this looked like a fine skirt when they came ashore. The only thing that could save the mermaid from her mother's fate was for her to marry a human being. Then she would also lose her tail. This is the reason why she tries on the shore to entice men to her through her beauty and enchanting music in order to make one of them marry her. A man must be strong to be able to resist her! Of course there was a prayer which might save them if they said it three times, but the problem was that they would become so dazzled by the mermaid that they could not remember one word of the prayer! Therefore there are numerous stories of men who had known the mermaids too well – their names were known – and 'his grandson is still living on the farm'.

Dennison said that he had Finfolkaheem described to him down to the least detail by those he spoke to in Sanday. It was a town so gorgeous that it might have come from the pages of the Arabian nights. Everything was built of gold and crystal, covered in pearls, and with rugs and hangings in the shimmering colours of the northern lights. There were those who had been there and could give eyewitness accounts.

The summer home of Hildaland was a group of lovely fertile islands with rich farms. They lay in the western ocean but only very rarely was a human being so fortunate as to see Hildaland. According to tradition, Hildaland later turned into the island of Eynhallow.

The Fin women have much in common with those who later were called witches. The Scottish Church came down hard on the witches, and particularly in the seventeenth century the witch fires often burned on Gallow Hill in Kirkwall. The Scottish inquisitors tried persistently to find witches who had sold themselves to the Devil, but, says Ernest W. Marwick (*The Folklore of Orkney and Shetland*, Batsford 1975), 'when he spoke, it was in a distinctly Scottish voice'. To most people the Devil was a theological hypothesis; trows and Fin Folk were everywhere.

The Selkie folk have no supernatural powers associated with them. They are ordinary human beings who for unknown reasons must live in seal skin. Selkie is a commonly used word for seal, but it is not used about the common seal which is so numerous; that is called tang fish. Selkie is used only about large seals like the grey seal or the Greenland seal. According to tradition it was only at certain times that the seal could take off its skin and become human again – as on Midsummer night or at high tide. Then they danced on the rocks along the shore in exuberant joy at their freedom – a sight that went straight to the heart of those who saw it.

The Selkie folk lived in the outskerries. There are many stories of how they would help people. Love between seal and human being is also a common theme. A story which is found in several versions tells of a man who hides the skin of a beautiful seal woman while she is dancing on the shore. She marries him, has several children and is a good wife to him in every way. But the longing for the sea is in her, and when she finds her skin many years later, she at once puts it on and runs down to the sea. She never returns.

It was said that especially unhappy married women got lovers from the Selkie folk. To meet a seal the woman had to cry seven tears at high tide. There is a story about a woman in Stronsay who loved a Selkie. Her descendants had thick horn skin on their hands and feet. Marwick says that he himself saw how one of these had hands with a greenish-white skin which cracked and smelled strongly of fish!

Many of the stories have been related until quite recently. How far the popular beliefs really had a grip on people and how much was told mostly for its entertainment value is impossible to know. Dennison says that his story-tellers believed fully in what they told him. In any case myths and legends make the popular imagination come to life for us in a way that mere historical knowledge does not.

12.   Customs and way of life

The winter gathered us into one room as it gathered the cattle into the stable and the byre; the sky came closer; the lamps were lit at three or four in the afternoon, and then the great evening lay before us like a world: an evening filled with talk, stories, games, music and lamplight.

Edwin Muir An Autobiography *(Hogarth Press, 1954)*

The old Orkney farm, which now is to be found empty and more or less derelict everywhere, had changed little since Norse times. It was long and narrow like the Norse longhouse. The furniture was simple, made of stone, perhaps of driftwood, for new wood was hard to come by. Therefore the inside of the house could almost be mistaken for the interior of Skara Brae. In the really old houses the beds were stone alcoves in the long wall. Such a house may still be seen on the Kirbister farm in Birsay.

The houses were mostly built to give room for both man and beast, who lived in close proximity to each other. This made the work easier when the wind was at its strongest in the winter darkness, and of course the animals also helped make the house warmer. The exterior of the house was one unbroken surface with as few openings as possible where the wind might find entry. Horses went in through the stable-door; cattle and people used the same entrance.

On his trip to Orkney in 1849, the Norwegian historian P. A. Munch visited the farm which gave the Ring of Brogar its name – Brogar, from *Brúargarðr*, the farm by the bridge. Munch's host told him that he would find most Orkney farms like the one at Brogar.

It was a long low clay or stone building, with a thatch roof. The entrance is in the long wall, near one end of it; one here enters an outer room which is used for cattle, sheep and pigs during the night and where the earth floor therefore is quite soggy and full of muck, especially during the rainy part of the year. The yard outside is also the same. Anyone who knows our ordinary mountain farms would realize how completely I felt I had come to one of them.

Reminiscences of Orkney

Most farms were built roughly to the pattern shown in Figure 6. The living quarters were really one big room, which was divided into two by a boxbed wall. This made two rooms, which were known as but-hoose and ben-hoose, or just *but* and *ben*. The ben was also called *salur*. The ben part of the house not only provided the sleeping quarters, but also served as a supply room. Among other things the home-brewed ale was stored there.

In the middle of the floor in the but part was the *back*, a wall which was about 3 ft 3 in. (1 m) high. Against this wall the fire burned day and night – it was considered very unlucky to let it die out. The smoke was supposed to drift out through the opening in the ceiling, the *lum* (O.N. ljómi). It did not always do so, however, so much of the time the smell of smoke hung in the room, while condensed moisture ran in stripes down the walls. It was also through the lum that the only daylight entered. The floor was flagged or made of dried earth. This is how P. A. Munch saw the interior:

In the house itself there is only an earth or flagged floor; in the middle of this there is a fireplace built of rough stones. From this the smoke goes out through a hole in the ceiling and this also supplies all the light. Along the walls are shelves and simple beds. It is understandable that the sight of this reminded me even more strongly of our mountain farms.

Reminiscences of Orkney

The roof was mostly thatched, apart from in a few places, like Rackwick in Hoy, where there was slate that might be used. It rarely became completely leak-proof. Stones were used to hold the roof in place – even so it happened that the roof was gone after a stormy night.

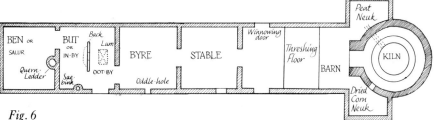

Fig. 6
Diagram of an Orkney farmhouse after a drawing by John Firth.

The space between the back and the door was called the *oot-by* and was the haunt of the smaller animals on the farm, such as calves, a pig with piglets, geese and hens, as well as cats and dogs. The hens would also perch on the rafters.

Behind the back was the *in-by*. Here the farmer and his wife, the *guid-man* and the *guid-wife*, had their high-backed chairs of bound straw – now known as Orkney chairs. The sides of the back are curved – to keep the draught out, they say. Grandfather's chair might even have a kind of roof. The children would sit on stools with a straw seat. The in-by was where the family gathered for meals and also when they were not busy with the number of farm tasks that demanded their attention. After dark an oil-lamp, called the *cruisie-lamp*, lit up the room in addition to the light from the peat fire.

A flat slab of rock ran the length of the wall beside the door; it was the *bink*. In the corner of the ben-wall was a curved stone shelf. It was the *sae-*

The in-by. Drawing by Ian MacInnes.

bink, called thus because the sae, or water-bucket, stood there. All water-carrying was woman's work. On the whole, women had not only a long, but also a hard working day.

- Food was cooked in a pot, which hung from a *swey*, a long iron chain, over the open fire. Everyday cooking was very simple. Bread and porridge made from the local grains bere and oats, together with cabbage, potatoes and turnips constituted, apart from fish and meat, the most important articles of food. On festive occasions bannocks and scones, baked on a griddle, were served.

An unbalanced diet low on minerals and vitamins has been a serious problem in the islands until quite recently. Fruit was earlier very expensive and often difficult to get hold of. Lettuce was considered to be food fit for rabbits, and most vegetables were boiled for too long. It is not so many generations since tuberculosis was the scourge of the islands. Nor was it unusual to see quite young people with artificial teeth.

Because the islands are treeless, peat has been the common fuel ever since Norse times. For those who can cut the peat themselves, it is still a good and reasonable fuel. Both coal and electricity are expensive, and besides, the smell of a peat fire has a charm of its own, even though peat gives off a lot of soot! Most farms have the right to cut peat in the old commons. How long it takes to cut enough peat for a year's consumption depends on where the peat hill is located. The lucky ones have a peat strip near their own farm or near a road. The peat is cut in May and June with a special tool which is called a *tusker* – from O.N. torf-skeri, peat-cutter. But the cutting is not always the hardest part of the work – usually it is more of a task getting the peat home. It can be taken home in July and piled in a stack, ready for use. But in wet summers it can be difficult to get the peat dry enough to be used.

Not all the islands have peat, and people have then had to get their fuel in other ways. In North Ronaldsay and Sanday they have partly got peat from Eday and partly made do with dried seaweed or cow dung. Driftwood has also played an important part both as a source of fuel and in making furniture. Thus mahogany was used in the islands long before it was known in the rest of Britain, because it was washed ashore by the Gulf Stream. To find wood on treeless islands was not easy, and the many shipwrecks taking

Peat stack, piled high, ready for winter use.

place in the dangerous waters around the islands were looked upon as heaven-sent gifts. It is said that the minister in Sanday even went as far as praying in church: 'O Lord, gin it be Thy will to cast a ship awa', send that bracken ship to the poor island of Sanday'.

From Westray comes the story of the Storm Witch which in a painful way shows how far the prospect of a rich shipwreck could make the islanders go. People stood on shore and watched while the storm tossed a strange ship towards a sunken rock. No one lifted a finger to help. Then the young Janet Forsyth sprang into her father's boat. She performed the feat of getting on to the ship and bringing it safely to port. Her seamanship in all kinds of weather had already made people call her the Storm Witch. The furious Westray people, cheated of a rich plunder, charged Janet with witchcraft. She was tried in the St Magnus Cathedral, was found guilty, and condemned to be burned at the stake. But the story of Janet Forsyth does not end on Gallow Hill. Her missing sweetheart, who had been seized by the pressgang and forced into the war against France, came home in the nick of time. He contrived to get her guards drunk, and the ship she had rescued took them away from Orkney. Understandably she never came back.

For a long time all finer wood utensils were brought from Norway, including kirns or wooden bowls for housekeeping use. An old verse illustrates this:

> An he wis twice at Drunton (Trondheim)
> For fraghts o tar an deals,
> An troughs an Norwa ladles,
> An skovy kaps an wheels.
> (Wooden cups and spinning wheels)
> L. G. Johnson *Lawrence Williamson of Mid Yell*, 1971

'There's plenty o wid in Norrowa' another song tells us.

Ale brewing was an old custom at all the farms, especially when a wake or a wedding was expected, but also in the spring when milk was scarce. Probably the ale brewing goes all the way back to Norse times. Holinshed's Scottish Chronicle from 1578 maintains that the Orcadians were the worst drinkers in the whole world; yet there was never a drunk man to be seen there. According to tradition the old ale was brewed with Pictish oats, a kind of wild oat, and it was possible to drink that brew without getting drunk.

At one time the making of both ale and spirits was prohibited. The Excise Board probably had their doubts as to whether it would be possible to enforce such a law in the islands; therefore it was decided that two people from each parish should be licensed to keep stills. These would then supply other people in the parish, against paying a certain tax on every pint they produced. This did not work out either. Smuggling, distilling and brewing went on everywhere, in spite of the zeal of the excisemen. Just to keep malt in the house gave cause for suspicion, and there are numerous stories of the ingenious hiding-places which were thought up for the malt. In the end the

The Storm Witch. Drawing by Ian MacInnes.

law was changed so that the farmers had the right to brew their own ale, and this custom of ale brewing still exists.

Life in the old community was ruled by the cycle of the year and the demands of daily life. Animals had to be fed, and seed had to be sown. Both the day and the year followed a regular rhythm. The cycle of life – birth, marriage, death – was surrounded by rites, which everybody accepted to a larger or smaller extent. They acknowledged that the turning points in life are both important and unavoidable. Maybe some of the old Norse belief in destiny, or *lagnad*, survived in this willingness to accept all aspects of life. The message of Ecclesiastes:

> To every thing there is a season,
> and a time to every purpose under the heaven:
> A time to be born, and a time to die;
> A time to plant,
> and a time to pluck up that which is planted;

is just the philosophy of life that gives life in a small community dignity and meaning.

A birth was a happy event, but it was important to guard against the trows and the peerie folk, who would exchange a new-born child with one of their own, if they only had a chance. A child who did not develop as it should might be such a changeling. A common precaution was to put a Bible and a piece of iron in the bed to protect mother and child against all evil forces. It was the custom for all the neighbouring women to come visiting to see the child. The gift they brought was called *hansel* and was usually money. The hansel money could make a nice little fund for a child. The women who called were given *blide-maet*, which was scones and the ale of the house.

The christening of the child was called *cirsening*. If several children were to be christened in the same water, it was essential for the girls to be christened before the boys, otherwise the girls might grow a beard and the boys remain beardless. The safest way would be to change the water. This strange idea once led to drama in Burray when the minister was to christen several children at the same time, and he thought the sequence did not matter. The local midwife, who was known for her interest in the children she helped into the world, rose in protest: 'You're no' gauan tae bapteeze this lassie oot o' the same water as the boy, or it'll be a living disgrace to her a' her life'. The minister, who was notorious for his temper, answered: 'I am a minister of the Kirk of Scotland, come here to administer one of its most solemn ordinances, an' if ye dinna lat me bapteeze this lassie oot o' the same water, I'll bapteeze you, ye auld limmer that ye are'. Then he threw the water in her face and stormed out of the church (W. R. Mackintosh *Around the Orkney Peat-fires*, Kirkwall 1938).

The wedding, like the courting that preceded it, was also surrounded by established customs. It might take some time before a couple could marry because the bridegroom was unable to support a family. But the young people enjoyed quite a lot of freedom, and the old Scandinavian custom of Saturday night courting flourished in Orkney too. The Scottish ministers raged against this custom, but to no avail. In the name of virtue it happened that a wooden plank was put lengthwise in the girl's bed to keep the sweethearts apart.

When the young man thought he had means enough to 'speir' his girl to marry him, her way of accepting him was to say; 'thu can spaek to me faether'. In the old days it was the custom for the young couple to go to the Odin stone to get engaged. This was a single standing stone with a hole in its middle near the Ring of Brogar. The sweethearts would grip each other's hands through the hole in the stone and swear to be true to their love for ever. Now the stone is gone. The story goes that around 1815 the Odin stone was removed by the local farmer; he was tired of all the people crossing his fields. Embittered young people later attempted to set fire to his farm on two occasions.

The wording of the oath which was sworn at the Odin stone is no longer known, but the oath was binding beyond death. In 1726 the pirate John Gow from Stromness was hanged in London. His fiancée went all the way from Stromness to London, to the gallows, where she held his dead hand while she freed herself from the oath of fidelity she had sworn at the Odin stone.

When the wedding had been decided upon, it was important to find a fortuitous day. Most weddings were held in the wintertime, as that was when people had more time. But if it took place in the summer, it must not be in May, as that could be very unlucky. Thursday was the luckiest day. It was essential, however, that the wedding took place between a new moon and a full moon and that the tide was in. This advice was followed in the North Isles until quite recently.

With the fiddler first, the wedding guests would assemble at the manse, where the marriage ceremony took place, and then they would walk to the church. This custom lasted until the First World War. The head-dress sometimes worn by the bride in the old days resembled the one worn by Icelandic women.

The guests were welcomed to the wedding feast with *hansel* – bread and cheese. The wedding cake was thrown above the bride's head, and then everybody had to try to get a piece of it. Inside the cake there was a cross ring to bless or *sain* the cake. The meal consisted of soup, meat and bannocks, with beer and whisky in large quantities. All the guests also contributed food or drink, and brought their own stools. A mixture of beer and whisky, warmed and spiced, was served to everybody in a wooden cog which passed from hand to hand numerous times. This custom still exists; it is customary for a wedding couple to pose for the photographer with the *bride's cog* between them.

The wedding procession. Led by the fiddler, the wedding party walked to the church. The custom lasted until the First World War. (Still from the film The Privilege *directed and written by Ian Knox, based on a story by George Mackay Brown.)*

Dancing and drinking alternated until dawn. It even happened that the wedding guests stayed until all the food was gone before returning home. The longest wedding was held at Notland Castle in Westray. It began at Martinmas, and three months later, at Candlemas, the host said: 'Lord kens what's to come neist! for we hae eaten last o' the bull, stoop and roop, the day' (Ernest W. Marwick *The Folklore of Orkney and Shetland*, Batsford 1975). Then the guests left.

The bride got *tocher geud* – a daughter's goods or dowry when she married. After moving into her new house, she would invite guests for *hame-fare* (O.N. heimferð) – the first party in her new home.

Death was accepted as the natural lot of man, but some strange beliefs were attached to it. There were many omens: the ticking of a worm in the woodwork, the rainbow reaching the ground in two places within sight, the cock crowing after dark.

Regardless of the kind of life the deceased had led or the manner in which he left this world, in death he was entitled to honour and dignity. He was laid on *lik-strae* in the best room of the house. All mirrors were covered up and all cats thrown out. The *lik-wak* began and it usually lasted eight days. The local young people took turns sitting with the corpse – three young men and three young women at a time. They were not expected to grieve, they could while away the time playing cards or drinking beer, and as often as not they thought more of each other than of the corpse. Many young couples first discovered each other at such a lik-wak.

When the deceased had been placed in the coffin, the procession to the church began. No women, not even the widow, were allowed to take part in that. The oldest men in the company walked first. The coffin must only be put down on the *wheelie-stanes* – the regular resting-stones – because anywhere else might bring bad luck. Nor must one mention the deceased by name, since it might raise his spirit – his *ganfer* (O.N. gandferð).

Those who died in the sea or died by their own hand were considered to be outside the community. Dead people who were washed ashore were buried on the shore where they were found. People believed that the sea claimed its own back for the rich gifts it gave; therefore ships sank and men drowned. To give those who drowned a Christian burial would enrage the god of the sea. Those who took their own lives were not to be buried in consecrated ground. On the borderline between the two parishes of Hoy and Walls a lonely hill-grave – Betty Corrigall's grave – bears witness to this custom.

The change of identity which the islanders had to go through during the transition to Scottish rule may not have been easy. It looks as if the old Norn-speaking peasantry, who had difficulty adapting to the new ways, were the losers to an upper class of Scottish incomers. At any rate that is the impression P. A. Munch had of the descendants of the Norsemen:

In the Brogar house we found only a couple of half-grown ragged children at home. Their facial features were so strikingly Norwegian that I, especially in these surroundings, once again was startled to hear them speak English. The greatest poverty seemed to prevail there, and unfortunately this is the case in most houses which are inhabited by the descendants of the Norsemen.

Reminiscences of Orkney

The old community was stagnant by today's standards. Before The Crofters' Act came in 1886, the tenants were almost without legal protection against the landlord, the *laird*. Even though there were lairds of all types, good and bad, the system in itself was unpredictable and wide open to misuse. Ministers and teachers were often appointed and paid by the laird, and it was therefore difficult for them to oppose him by supporting those who were being misused, and so it is not so strange that many lairds felt that they owned their tenants. 'The cep abune the door' was a warning to the husband and others that the laird was visiting the wife on the farm, and that they therefore ought to stay away.

Apart from the croft, there were not many possibilities open to a young man. It was possible to emigrate and many did. Whaling could provide a profitable living, but it was hard. It happened that sick or injured whalers were simply thrown overboard, because they would be an impossible burden to those left behind.

The Orcadians have a reputation for being people of few words. Whether this is a Norse heritage or whether the change of language at some point made them inarticulate, is impossible to know. Perhaps it is the way of islanders. The writer George Mackay Brown relates this story to illustrate that Orkney people say what they have to say in few words:

Two brothers worked a croft together. One day the younger brother went out into the world. After twelve years he was back again. The elder brother asked: 'Whare are thu been?' His brother answered: 'Oot'.

At the same time there existed a rich story-telling tradition. At a time when people had to supply their own entertainment, the family members used to take turns reading aloud. It is no coincidence that the library in Kirkwall is the oldest in Scotland. The lively interest of the Norsemen for family background lived long in Orkney too. 'Kin-redders' the people were called who knew the various families and could even keep track of those family members who had emigrated.

The old life, for better or worse, is gone for ever. It was a life lived at a slow pace, with simple pleasures and hard work, a subsistence economy where the work was not reckoned in hours but in achievement. Today the poverty is gone. Orkney is a modern community with more telephones and cars per number of inhabitants than any other district in Scotland. But even though the houses now are new and roomy and well insulated, they still seem to be merging with the ground as if to hide from the wind – the lazy wind – so-called because it takes the shortest way, right through everything.

13.
The story of the place names

It is not to be wondered at that a Norwegian, and especially a Norwegian historian, will with curiosity, care and some sadness observe these classical places, whose names are so inseparably linked with the memory of our country's strength and former greatness.

P. A. Munch *Reminiscences of Orkney* 1849

Even today Norwegians will agree with what P. A. Munch said in the middle of last century, for nothing has remained as Norse as the place names. Most of them are easily recognizable as such. This is especially true when the names are pronounced by the islanders themselves – then we can only wonder that the original pronunciation could last for so long.

In their written form, the place names have an English pattern imposed on them, and the original Norse form is apparent in varying degree. As Norn did not survive as a written language, the place names as we know them today were written down comparatively late by English or Scottish cartographers who did not know the background of the names. Nor did they understand their meaning. No attempt has ever been made at standardizing the spelling of Orkney place names, and the results are therefore quite confusing. Sometimes the names have been quite distorted, as when Varða-fjall has been turned into Farafield. Some place names defy interpretation.

Norwegian place names have attracted great attention from historians and linguists, and it was natural to extend this interest also to the old Norse dominions in the west. P. A. Munch was the first scholar to do so; with his great historical knowledge he tried to look through the Anglo-Scottish spelling to the Norse core behind it. He was succeeded by other Norwegian scholars, but the Orkneyman Dr Hugh Marwick was the most thorough of them all. In his book *Orkney Farm Names*, which was published in 1952, he analyses the names linguistically and historically. There are historical fossils hidden in the place names, for in them words can be preserved long after they have gone out of use and events hidden which have otherwise been forgotten. With the aid of the place names, linguists can unravel the story of the Norse colonization; but we must bear in mind that all conclusions are not equally certain, and it is necessary to have them confirmed through other sources as well.

The place names show first of all that the Norse landtaking and settlement were complete. Every outcrop of rock, every little brook has got its name. Dr

Marwick considered 10,000 as a probable number of names for commonly known places, but this number would be much higher if we were also to include the names which are of interest only to each farm, such as the names of fields. There are surprisingly few place names of a later Anglo-Scottish origin. The question of place names from pre-Norse, that is Pictish times, is difficult and controversial, and scholars do not agree as to which, if any, go back that far.

The only name we can with any certainty trace back to the time of the Picts is *Orkney* itself. *Ork* meant wild boar in Celtic – an animal which was highly rated because of its strength and ferocity. The boar was the totem for the Pictish tribes in Orkney, and these were also called the Orks. Irish historians wrote of the islands as *Insi Orc* (insi – islands). In Latin this became Orcades or Orcadia. The name of Ork must have been commonly used, for the Norsemen adopted it in *Orkneyjar* – the Orkn islands. In Norway *orkn* or *orknselr* was the name of the grey seal (Halichoerus grypos). We find it used that way in the Norse text *The King's Mirror* from the thirteenth century. Therefore the old name would seem quite a natural one to the Norsemen. They also called Maeshowe Orkahaugr – the Ork mound. One of those who broke into Maeshowe in the twelfth century wrote his name as Orkason. There are other place names as well with the Ork element.

Today *Orkney* is the name the islanders themselves want to use. They will also accept The Orkney Islands, but do not like the form The Orkneys, in spite of its being closer to the original name.

Let us consider what the names of the various islands were in Norse times, and what they mean. (P) means the present form, and (N) the Norse form.

North Ronaldsay (P) and Rinansey (N): locally the name has till quite recently been pronounced Rinnelsey. A possible explanation of the name is that the island is named from the British missionary St Ninian, because one variant of his name is Ringan, another is Ronan. But this is just guess work, and we must accept that the background of the name is uncertain. North Ronaldsay is a comparatively new name which has probably arisen as a misunderstood parallel to South Ronaldsay.

Sanday (P) and Sandey (N); Westray (P) and Vestrey (N); Papa Westray (P) and Papey (hin) meiri (N), that is Big (Greater) Papey: the Norsemen evidently found this island inhabited by Celtic monks. Locally the island is still called Papay. Eday (P) and Eiðey (N): this island has a narrow *eið*, or isthmus, in the middle. Stronsay (P) and Strjónsey (N): the background of this name is uncertain. P. A. Munch thought it was formed of *strjón*, the same word as in the Norwegian place name Stryn, a word meaning property or profit. A more romantic explanation is that the island is named from all the springs to be found there. The water from one of them, Kildinguie, has till quite recently been said to have the power to cure.

Papa Stronsay (P) and Papey (hin)litli (N) – Little Papey; Rousay (P) and Hrólfsey (N); Egilsay (P) and Egilsey (N): this seems to be a parallel to

Pomona Inn, Finstown. Though the mainland of Orkney was often called Pomona by writers of days gone by, the name was never used by the islanders themselves.

Hrólfs ey, formed from the name Egil. But it is possible that the Celtic word *eaglais* for church in the vernacular has been confused with the genitive of the name Egil. It is not impossible that the first settlers found a church in Egilsay. In a description from 1529 the name is explained as *insularum ecclesia*, that is church island.

Wyre (P) and Vígr (N): this word meant a javelin in Norse. It is the name of a Norwegian island, Vigra in Sunnmöre, as well as of one in Iceland. Possibly the shape gave the island its name. Eynhallow (P) and Eyin Helga(ey hin helga) (N) – the holy island: this name probably contains echoes of Pictish times, for the monastery ruins we find there today are from the twelfth century.

Gairsay (P) and Gáreksey (N) – from the man's name Gárekr; Copinsay (P) and Kolbeinsey (N); Shapinsay (P) and Hjalpandisey (N): P. A. Munch thought that the basic element of the name is *hjalpandi* – helping, and that this name is given because the island has a good harbour which helped those coming in from the sea.

Mainland (P): this is the island the Norsemen called Meginland – the main island. They also gave it a more specific name: Hrossey – the island of horses. In written usage the island was later often called Pomona – a form which was completely unknown to the islanders themselves. It was P. A. Munch who, around the middle of the last century, pointed out with irrefutable logic that the name had originally occurred in the writings of a Scottish author because he had misinterpreted a mention of the island in a text by the Roman author Solinus. This mistake was then repeated by later writers. It is worth noting that the Scottish mainland is never spoken of as Mainland, but always Scotland.

Graemsay (P) and Grímsey (N); Cava (P) and Kálfey (N); Flotta (P) and Flatey (N); Burray (P) and Borgarey (N): *borg* meant castle or fortification. The remains of two brochs are still to be found in Burray. South Ronaldsay (P) and Rǫgnvaldsey (N); Hoy (P) and Háey (N) – the high island, from há – high; Swona (P) and Svíney (N) – pig island; Stroma (P) and Straumsey (N) – the island in the current: there is a Straumsey in the Faeroe Islands as well. Stroma is now part of Caithness.

Many of the place-name elements are so common elsewhere that they do not need much explanation, such as -ness (promontory) and -wick (bay). Note, however, that the *w* in -wick is pronounced, contrary to what is common in standard English. Other place name elements are uncommon enough to require explanation:

brough – from O.N. borg. It is pronounced like broch, which is also derived from borg. This word is used about the little island which is made when the sea wears away the isthmus of a peninsula. The best known is Brough of Birsay (O.N. Byrgisey). Such an island makes a natural fortification and often has the remains of pre-Norse buildings.

geo – from O.N. gjá or gjó – is a deep, narrow cleft in the coastline. The cleft is made when the sea wears down a soft strip in the rock. Such a geo is impressive and sometimes frighteningly steep.

gloup – from O.N. gljúfr. When the sea thunders into the opening of a cave, it can press against the top of the cave so that it collapses. The abyss which is then formed is called a gloup. It can be quite large, and it can also be quite dangerous, because without warning we can find ourselves on the edge of a perpendicular rock wall. There is a well-known gloup in Deerness in east Mainland, another near Halcro Head in South Ronaldsay.

roost – from O.N. rǫst, a maelstrom. When an outgoing current meets the waves of the Atlantic on the way in, the water swirls in a series of whirlpools, as in the rapids of a shallow river. Such roosts are seen in Hoy Sound and in Eynhallow Sound.

hope – from O.N. hóp, which means a bay, as in St Margaret's Hope, or in Mathopen, near Bergen.

voe – from O.N. vágr – a bay – as in Hamnavoe.

wall – this is a strange distortion of vágr which appears in some place names, for example Kirkwall from Kirkjuvágr, and Osmondwall from

The gloup, Deerness. When the sea thunders into the opening of a cave it can press against the top of the cave so that it collapses. The abyss which is then formed is called a gloup.

Ásmundarvágr. Walls is derived from the plural form Vágar, as is Vågan in the Lofoten Islands. The final sound -gr fell away in the Middle Ages; in 1274 Kirkwall had become Kyrkewa in the *Chronicle of Man*. When the town became a burgh it was given the documents in the name of Kirkwall, because the Scots believed that *wa* was just a local pronunciation of the word wall. The old pronunciation lasted till the beginning of this century – but the power of the written word is great, and Kirkwall has now become the accepted pronunciation. Note that the name Tingwall in Evie has no connection with these other -wall names. It is derived from O.N. þingvǫllr and means a field where the assembly would meet.

oyce – from O.N. óss – the mouth of a river.

taing – from O.N. tangi – a tongue of land.

fea, fiold – from O.N. fjall – mountain or hill, as in Binga Fea in Walls in Hoy and Hindera Fiold in Harray on Mainland.

shun, chun – from O.N. tjǫrn – a tarn or small lake, as in Loch of Loomachun in Rousay. Loomachun means the tarn of the loon, but the meaning was forgotten, and the Scottish word loch was added.

The place names also show that the majority of the settlers undoubtedly came from Norway. Elements like *gil*, *brekka* and *klettr* were notably Norwegian. So were the farm name elements *bolstaðr* and *skáli*.

Orkney, unlike Iceland, does not have a Landnámabók – a book of settlement which describes in detail how and when the landtaking begins. The Orkneyinga saga is not necessarily wrong when it asserts that it was when King Harald Fairhair first welded the small kingdoms of Norway into one realm towards the end of the ninth century that the migration to the west began. But it is possibly the second, even the third wave of migration which was caused by the battle of Hafrsfjord in 872. The Faeroese linguist Jakobsen was struck by the many southwestern Norwegian characteristics of the dialects in Orkney and Shetland. A brief Swedish occupation of southwestern Norway early in the ninth century may have caused a wave of emigration from Agder and Rogaland.

We see that the place names supply overwhelming proof of the Norse colonization. Scholars have emphasized different elements and for that reason they have not reached the same conclusions about when the settlement took place. The most extreme conclusion concerning early dating has been put forward by C. J. S. Marstrander, who thought the Norse settlement in Orkney began as early as the sixth century. Today scholars try to compare the place–name conclusions with archaeological finds, and seen against this background it looks as though the early ninth century is the most likely period for the main weight of Norse settlement.

It is the farm names that contain the most historical information. We can assume that the best and most easily available land was taken first. Apparently the farm names have also followed certain fashions; thus, for example, the -vin and the -heimr names had gone out of fashion even before the Viking Age began. When some scholars thought they could identify -vin names in Orkney, a sharp conflict about dating started.

As already mentioned, it is Dr Hugh Marwick in *Orkney Farm Names* who has really studied the farms thoroughly. He tries to establish a chronological sequence in the names, and on the whole uses the method set forth by the Norwegian scholar Magnus Olsen in *Farm and Fane* (1926). Marwick picks out nine farm-name elements: *bú* and *býr*, *skáli*, *staðir*, *bolstaðr*, *garðr*, *land*, *setr* and *kvi*. Marwick's method is to study these elements from an historical and topographical angle. He compares the information he finds about the farms and what they paid in tax in the old rentals with conditions today; he considers where the most fertile soil is and how the farms are placed in relation to the sea and each other. Even if other scholars may question some of Marwick's conclusions, his main results will probably not be refuted.

bær/býr – a dwelling place. The word is connected with O.N. *búa* – to live. This is a very old type of name in Norway, and it could mean the farm houses, the farm itself and a cluster of farms. In Orkney we find the name by itself: Bae or Bea, or as an ending: -by, -bay, -bie and -bae (examples: Houseby, Trenabie, Midbea). All these variants are typical of the earliest settled farms so that whenever we find a name with an ending like this, we can assume this to be one of the major farms of the early settlement or built on land belonging to one.

The Huseby names – O.N. Husabyr and Husabær – make up a very interesting group. Huseby was used in Norway about a royal farm which had both an administrative and a military function. The king's ombudsman stayed there, and a military unit of armed men was stationed there all the time. This form of administration arose first in Uppland in Sweden in the first half of the seventh century. The dynasty of the Ynglings brought it to Norway when they became kings there, and then it was introduced into the dominions in the west. A similar system is known both in the Isle of Man and the Hebrides. We know of four huseby-farms in Orkney: Houseby in Stronsay, Housebay in Shapinsay, Houseby in Rousay and Housebay in Birsay. The Norwegian historian Asgaut Steinnes has tried to reconstruct the administrative division in Norse times on the basis of the location of the huseby-farms. Steinnes deduced six probable huseby districts. This also agrees with the number in Man and the Hebrides. We may perhaps also conclude that each huseby district had approximately the same number of inhabitants and basis for tax. Thus the huseby system can give us an idea of how the population was spread in the various islands in Norse times.

The location of the bær and býr farms points to their having been taken by the very first wave of settlers. In addition we find the interesting fact that we never find any combination with kirk or kirkja in this type of name. Does this show that these farms were taken so early that the Norsemen were as yet untouched by Christianity?

bú – farm, a place to live. This is a common farm name in Orkney, but it is used more as a generic term than as an ordinary name. It is always used with the definite article: The Bu of Wyre, The Bu of Skaill, The Bu of Rapness etc. Locally these farms are referred to only as The Bu. The strangest thing about this name is that as a farm name it is used almost only in Orkney. There are none in the Faeroe Islands, Iceland has three, and Norway has some very few. But nowhere have they got such a form as in Orkney.

According to the old rentals, a *bú* was a large farm which was run independently of the other farms. In Norway some of the king's estates were known as *konungsbú* – the king's farm, and possibly a bu in Orkney in Norse times was the seat of a *göðing* or a man of chieftain's rank. Some of the farms of the earl were perhaps given to trusted men in veizla – a kind of feu. It is possible that this may be behind this special use of bu.

skáli – in Norse this meant either a small shed or the main house of a farm. But in Orkney it has acquired a more special meaning, for it is used more in the sense of a large banqueting hall: these are known as Skaill or Langskaill. Svein Asleifarson, 'the ultimate Viking', built his farm in Gairsay, and it is still known as Langskaill. But we also find combinations like Netherskaill and Breckaskaill. These names are not among the oldest ones. The Orkney historian P. L. Thomson suggests that the Skaill-farms may originally have served as the earl's storehouses. 'Skaill names are usually to be found at a prime site, in the centre of the district, with a good landing place and are often adjacent to an early church site.' The Skaill farms seem to have had little land, and this may perhaps also be taken in support of this theory.

staðir – the plural form of staðr – place. This ending appears today as -sta and -ster, but mostly as -ston (example: Tormiston from þormodstaðir). When Iceland was built, this was the most common of all place-name elements, and in Norway there are also a lot of such names. In Orkney there are 23 instances of these names; most of them are on Mainland, around Lochs Stenness and Harray. These names have in common that they are combined with a man's name and that none of the staðir-farms belongs among those first settled. That they are not primary farms appears also from the fact that there is not a single farm with a staðir-name in the North Isles, which were settled from Norway first. In this way the evidence of the place names also shows that the colonization of Orkney took place long before the settlement of Iceland, and that we can actually speak of a new wave of immigration at the time the staðir-names were used.

bolstaðr – farm, a place to live. This was a place-name element special to Norway, and occurs mostly in the northwest, in the districts of Möre, Romsdal, Sogn and Fjordane. It is one of the most common and most characteristic place-name elements in Orkney. We find it evenly distributed, as -bister, -buster, and -bist. Examples: Isbister, Kirbuster. These names are considered to be of the same age as the -land and -garðr names and are very old, but not among the first. Probably they are from the ninth century. There are ten bolstaðr-names with kirk as a prefix. This must mean that many Norsemen were Christians long before the islands were officially Christianized.

garðr – farm (Suthergarth, Midgarth, Garso). These names are unevenly distributed, but there are quite a few of them in Sanday.

land – this ending is also Scottish. All the same, we can say with certainty that the major part of the land names are Norse, as they appear in pre-Scottish sources. The land-farms are evenly distributed. As many as nine of them have been called Holland, from há – high and land.

setr – a place to stay or live. This is a common ending in Norway, especially in the northwest, but it is not found in Iceland. It is probably derived from sitja – to sit. The ending appears sometimes as a name by itself: Seater or Setter, but it is found mostly as a suffix: -setter, -ster, -set (examples: Morsetter, Cursetter). These farms are mostly rather small, secondary farms, and we must therefore conclude that they were built relatively late, after the best land had been taken.

kvi – an enclosure of animals. This word was used about places where animals gathered, and it is a very common place-name element. It is now spelled *quoy* and pronounced *kwai*; earlier it was pronounced *kwi*. This is the Norse place description which has remained the longest in active use. Till quite recently older people have used it about a field.

To deduce historical development on the basis of place names is difficult and uncertain, but it may be possible to draw some cautious conclusions. Not all Norse settlement occurred at the same time – it was scattered over at least a century. The first settlement took place earlier than generally assumed, probably around 800. The Norsemen did not come to empty land; at least groups of Picts survived – the place names combined with the genitive plural form *petta* bear witness to this. There are very few examples of names from pagan times, but we find Tor Ness and Odin Head in Stronsay – in the east, where the settlers would first make a landfall. The Kirbister-names – kirkja and bolstaðr – probably date back to the ninth century. That may mean that the Norsemen lost their pagan beliefs early on and that the contact with the Christian Picts gave them a new faith, if little else.

We must be pleased that so much work has been devoted to the study of Orkney place names. When interpreted along with written sources and archaeological finds they give us a good idea of how the Norse settlement took place. It is a source material that will shrink as time goes on. The Orkney countryside is changing character; farms disappear, and in many places there are as many empty houses as there are occupied ones. All the time the door is being closed on farms for the last time as the old Orkney families move out. How long will the old farm names then remain part of living memory?

14.   The language

The men spoke for the most part in a slow, deliberate voice, but some of the women could rattle on at a great rate in the soft sing-song lilt of the islands, which has remained unchanged for a thousand years ... It is a soft and musical inflection, slightly melancholy, but companionable, the voice of people who are accustomed to hours of talking in the long winter evenings and do not feel they need to hurry: a splendid voice for telling stories in.

Edwin Muir *An Autobiography* (Hogarth Press 1954)

When the Norsemen first came to Orkney there were probably two different languages in use among the Picts: an old Pictish language which is forgotten today, and a Celtic language. The papae – the missionary monks – also spoke a Celtic language. The papae could have had some linguistic influence on the Norsemen through the new faith. On their expeditions for trade or plunder to the areas around the Irish Sea, the new Orkneymen met Celtic-speaking Irishmen and Scots. It is not possible to know whether the Norsemen picked up words from the old Pictish language. Much would depend on how the settlement took place, for experience seems to show that the cultural influence rarely goes from thrall to master when an area is conquered.

Of the few Celtic words which have been used in Orkney through the years, it is difficult today to ascertain which may have been later loanwords from Scots-Gaelic. By comparing with Celtic words used in Icelandic and Faeroese, where later contact with Celtic words has been slight, it has been possible to deduce that certain common words have been borrowed in the early Norse period, but these conclusions are far from certain. One such word is *krue*, which means an enclosure for sheep. This word is also found in old Irish.

By the Viking Age in the ninth century the language in Orkney was Norse. Linguists agree that the language must have had some of the characteristics of West Norse, more specifically of the speech of southwestern Norway, and it is therefore reasonable to believe that the settlers came mostly from the areas of Vest-Agder, Rogaland and Sunnhordland. The language later became known as *Norn*, a contraction of *norrænn*: northern, the adjective commonly used about old Norway and her North Sea dominions, best translated with *Norse*.

Some runic inscriptions have been found in Orkney. The richest collection is inside Maeshowe, which the Norsemen called *Orkahaugr*. A band of crusaders broke in there, probably in the winter of 1152, and most of the inscriptions seem to have been made then. They amused themselves by scribbling down anything that occurred to them. One of them calls himself Orkason, and one inscription reads: *Þisar runar rist sa maðr er runstr er fyrir uæstan haf* – 'these runes that man cut who is most skilled in rune-craft west over sea' – so it is possible that one or more of those who broke into the tomb were Orkneymen.

The saga literature gives few, if any, clues to the language spoken in Orkney in Norse times. The Orkney Bishop Bjarni Kolbeinsson is the author of *Jómsvikingadrápa – The Lay of the Joms vikings*. In this work we find a special Orkney word, *göðingr*, which was used in Orkney about a chieftain or a man of outstanding family. In the poem *Málshátta kvæði*, which is also believed to have been written by Bishop Bjarni, there are several word-forms deviating from standard Norse; these may therefore be considered Orkney words. The word *gagarr* for dog seems special to the islands, it is used in other Orkney writing as well. But in the work of the two Orkney poets Sigmundr Ǫngull and Thorbjörn the Black there are no dialect words, the form being standard Norse.

The oldest preserved public document from Orkney, dated 4 April 1329, is still in pure Norse language, whilst another document, from 1424, shows a certain Danish influence in the spelling, with Low Scots words and names adopted (though otherwise the language is still Norse).

When the line of Norse earls became extinct the earldom passed first to the Angus family, and then from them to the Stratherne family. These were

Runic inscriptions, Maeshowe. The richest collections of runes are found inside Orkahaugr, the name the Norsemen gave to Maeshowe.

both Gaelic-speaking families, and it is therefore natural that some Gaelic words would be adopted during this period. However, this influence was short-lived, as in 1379 the title of earl passed to the Sinclair family, who were Lowland Scots. With the Sinclair family the Anglo-Scots influence began in earnest. The transition to Scots was gradual and thus began even before the islands were pledged to Scotland in 1468. Under the Lowland Scots earls all administrative language was Scots, they appointed a Scottish bishop, and all legal documents were also written in Scots. The transition to Scots as a written language, therefore, did not take long.

Among the common people Norn lived on. We can only marvel at its being as tenacious as history tells us that it was. It was a language without written form, without social status – and thus doomed to extinction.

One of the reasons why Norn could survive as long as it did, was that the ties with Norway were not completely broken even after the islands were pledged to Scotland. For a long time there was a lively trade with Bergen, and quite a few Orkney youths also went there to find work. It is reasonable to believe that the islands were mostly bilingual throughout the sixteenth and most of the seventeenth centuries.

In 1700 James Wallace wrote this about the old language in the islands:

All speak English, after the Scots way, with as good an Accent as any County in the Kingdom, only some of the common People amongst themselves, speak a Language they call Norns; which they have derived to them, either from the Pights, or some others, who first planted this Country; for by the following Lord's Prayer in that Language, it has but little of the Danish or Norwegian Language, to which I thought it should have had more affinity, considering how long time they were possessors of this country.

An Account of the Islands of Orkney, 1700, London

The good Wallace was no linguist, or he would have realized that the version of the Lord's Prayer that he wrote down at the time was quite similar to that used by the Norsemen – with a few exceptions of Anglo-Scots words:

Favor i ir i Chimrie, helleur ir i nam thite. Gilla cosdum thite cumma, veya thine mota vara gort o yurn sinna gort i Chimrie. Ga vus da on da dalight brow vora. Firgive vus sinna vora sin vee firgive sindara mutha vus. Lyv vus ye i tumtation, min delivra vus fra olt ilt. On sa meteth vera.

An Account of the Islands of Orkney, 1700, London

Naturally enough Norn survived longer in the more remote islands, and strangely it is no other than Sir Walter Scott who can tell us about this. He once travelled in Orkney, and this inspired him to write the novel *The Pirate* in 1821. In some notes for this book, 'Norse Fragments', he wrote that in the eighteenth century the Norse language was still not forgotten in North Ronaldsay. This is how Scott tells about it:

A clergyman, who was not long deceased, remembered well when some remnants of the Norse were still spoken in the island called North Ronaldsha. When Gray's Ode, entitled the 'Fatal Sisters', was first published, or at least first reached that remote island, the reverend gentleman had the well-judged curiousity to read it to some of the old persons of the isle, as a poem which regarded the history of their own country. They listened with great attention to the preliminary stanzas:

> Now the storm beings to lour,
>> Haste the loom of hell prepare;
> Iron sleet of arrowy shower
>> Hurtles in the darken'd air.

But when they heard a verse or two more, they interrupted the reader, telling him they knew the song well in the Norse language, and had often sung it to him when he asked them for an old song. They called it the Magicians, or the Enchantresses.

It was the old *Darraðarljoð* the clergyman heard, a poem from the late Viking Age. It is sung by the valkyries, who choose those to die in battle, over the loom where they are weaving the fates of the men fighting in the battle of Clontarf in Ireland, on Good Friday 1014. It is probable that this poem originated in Orkney, and has survived through the centuries in the oral tradition. The poem is part of *The Saga of Burnt Njál*.

Thomas Gray's poem 'The Fatal Sisters' is an English version of *Darraðarljoð*, based on a Latin translation by Thormod Torfaeus, the Icelandic historian. Although Gray's poem as captured some of the intensity of the Norse original, it lacks its grandeur, and is a rather pale imitation.

During the eighteenth century the decline came quickly. The main cause of this was that people were taught Scots both through the Church and through the schools, which were increasingly becoming open to everybody. The ministers considered Norn sinful, and a great deal was done to suppress it. And, of course, belonging to a linguistic minority often gives a feeling of inferiority. It is said that the last persons to speak Norn were looked upon as strange eccentrics – such a person was spoken of as 'an auld Norny body'.

In 1774 the minister George Low published a book about a journey he made through Orkney and Shetland. About the language he says that

It was called here Norn but is now so much worn out, that I believe there is scarce a single man in the country who can express himself on the most ordinary occasion in this language. Even the Songs, which are commonly longest retained of any part of a language, are now (except a few of the most trifling) altogether lost, tho this little more than half a century ago was the prevailing tongue of two parishes in the Mainland.
A tour through the islands of Orkney and Shetland in 1774 (ed. Joseph Anderson 1879)

When a language dies gradually, as Norn did, the process seems to follow certain laws: first the inflected forms fall away, then the most common words, such as numerals and prepositions, are replaced by new words. But when the most commonly used words have disappeared, there may still remain a core of those words, especially those connected with people's life and work. Often the new language does not have suitable or adequate terms to express these concepts. The old sentence structures and intonation also tend to merge into the new language.

This process is also borne out by another of Low's observations:

They now altogether speak English, but with a great deal of Norwegian accent, and even with some words of that language intermixed – to this day there are many sounds in the English language which the Orkney people cannot master, but pronounce according to their old Norn dialect, for example, qu in queen, question, quarrel &c.&c. is universally pronounced as if it was written wh, hence to a man, they say wheen, whestion, wharrel &c. th they pronounce without the aspiration, as thing, ting; three, tree; thumb, tumb; thousand, tousand; and in many other particulars this corruption of their English is observable . . .

But much of what seems typically Norwegian in pronunciation, such as the r-sound, the long vowel instead of the dipthong in *oot* for *out*, and *hame* and *stane* for *home* and *stone*, is at the same time Scottish pronunciation. The Orkney dialect is also a rich Scots dialect – the Scots Lowland speech has survived better here than in most places in Scotland. One example is the consistent use of *no* for *not: Why did they no tak' it?*

Orkney speech has retained other phonetic characteristics besides intonation that affirm its Norse background. The Scots sound *ch*, as in loch, is rarely used. The sound *th* was earlier pronounced mostly as *d* or *t*, that is the unvoiced *th* as in *think* was pronounced as *t*, *tink*, and voiced *th* as in *mother* became d(d). This pronunciation was used as recently as after the Second World War, but is now becoming rare. In a final position, *rs* has a clearly discernable *h* added on, so that this sound combination is pronounced as in eastern Norwegian speech. The Norwegian ö-sound is used in a number of words: *gös* (goose), *döck* (duck), *shö* (she), *dö* (do), but this sound is also losing ground. About to die out also is the y-sound in *kettle*, which is pronounced *kyettle*; on the other hand it is quite common for *j, g, dg* to be pronounced as unvoiced sounds. This also applies to the voiced *s*. *A zebra in the zoo* will usually be pronounced with the unvoiced *s*.

The Norse present participle ending *-andi* has been retained in the pronunciation as *-an*. Whereas the present participle in modern English, and mostly also in Scots, both in written and oral usage, is identical with the verbal noun, and therefore has the ending *-ing*, the Orkney dialect still distinguishes between these two forms: *He was drinkan all night; he would never stop his drinkin. I'm been speakan at the meeting, but I'm no much good at the speakin.* This form is also used adjectivally: *glitteran stars, greetan bairns* (crying children). The distinction between *-an* for the present participle and *-in* for the verbal noun is still common usage.

Another distinctively Orcadian characteristic is using *to be* instead of *to have* to form the perfect tense. *I'm walked a piece the day*, and *are ye been there? Better* is used in the meaning of *more: thir wir better ur five men there.* *Ur* (or) is used instead of *than* in comparisons: *better ur any man.* This is especially interesting, because it is a characteristic the Orkney dialect has in common with the Rogaland and Vest-Agder dialects. The same is true of the reflexive use of pronouns in a way unknown to standard English: *sit thee doon.*

As is to be expected, most of the Norn words and expressions still in use in Orkney concern people's daily life and work. These are words connected with fishing and farming, peatcutting and weaving, seabirds and boats. As the way of life changes, many of these words disappear. Sometimes a word has acquired a slightly different meaning. *Noust* – O.N. naust – is used about a landing place instead of in the Norse meaning of boat-house – maybe because a boat-house is rarely used – the boats are just pulled up on the beach. Nevertheless, we must acknowledge that the language has been transformed during the last 50 years, as so many words have disappeared. In 1920 the Orkneyman John Firth wrote his reminiscences of a long life spent in the parish of Firth in Mainland. He includes in his book a number of words that are characteristic of his own dialect.

The Orkney writer George Mackay Brown, who was born about the time John Firth wrote down his collection of old words, finds few words there still in use. '. . . some of the words I've never heard. Others were familiar in my childhood, when the old folk used them with style and relish. But now you hear them only very occasionally. As for the new generation, these are words from beyond a great divide. More and more our speech is approximating to standard English; with, it's true, the music of the islands in them still.

'What lovely words have gone into the silence! "Vore", the springtime, for example. Another is "ice-lowsing", meaning the thaw – a marvellous word that . . . Still, in lonely crofts, there is the "sae-bink", a stone shelf for water vessels to be set. There is excuse for the vanishing of such a fine word, for now there is little need for the "sae-bink".

'Will there come a day, maybe in the last years of the century, when the most tenacious Norn word of all, "peedie" or "peerie", is a ghost – when we all purse our lips and say "little" or "small", which doesn't mean the same as "peedie", with its undertones of joy and affection?

'This is how the rot sets in; though it had begun long before. It is only when you see such a word-list that you realize what a treasure has been lost.' (Article in *The Orcadian*).

Strangely enough, the decline has coincided with a growing interest in language and historical roots. Orkney's Norse past and cultural kinship with the Scandinavian countries are often emphasized today. Every Orcadian is brought up on the Orkneyinga saga and its heroic stories, and this has made the names from the past familiar and commonly used – names such as Ingrid, Sigrid, Thora and Inga, Thorfinn, Olaf, Magnus and Erlend.

1 *Stack Skerry with gannets*

2 *Orphir: fields all over Orkney turn yellow with buttercups in June*

3 *Silage cutting makes the landscape turn to every shade of green during the summer months*

4 *Skara Brae: this Stone Age village emerged during a storm in the middle of the last century*

5 *Rackwick, Hoy: the most isolated place in Orkney*

6 *Loch Stenness: a favourite place for swans and other birds during the winter. The hills of Hoy are in the background*

7 *Puffins, Suleskerry: more than 50,000 of this distinctive bird breed here*

8 *A herd of cows beside the Loch of Swannay*

9 *Primula Scotica: this flower is special to northern Scotland, and its whereabouts are a well-kept secret*

10 *Kame of Hoy: a dramatic cliffscape*

11 *Sanday has long white beaches where sand is sometimes blown into large dunes*

12 *Kirkwall: looking towards the northern isles*

13 *Broch of Gurness: one of the best preserved brochs in Orkney*

15. The cultural heritage

Although most of Norse literature was made and written down in Iceland, some skaldic poetry was clearly composed in Orkney. Other literature is in various ways associated with the islands, and some of it is of particular interest.

The Orkney earls seem to have been gifted in many ways, some of them also with a talent for poetry. One of the first earls, Turf-Einar Rognvaldsson, left behind him a legacy of dry irony, apparent both in his verse and in the remark to his father: 'I can promise you the greatest favour you could wish for, and that's never to have to see me again'. Five short verses, known as *lausavísor*, loose verse, are all that is left of his writing, and we do not know whether he wrote any more.

Einar's verses are among the best skaldic poetry. They are written in the characteristic *drottkvætt* metre, which was the favourite metre of the *skalds*, as the poets were called. The stanza consisted of eight three-stress lines, and the last word of each line always had the same metrical form. Drottkvætt verse also had complicated rules about internal rhyme and alliteration. The skalds were especially interested in the metrical technique of verse, aiming at making poetry which would be impressive in recitation. This they achieved in the drottkvætt metre, which suited the emphasis of Norse speech. Einar does not excel in form nor in his use of *kenningar* – the Norse metaphors – but there seems to be real feeling underlying the heavy sadness of his verse.

Einar's verses were composed towards the end of the ninth century, in the middle of the Viking period. The strange *Darraðarljoð* – also known as the Spear-song – was probably written in Orkney by an unknown writer just after the Battle of Clontarf in 1014, an event which marked the end of Norse expansion in the west. The poem is completely pagan, and both in style and idea it is reminiscent of the heroic verse of the Elder Edda. Still, its visionary contents are in a class to themselves: it tells no story but is a wild and bloody battle song with an almost hypnotic effect, sung as it is by the valkyries, the choosers of the slain in the field of battle, to the rhythm of their loom: *Vindum, vindum/vef darradar* – wind we, wind we/the weave of spears.

Arnor Thordarson, called the Earls' Poet, may not be much later in time than the writer of *Darraðarljoð*; like him he belongs to the eleventh century, but as a Christian and a court poet he belongs to a completely different tradition. He was an Icelander by birth, the son of Oddny 'Ey-kyndill' – the island torch – the girl who was loved by the two skalds, Thord and Björn. The story of their fight for Oddny is described in one of the less-known sagas.

Arnor started on his travels when he was quite young. He married into the family of the Earls of Orkney and for a long time made his home in the islands. But he also spent some time at the royal court in Norway, and he probably returned to Iceland in his old age. He was a prolific writer, but some of his poetry survives only in fragments. This is true of his *Rognvaldsdrápa*, which was written to honour Earl Rognvald Brusason. A drápa was a long poem which was written especially for kings or chieftains and was meant to be recited ceremoniously. It had a refrain of two or four lines between every two, three or four stanzas.

In the winter of 1047, Arnor was in Trondheim on a visit to the two monarchs Magnus the Good and Harald Hardrada, who ruled the country together. Arnor recited a drápa for each king. Of the *Magnusdrápa* 20 stanzas still survive, whereas the drápa written for King Harald is lost. The *Magnusdrápa* is Arnor's best work. It was written in a new and exciting metre; the poem was striking in its freshness and originality. Its style was simple, with fewer kenningar than were usual in skaldic poetry – the king stands 'like a hawk' in his ship which shines 'as when the sun rises or beacons burn'. This drápa is also an important historical source, in spite of its tendency to exaggeration which made King Harald exclaim in annoyance 'what violent expressions the man uses'. King Harald also said that the poem about himself would soon be forgotten but the drápa about King Magnus would be recited 'as long as the North is built'.

Arnor also wrote a *Thorfinnsdrápa* on the death of Earl Thorfinn the Mighty. Like all his poetry it is remarkable for the sincerity underlying it. He was a deeply religious man of peace, and the writer of *Geisli*, perhaps the greatest religious work of the Norse period, was influenced by Arnor's poetry.

Like Arnor, Earl Rognvald Kali Kolsson wrote easily and well – writing poetry seemed almost a game to him. His lausavísor are a light-hearted part of the Orkneyinga saga. He was capable of improvising verse, as when he sees a shivering servant girl coming into the hall, and people cannot make out what she is saying as her teeth are chattering so:

> You sit steaming, but Asa's
> s-soaked to the skin;
> f-f-far from the fire . . .

Only one long work by Rognvald has survived, and we do not know whether he made any more. This is *Háttalykill* – a metrical key to Norse prosody – which Rognvald wrote together with the Icelandic skald Hall Torarinsson who stayed at the earl's court some time after 1140. It tells of myths and monarchs; the contents are not important, but the form is. It is a long illustration of various metres and poetic effects. They were not content to include only samples of Norse metre as used by the skalds, but also tried to introduce Latin and French variations, perhaps in an attempt to renew skaldic poetry. Snorri Sturluson learnt from this work and perfected the idea in his *Háttatal*.

The greatest of all Orkney skalds was Bjarni Kolbeinsson, Earl Rognvald's kinsman and the son of the Norse chieftain Kolbein Hruga from Sunnfjord, who settled in Wyre. Bjarni Kolbeinsson was Bishop of Orkney from 1188 till he died in Bergen in 1222 while attending a meeting to settle Hakon Hakonsson's right to the throne. He was responsible for getting Earl Rognvald canonized, and he continued the building of the St Magnus Cathedral, so that only the west front was lacking when he died. Bjarni was a well-educated man, familiar with English tradition and also closely connected with learned circles in Iceland.

Only one poem can with certainty be said to have been written by Bjarni – *Jómsvikingadrápa*. It is included in the last pages of a manuscript of Snorri's *Edda* from about 1325, along with *Málshátta kvæði*, whose author is not known. For that reason, and because of certain similarities of style and content, this poem is also commonly ascribed to Bishop Bjarni. The *Jómsvikingadrápa* tells about the vow of the Jomsvikings to capture Norway. They sail north in the middle of winter and are thoroughly beaten by Earl Hakon in the battle of Hjǫrungavágr in 986 and must return in disgrace. It is possible that Bjarni here actually makes covert fun of the 'island beardies' – the men from the islands who were beaten by King Sverre near Bergen in 1194. Bishop Bjarni was closely involved as an intermediary in the reprisals which followed. Both the *Jómsvikingadrápa* and *Málshátta kvæði* contain material not found elsewhere, which perhaps shows that Orkney had its own tradition of myths and stories.

Bjarni uses the drottkvætt metre of the skalds, but even in his opening lines he breaks with literary tradition, and his poem seems to be a subtle parody of the heroic poem. He introduces a theme of unhappy love which perhaps is intended as a satire of romantic English troubadour poetry. It is a clever poem full of puns and double meanings; at the same time it is written in a simple and flowing style; it is not the words but his use of them that is exceptional.

Bishop Bjarni has also been suggested as the author of Orkneyinga saga, or *Jarlasǫgur* – the Earls' Sagas – as its original name is. This work is known as a fragment from the early thirteenth century and was later included in *Flateyjarbók*. The original is kept in Stofnun Árna Magnússonar in Reykjavik. The Orkneyinga saga was probably written in the first decade of the thirteenth century and was used by Snorri Sturluson when he wrote *Heimskringla*, the sagas of the Norse kings.

The last part of the Orkneyinga saga describes contemporary events and especially the exploits of the Gairsay chieftain Svein Asleifarson, who was closely connected with Bishop Bjarni. There is also information of little

Langskaill, Gairsay. The Orkneyinga Saga describes the exploits of Gairsay chieftain Svein Asleifarson who built his hall and farm here.

interest outside Bjarni's family, and it is therefore probable that Bjarni had a hand in the writing of the Orkneyinga saga. The author knew Orkney well; at the same time most modern scholars are convinced that it was written by an Icelander. The Norse scholar Anne Holtsmark suggested that it was written by Hrafn Sveinbjarnarson under Bjarni's supervision – a theory which seems logical. Bishop Bjarni is known to have sent very generous gifts to Hrafn in Iceland.

The Orkneyinga saga did for Orkney what Snorri Sturluson's *Heimskringla* did for Norway: it opened a door on a heroic past and gave the Orcadians an awareness of a separate and unique identity. It served them their history on a platter. It was unknown for a long time; the translation was slow in coming, but in 1873 the first English version finally appeared. It was translated by the Icelander Jon A. Hjaltalin and the Shetlander Gilbert Goudie. Altogether there have been four translations in little more than a century. The newest version, by Hermann Pálsson and Paul Edwards, is perhaps closer to the original than any of the others.

The Orkneyinga saga became the secular scripture of the islands:

'there was a hunger on the part of the Orcadians to read the stormy and glorious record from all those hundreds of years ago. These were the kind of men our ancestors were. Familiar names cropped up everywhere. In these present days of ghastly narrative styles, here was prose simple, direct and dramatic'.

This is said by the contemporary Orkney writer George Mackay Brown (*Letters from Hamnavoe*, Gordon Wright Publishing, Edinburgh) whose own work has been strongly influenced by a long study of the saga. It has also fired the imagination of Orkney writers like John Gunn and J. Storer Clouston, in books like *Vandrad the Viking*. Its style was imitated by Eric Linklater in *The Men of Ness*. Parts of it were included in *The Orkney Book*, and thus are read by every school child.

The Orcadian Samuel Laing (1780–1868) also contributed actively to bringing Norse literature to the British public. In 1844 he published his translation in three volumes of the *Heimskringla or Icelandic Chronicle of the Kings of Norway, with a Preliminary Dissertation*. It was an important achievement, as at that time Norse literature was practically unknown in Britain. His simple, clear prose made it readable also for modern readers, so that it remained the accepted English version for more than a century. Laing translated the *Heimskringla* while living in Kirkwall where he was provost for 14 years. At that time he had many years as a soldier and traveller behind him.

With the economic changes in Orkney in the second half of the nineteenth century came also a cultural flourishing. Two local newspapers were founded: *The Orcadian* in 1854 and the *Orkney Herald* in 1860. The latter championed the Liberal cause and existed until 1961. It had several outstanding editors, among them Daniel Gorrie who wrote *Summers and Winters in Orkney*. George Mackay Brown started his writing career as 'Islandman' in the *Orkney Herald*, and the Orkney scholar Ernest W. Marwick had a very popular weekly column called 'Sooan Sids'.

The Orcadian is still on sale every Thursday, and as the only newspaper in the islands its circulation has reached 10,000. It is owned and operated by the family of its founder, James Urquhart Anderson. He started out as a printer and created Kirkwall Press in the 1820's. His son-in-law W. R. Mackintosh was the author of the well-known collection of anecdotes and stories, *Around the Orkney Peat-fires*.

Another Orkney paper which existed for four years during the Second World War was the *Orkney Blast*. This paper for the forces was edited by Gerald Meyer, a Londoner serving with the army. He subsequently married a local girl and edited *The Orcadian* for 36 years.

Kirkwall Library began its days as the Kirkwall Biblioteck as early as 1683. It was founded by William Balfour Baikie who said 'Keep your sone diligent reading'. Evidently this admonition was taken seriously, for there was a high level of literacy in Orkney even before the Education Act of 1872 made school attendance compulsory. Many new schools were built in the first few years after the passing of the Act, but putting compulsory attendance into practice proved difficult, as the farmers often considered their crops more important. This made the headmaster of Stenness school write in 1879:

When there is a fine day the larger scholars are kept at home for fieldwork, and in a bad day it is not weather to come, so I rarely see some of them.

With rare foresight, a group of young Orcadian scholars published *The Orkney Book* in 1909 for use in local schools. It contained extracts from the Orkneyinga saga, nature essays, myths and legends. The book fostered interest in the islands, long before it was commonly accepted that 'knowledge ought, like charity, to begin at home'. It was brought out in a new version in 1966 and is still studied by Orkney school children.

How to combine a love for the local community with the need to reach out beyond it is the eternal dilemma of the regional writer. The choice lies between a dialect which alone expresses the eloquence of local speech and a standard language which in comparison seems remote and sterile. Thus the Orkney poet Robert Rendall wrote some of his best lyrics in dialect; one of them is 'Salt i' the bluid':

> A'm bydan heem, 'at geed for lang
>> Ruggan afore the mast,
> Yet times me thowts they taak a spang
>> Aff tae the wild Nor'wast.

> On winter nights I whiles can feel
>> Me cottage gaan adrift,
> An' wance again I grip the wheel
>> Tae the sea-swaal's aisy lift.
>> *Orkney Variants and Other Poems* (Kirkwall Press, 1951)

Still, the three great Orkney writers of our century – Edwin Muir, Eric Linklater and George Mackay Brown – all write in a language which only now and then is coloured by island speech. But in various ways they all bear the island stamp.

Edwin Muir (1887–1959) grew up in Wyre where his father farmed the Bu. In a shiningly beautiful book *The Story and the Fable* he tells of the island community he knew as a child. He was brought up in a life 'which had still the mediaeval community feeling. We had heard and read of something called "competition", but it never came into our experience. Our life was an order.'

When Edwin Muir was 14 years old, his father had to give up farming, and the family moved to Glasgow. The young boy found work in a factory which made soap from mouldy maggoty bones. Within a year's time his two elder brothers died. Muir hated Glasgow: 'The slums seemed to be everywhere around me, a great spreading swamp into which I might sink for good'. He managed to work his way out of poverty to become a well known and respected literary critic and translator of European writers, especially Kafka. But in spite of a late start, it was as a poet that Muir achieved fame;

Eric Linklater's grave, Harray Churchyard. It overlooks the parish of Harray where the well-known writer had his home.

he is perhaps the best known Scottish poet of our century in the rest of the English-speaking world.

His Orkney childhood was Muir's most important source of inspiration. He felt that having to leave the islands was an expulsion from paradise, and lost innocence is a recurrent theme in his poetry. So is the relativity of time. Towards the end of his life he saw a purpose also to his Glasgow life: it was the dark shadow necessary to throw his childhood into even sharper relief. In his poem 'One Foot in Eden' in the book with the same title, from 1956, this idea is clearly expressed; the darker shadowy sides of life help give us a deeper understanding:

> But famished field and blackened tree
> Bear flowers in Eden never known.
> Blossoms of grief and charity
> Bloom in these darkened fields alone.

At the Royal Wedding in 1981 the Archbishop of Canterbury quoted a poem by Edwin Muir ('The Annunciation' *Collected Poems*, Faber 1960 in his homily:

> ... Where each asks from each
> What each most wants to give
> And each awakes in each
> What else would never be ...

Eric Linklater (1899–1974) was born in Wales, spent his childhood summers and much of his adult life in Orkney, and was cosmopolitan by nature. He thought of himself as an Orcadian, and was proud of his Norse roots – the first known Linklater in Orkney is mentioned in a document from 1424. By the Scottish writer Hugh MacDiarmid he was called 'a Norse berserk', by others 'a misplaced Viking'. Linklater was a versatile and prolific writer. In 38 years he wrote 23 novels; in addition there were plays, short stories, children's books and documentary literature. He also wrote no less than three autobiographies.

Eric Linklater rarely uses the same theme twice. His imagination is so rich and his zest for life so great that he breaks new ground in every book he writes – a journey of exploration both for him and for us. He was like Renaissance man in his embrace of everything, and we also must go back to the Renaissance to find his sense of humour – it is often luxuriantly grotesque, but never caricatured.

Linklater's characters are modern wanderers, like Linklater himself. In this way he could hold a mirror up to other societies, and thus indirectly also to conditions in Britain. His wittiest and most popular book *Juan in America* describes the USA during Prohibition in the 1920's. *Private Angelo* is based on Linklater's own experiences during the Italian campaign at the time of the Second World War. In *The Men of Ness* the story takes place in Orkney, and Linklater goes to the sagas for his material. He had gradually come to see a superior motive inspiring the Viking raids – what drove the saga characters to action was not primarily a prospect of material gain, but the action itself – to complete an action that was artistically satisfying was a goal in itself.

Linklater said himself that his love of Orkney had dominated and perhaps distorted much of his life. But it is when he writes about Orkney – as in his famous short story *Sealskin Trousers* – that Linklater is serious. And it is then, when the masks fall, that his prose style is among the best in English literature.

George Mackay Brown (1921–) is the poet who stayed in the islands because he found at home his style and what he wanted to write about. His simple but striking style is sometimes called 'the Orkney style'. His images are vivid and concrete.

Brown is a fine and original poet, although he has become better known for his short stories, and perhaps it is true to say that his prose is even more poetical than his verse. Like Muir he is concerned with the element of time, or rather timelessness. His stories are set in an eternal Orkney where everything is part of 'the unchangeable fabric of time'. Many of the stories are woven around old myths and legends, and in that way Brown helps bring new life to Orkney folklore.

Brown is a familiar part of life in Stromness, where he has always lived apart from periods of study in Edinburgh. He likes a simple life and identifies with Orkney in spite of fame as a writer. His door is never closed to visitors, who keep coming to see a man with a warm smile and a rare gift for friendship.

In the last few years the composer Peter Maxwell Davies has been among the friends who have found their way to Brown's house in Stromness. They first met when Davies came to Orkney on holiday in 1970. Davies was even then an internationally-known composer and conductor of his own ensemble, the Fires of London. He had composed an opera, *Taverner*, but was known abroad mostly for *Eight Songs for a Mad King*, which has been described as musical theatre.

Orkney made a strong impression on Peter Maxwell Davies. He restored a derelict croft in the hillside above Rackwick in Hoy, and here he composes all his music, with only the sounds of nature to influence him. According to Davies, coming to London from Hoy is like being flung into an inferno. Davies' years in Orkney have been very productive. Most of his work has been inspired by Orkney, partly by George Mackay Brown's writing, and partly by the magic of the islands. His first Orkney work was *From Stone to Thorn* in 1971, a setting to music of a poem by Brown in his book *An Orkney Tapestry*. Since then their collaboration has produced a variety of works.

Davies felt that he owed to Orkney and the people there an artistic debt and he wanted to give something in return for everything he had received: a festival of and for the islands. Since the first St Magnus Festival was held in 1977, it has become an annual event which has been built largely around Davies' organisation and compositions. The festival programmes involve

'*What lovely words have gone into the silence!*' George Mackay Brown.

everyone from amateur actors to school children – as in 'Songs of Hoy' which were sung by all the children attending North Walls School. Although the St Magnus Festival has become popular and attracts visitors from far and near, the local music is still close to Orkney hearts. The Orkney fiddlers are largely self-taught; they have perhaps long played second fiddle to the Shetlanders, but they are now coming into their own. The Orkney Strathspey and Reel Society has done much to make fiddle music popular. The first Orkney Traditional Folk Festival was held in May 1983. It was a great success and promises to become an annual event.

During the few years that the Pier Arts Centre in Stromness has existed, it has become a centre for much of the cultural life in Orkney. It serves to stimulate further the interest in the arts that has been growing in Orkney ever since the Second World War. The time just after the war saw the return of Orkney's leading painter, Stanley Cursiter, who from 1930 had been Director of the National Galleries of Scotland. He was at one time well known as a society portrait painter; but he would spend his summers in Orkney, and all the time it was the island scenery that provided his main themes, as in 'The Sea at Yesnaby' from 1939. Other outstanding Orkney painters today are Sylvia Wishart from Stromness and Ian Scott who lives and works in North Ronaldsay.

The Orkney Press has been established to encourage the production of Orkney books and help new writers to get their works published. Another recent initiative is the Orkney Heritage Society, whose objectives are to help preserve for posterity everything of beauty and interest and to encourage a high aesthetic standard in anything new. The Heritage Society led the campaign in support of the Orkney Islands Council's ban on uranium mining. It also employs a resident field archaeologist to coordinate all archaeological excavation carried out in the islands.

Radio Orkney first went on the air in May 1977 and since then has become an important part of everyday life. It brings the news of everything which happens in the islands – from the whereabouts of a runaway cat, to the state of the roads, and a whist drive in one of the community centres – thus serving as an effective calendar of events. At the same time it is the island voice, because the Orkney dialect is used most of the time. And by bringing programmes about a variety of local topics, it helps keep interest in Orkney culture alive.

16. Agriculture

To a Norwegian who in Denmark, Germany, France and England has grown accustomed to seeing those villages so unknown in Norway, the sight of the scattered farms in Orkney is bound to remind him of his own country and proves conclusively that the settlement took place in the Norwegian way.

P. A. Munch *Reminiscences of Orkney* 1849

The Orkney countryside inspired Munch to say this – the sight of farms lying in the centre of their fields and meadows, in contrast to the clustered farms of the feudal society. But much of what Munch saw then in the middle of the nineteenth century was relatively new and the result of the first agricultural revolution.

When we fly in over Orkney, we see clearly that it is first and foremost a farming society. Green fields meet the sea, as far as the eye can see. The soil is so fertile that even the primitive tools of Stone Age man could produce a crop.

Back in Norse times, the odal (from O.N. óðal – property) law was in force. An odaller paid a tax to the king, but otherwise he ruled like a petty king on his farm. His right to the land extended as far as the low water mark on the shore, and this is customary in Orkney even today – the shore is not considered Crown property as it usually is elsewhere in Britain. The greatest drawback to odal law was the system of inheritance. All sons inherited equal shares, whereas daughters got half shares. One can see the justice inherent in everybody sharing equally, but it was nevertheless a ruinous arrangement for a farming community. Gradually the land became split up into small unprofitable strips, and poverty for everybody was the logical consequence.

This is part of the explanation as to why so much of the land was bought up by rich Scottish incomers within a short time after the pledging in 1468. The fact that the farmers were confronted by new laws, in a language they did not understand, also opened the way for fraud and swindle. Most of the land gradually passed into the hands of big landowners – known in Orkney as the lairds. In the beginning of the nineteenth century 90 per cent of all land belonged to 33 landowners. A few farmers were still freeholders, but by far the most of them were tenant farmers.

The lairds might be good masters and then again they might not. Not all were as hated as General Burroughs in Rousay, who enjoyed a dubious reputation as the worst landowner in the nineteenth century, but they were often hard businessmen who took what they could get and gave little in return. Many were absentee landlords who spent most of their time in London or Edinburgh and were rarely at home. Much of the possible profit from farming was therefore taken out of the islands.

From the old days, all farms within a cultivated area were part of a *tun* or *tunship*, and all this land was surrounded by a 3 ft (0.9 m) high stone fence. The uncultivated land outside the fence was common land.

The cultivation methods were extremely primitive and the division into strips of land was unprofitable and inefficient. Usually there were no fences within the tunship, so the crops were often trampled by cattle. For the most part only oats and barley were cultivated. The barley was a special Orkney variant which is called *bere* – the Arctic barley. The same barley was grown during the Stone Age – bere grains were found in the Unston cairn from 3,500 B.C. Crop rotation and drainage were unknown, and the land never lay fallow, so the fields were full of weeds. On the whole the soil got its only manure from the cattle. The crops were therefore small, so the autumn slaughter of a great deal of the livestock was usually necessary.

The average size of a farm was about 8 acres (3.2 ha). The tenants had to pay the rent with grain and malt, but also in work such as fishing and kelp-gathering. During the Napoleonic Wars fishing prospered, as the demand grew. The kelp was burnt to potash which was used for making glass and soap.

As long as the lairds made large profits from the sale of fish and kelp, the land was a secondary source of income. The land was cultivated for the purpose of keeping alive those who lived on it, and therefore inferior grain was produced. This was despite the fact that the climate put cereal crops at risk at harvest time and made the growing of grass more desirable. The rent paid for the land was unreasonably hard. If crops failed, the farmer had to pay in cash the part of the rent he could not supply in grain. As the price of grain would rise in a bad year, the sum the farmer had to pay would be impossibly high. Were it not for his income from kelp-gathering he would never have managed to pay.

In the summer of 1839 Christian Plöyen, who was the Danish commissioner of the Faeroes, visited Orkney, and had this to say:

The dwellings of the wealthy are pretty, some of them even elegant, but the peasants' houses are miserable in proportion. It is strange that they are such poor structures, when it is considered that excellent building materials, a coarse reddish sandstone, easily broken and squared, is everywhere found in great abundance. If the Faroese possessed such material they would employ it much better; they have the desire and the taste for a good dwelling, when their means are sufficient to procure it; but then they are all either freeholders or hereditary tenants, whereas most of the Orkneymen, like the Shetlanders, are the tenants, or more correctly, the slaves of the proprietors.
Reminiscence of a voyage to Shetland, Orkney and Scotland (trans. by Catherine Spence) T. & J. Manson, Lerwick 1894

Plöyen saw clearly that the rent system was detrimental and did not invite improvement. The rents were far too high and the leases too short for that. Any improvement made by the farmer on his land just raised the rent. It must also be said that the farmers resisted any change, and any landowner who tried to reform his estate was intensely disliked. Therefore a reform attempted in the 1760's was unsuccessful.

When change finally came, it was explosive. The economic depression after the Napoleonic Wars made all trade difficult. The income from the kelp-burning stopped suddenly in the early 1830's when it proved possible to get the potash cheaper and better from Spain. The landowners were left with nothing but the land, and they had to rationalize or give up. Thus between 1830 and 1860 the foundation of modern agriculture was laid.

First of all a planking of the land had to take place – that is, the hopelessly small strips of land, lying intermingled with one another, had to be exchanged, so that one farmer's land might be made into one field. If we look at the map of Shapinsay, we see an island where planking was carried out systematically. The land is divided into rectangles, not all of the same size. The landowners divided the land into farms of different sizes, and appointed tenants who were willing to try new methods of farming. Those who then lost their farms got around 25 acres (10 ha) of the common grazings which, until then, everybody had been able to use freely. New breeds of cattle were introduced, new tools were adopted and new farm buildings were built. It was as if the countryside woke from a long winter sleep, and in 25 years more happened than in centuries before.

New land was ploughed up, and the population rose to 32,000 in 1861. But the living conditions did not improve very much for the tenants, and in 1883 The Napier Commission was appointed by the British government to examine how the tenant farmers really lived in the Scottish Highlands and in the islands off the west and north coasts of Scotland, where the tenant system, or crofting, was customary.

One of those who was affected by the planking and had to leave the farm in Rousay he used to rent, declared to The Napier Commission:

I then got permission to build a dwelling on the hillside where I now live, where there was no cultivation of any kind, nor houses. I began to build, and got up with much trouble a humble cottage and outhouses suitable. I ditched and drained more than I was able and got a little of the heather surface broken up. At this time I paid twelve shillings; but again, as I improved, more and more rent was laid on until I am now rented at a sum which is five times the rent I paid at first for a house I built myself. At the same time the common was taken away from me, as from all others ...
Lord Napier: Royal Commission of Enquiry into the conditions of crofters and cottars in the Highlands and Islands, 1884

Then, in 1886, The Crofters' Act was passed. It was also known as the crofters' Magna Carta, and it really was their letter of freedom. The pendulum now swung so far in the opposite direction that the tenant was in many ways better off than the freeholder. The tenants could remain securely on their small farms with a reasonable rent, and the right of tenure was hereditary. A tenant who had improved his farm, received compensation for this if he left.

The period after the 1914–18 war, with high prices and taxation, drove almost all the landowners into selling their land cheaply to those who rented it. Some of the small farmers chose to go on as before, but the majority of farmers bought the land. The circle was closed – the Orkney farmer was once again an odaller.

Of course the new freeholders are not odallers in the original sense of the word – that is reserved for the few who till now have paid 'the king's skatt' for their farm. After the pledging in 1468 the farmers also had to pay a land tax to Scotland. The freeholders therefore had to pay tax twice. Protests through the centuries went unheeded. In the 1920's those odallers who were still left were given the option of buying their way out of the king's tax once and for all. Some chose not to do so and are therefore every year required to pay the old odal skatt, which today is one of the few relics of Norse rule.

Freeholding led to great improvements, but there are disadvantages to that system as well. It is almost impossible to take over a farm unless it is inherited, as the purchase price of a farm is out of proportion to the profit made on it. It is true that the price of land in Orkney may be about half what

Milking time, Swannay Farm, Birsay. By means of this movable 'walk on, back off' system, 240 cows can be milked in an hour and a half.

it is further south, but the transport costs must be added on all goods. Leasing a small farm was not difficult in the old days, and an enterprising young farmer could soon move on to something bigger and better.

The wild white clover was introduced into Orkney in the 1920's. It was well suited to local conditions and it greatly improved the quality of the pastures. White clover is rich in protein, phosphorus and calcium, and the cattle also like eating it. It adds combined nitrogen to the soil, so that crop rotation is no longer necessary. The improved pastures led to an increase in the number of beef cattle, which is now the mainstay of the farming economy. The use of silage has become common. In the 1970's the number of beef cattle was around 90,000. The Aberdeen Angus breed has been very popular for a long time, but it grows slowly, and is therefore usually crossed with breeds like Hereford to provide the larger beef animals the market wants. Perhaps the question of breeding has not always been given serious enough consideration, so that the bulls have been used indiscriminately in order to obtain a wider variation in breed type and quality. This has led to calving problems, among other things.

Because there is not much natural shelter and the ground stays very wet in the wintertime, the cattle cannot be left outside. The cattle have to be housed for about half the year and this requires expensive cattle buildings. It has been the custom to send the cattle to Aberdeenshire for fattening before being slaughtered. Some 30,000 heads of cattle have been sent every year. The transport price is much higher for live animals than for beef, and therefore it was long felt that Orkney ought to do more than just produce the raw materials for this industry. An abattoir built according to EEC standards is now operating in Kirkwall. With grass in silage it should be possible to have winter keep enough, so that there will be cattle available for slaughter all year round.

During the Second World War the Orkney population was for some time more than doubled because of all the servicemen who were stationed there, and this led to a great demand for milk. The number of cattle was therefore adjusted accordingly, so that some 40 per cent were dairy cattle. After the war the Claymore Creamery was established in Kirkwall to receive the surplus milk production. Most of the cheese which is produced at Claymore and the big Swannay farm in Birsay is sent to the mainland. The number of dairy farms has now fallen to about 50. Many have switched to beef cattle because it has been necessary to reduce the mountain of butter and cheese within the EEC countries.

Poultry keeping used to be common on all farms – at least for the owner's consumption. Stories are still told of how hens were simply swept out to sea in stormy weather. In the period during and after the Second World War there was nevertheless a flourishing egg industry for export to the mainland. Its export at one time exceeded £1,000,000. It put many a farm back on its feet, and for the first time farmers' wives had spare money to spend in their purses. But later on this production could not compete with the large-scale

Cheviot sheep crossing the Hunda Barrier, Burray. There are about 30,000 sheep in Orkney, most of them of this breed.

mechanized egg production in the south. It also relied on imported feed coming in as well as the finished product going out, so that freight charges are another reason why it would be unprofitable today. Moreover Orkney has no natural advantages that make the area especially suited for poultry keeping.

The number of sheep has increased in the last few years, but they are still of secondary importance on most farms. The number of sheep lies around 30,000 – mostly of the Cheviot breed. In North Ronaldsay there are descendants of the original Norse sheep – one of the rarest breeds in the world. It is almost like a goat to look at, and the average weight of the ewe is only 44 lb (20 kg). Most of the year the North Ronaldsay sheep live on seaweed and are shut out from the pastures by a stone dyke which runs round the whole island. Only during the lambing season are the ewes let into the pastures. There are some 4,000 of this breed in North Ronaldsay, and they have lately been the object of great scientific interest. To prevent the breed dying out from disease or poisoning, some of them have been moved to small uninhabited islands.

Most of the (approximately) 1400 farms in Orkney are now owner-occupied. Some of the small farms are still run by tenant farmers, but according to a new land law, the Crofting Reform Act from 1976, a tenant has the right to purchase the farm he occupies from his landlord at a price corresponding to 15 years' rent. Even though leasing a farm offers many advantages today, there is still the drawback that the farm cannot be used as security for an improvement loan in a bank. As the egg production is no longer viable, the smallholders have lost an important source of income, and they are forced to have jobs outside their holdings. In the disastrous years of 1979 and 1980 Orkney farming was hit by the worst weather conditions for a century, and it was amazing that the farmers managed to keep going. The government, the EEC and the Orkney Islands Council came to the aid of the Orkney farmers when their crops failed completely.

As increased mechanization leads to further rationalization, the agricultural units are growing bigger and bigger. The average size of the farms has doubled since the Second World War and is now around 130 acres (52.6 ha). At the same time the number of people employed in agriculture has fallen by 20 per cent in the last decade. A farm has to be around 100 acres (40 ha) to be economical. During the 1970's it was relatively easy to get government subsidies for the amalgamation of farms, and the consequence of that is evident everywhere – derelict farms meet the eye all over the countryside. But the Orkney landscape is greener than ever, for new methods of cultivation and new machinery make it possible to reclaim more and more of what used to be unproductive hill and moorland.

17. Fishing

It has often been said that, whereas the Shetlanders are fishermen with ploughs, the Orcadians are farmers who fish. Even though this is a simplification, it is still true; at least the old pattern was like that. People in Orkney used to fish mostly for their own consumption, and not on a commercial basis.

From their Norse ancestors the Orkneymen inherited good seamanship, and they are known as first-rate sailors. This was necessary since, though the waters around Orkney are full of fish, they are not easy to navigate. A gale may strike without warning; the tidal currents between the islands are always dangerous, and the tide also makes the mooring of a boat difficult. And at any moment a fog may come down and wipe out all familiar landmarks.

During a period of investment in the nineteenth century, a flourishing fishing industry grew up in Orkney, based on herring fishing. But lack of capital made it difficult for Orkney fishermen to acquire big enough boats. Orkney boats therefore fished only a small share of 'the silver darlings', as the herring was called. Most of the catch was taken by outsiders, and the only work which the fishing provided locally was gutting and salting.

Stromness and Whitehall in Stronsay became the main receivers of the herring. Both places had good harbours, which were now developed with piers and sheds for gutting and curing. Whereas Stromness received the early herring, the summer fishing was done from Stronsay. During the six weeks the herring fishing lasted, the population of Stromness would multiply, and for a while there were as many as forty pubs.

But the herring moves on. At the turn of the century Stromness had 38 curing stations, but by the beginning of the First World War the winter herring was gone and the good days were over. Stronsay became the centre of fishing.

Today fishing can no longer be carried out as a part-time occupation; it has become a big industry and a serious business. The trend in fishing has all the time been towards bigger and more sophisticated boats, and until recently it was difficult for Orkney fishermen to obtain enough capital to buy trawlers. But they have now received support both from The Highlands and Islands Development Board and from the Oil Reserve Fund of the Orkney Islands Council. This capital has enabled the local fishermen to get larger

Herring barrel stencil. A brazier forms the trade mark on a stencil from one of the Stronsay curing stations. (Stromness Museum)

boats and revitalize fishing in the islands. As yet, most boats are between 30 and 40 ft (9–12 m), but some time ago the fishing industry also got a 110 ft (34 m) purse seiner, the *Orcades Viking*.

The fish stocks in the North Sea are under severe pressure. A modern purse netter can catch as much in a week as was caught in a whole season not so long ago. Up to 1965 the annual herring fishing in the North Sea was normally some 600,000 tons. But in that year Norwegian fishermen started using the purse seiner, and fished the same quantity on their own. Others followed. But soon the consequences of the increased fishing became obvious to everybody: the fishing grounds were becoming empty of fish. In 1977 came the end of an era – a ban was imposed on herring fishing in the North Sea, and there is a risk that the story may be repeated with other species.

In recent years fishing in Orkney has increased, despite the nationwide slump in the fishing industry, and local fishermen have landed annual catches worth as much as £1,500,000. As there is now little room for expansion in farming, fishing is important for future employment in many directions, especially if more of the fish could be landed and processed in the islands. It was, therefore, with annoyance that local people saw boats from other EEC countries fishing close to the shore. They felt that the fishing in northern waters was given away to get British membership in the EEC. They had no control over how much other nations fished and believed that a restriction on the fishing rights of other fishermen operating in Orkney waters was called for. Local fishermen hardly took more than ten per cent of the fish caught in their own waters.

Winifred Ewing, who represents the Scottish Highlands and Islands in the European Parliament, thinks that the rights of communities relying on fishing have been ignored for too long:

> Our fishing waters were given away as a bargain for getting into Europe, and it was a very bad exchange. Now we are trying to get 12 miles of them back while the rest of the world with a coastline has 200 miles – that's what we gave away. My constituency has the richest fishing in Europe and yet it has no rights over it.
>
> Article in *The Orcadian*

The fishermen of Orkney and Shetland worked out a joint fisheries plan, aimed at preserving the fish stocks and protecting the local fishermen, by giving special rights to the Orkney and Shetland fishing industries. Many fishermen live in areas where there is nothing for them to do except fish; if that fails there is nothing to fall back upon and no alternative but to leave.

First of all, the fishermen demanded a 12 naut. mile fishing limit around the islands; inside this only local fishermen would be able to fish, with boats of up to 80 ft (24 m). Outside this limit they suggested a 50 naut. mile zone where various safeguards must be taken, such as a restrictive licensing scheme based on a quota system, and control of equipment. Also within this zone the local fishermen would have special rights.

The proposal for a protected area round Orkney and Shetland was at first met with massive opposition in Brussels. The French in particular will not give up the right to fish close to the shore. They claim they have a historic right to do so, as they have traditionally taken sizeable catches from Orkney waters. But the Government in London finally seemed to understand that the islanders meant what they said. The British EEC delegate declared in Brussels that if Orkney and Shetland did not get a 50 naut. mile protection zone in their waters, then it was possible that they would break with the EEC and even with the rest of Britain and declare their own 200-naut. mile fishing limit like the Faeroes and Iceland have done.

The area proposed to be subject to licensing for fishing became known as the 'Orkney and Shetland Box'. But following the 1983 Common Fisheries Policy negotiations in Brussels the box was reduced considerably – a reduction condemned by both Orkney and Shetland. There is now an inner 6 naut. mile zone reserved for local fishermen and an outer 6 naut. mile zone where only fishermen with 'historic rights' have entry. But rather liberal specifications on the size of boats which can operate in the area have meant that far more boats than originally intended can fish in the region unchecked. In addition, an increased number of vessels have been given licences to fish in these waters.

This Fisheries Policy was accepted by all the EEC members except Denmark. According to the new rules, the Danes cannot fish at all within the 12 naut. mile limit, because they cannot claim historic rights. They were bitter about not getting a single licence to fish cod and haddock in the protected areas around Orkney and Shetland, and refused to accept the Fisheries Policy, claiming they would cross the 12 naut. mile limit anyway. All protection vessels, HMS *Orkney* among them, were put on alert, but the situation quietened down.

There is still concern in the islands about over-fishing, not only by foreign vessels but by the number of British vessels that may fish around Orkney and Shetland. Fear that the fish will disappear has also made the Orkney Islands Council encourage fish farming for many years. It was believed that the waters around Orkney would be well suited for the farming of various kinds of fish, especially salmon. It was hoped that the twinning of Orkney with Hordaland County would lead to co-operation in this field, as salmon-rearing is well-established in West Norway.

It turned out, however, that there were very few sites in Orkney with water conditions suitable for salmon rearing. One of them was at Lamb Holm, close to the Italian Chapel. A proposed lobster and salmon complex at Lamb Holm therefore became a source of controversy, as many felt it would impair the beauty of the chapel setting. The plans went ahead despite these objections.

There used to be oysters of high quality, especially at the Bay of Firth, and originally Orkney had a thriving natural oyster fishery. The oysters disappeared some time around the turn of the century, probably as a result

Oyster farming is an escalating industry. On this new farm in Burray 'Orkney Oysters'
hope to have 2,000,000 ready for the table in three years time.

of over-fishing. As early as 1912 a company tried to carry on oyster farming at the Bay of Firth, but the attempt failed. In 1979 the Council set up an oyster cultivation project and as the tests with oyster farming were successful, people were encouraged to take up oyster farming on a part time basis. Since then the industry has escalated and by 1986 it is hoped that 1,000,000 oysters will be shipped out of Orkney annually.

The use of some of the lochs for farming trout has also been discussed. Traditionally fishing in the lochs has been free, but the rule has been one man – one rod. This rule is being broken all the time by people using illegal methods such as netting or fixed lines. Stories are told of tourists, 'ferryloupers', heading back south with their cars loaded with trout. But whoever is behind it, this illegal fishing is affecting the fish stocks in the lochs and it is doubtful if they will survive in the long term. If the trout fishing disappears, Orkney would lose a valuable asset.

It has also been argued that only full-time fishermen should be allowed to catch lobster. As an experiment the Orkney Fisheries Association put out berried lobsters in Scapa Flow, in an attempt to increase dwindling stocks.

18. Industry

In the traditional economy, agriculture was by far the most important factor, and so it still is. In fact agriculture makes up more than half of the gross county product. But the number of people employed in agriculture has been decreasing, both absolutely and in relation to the size of the population.

Rather unexpectedly, whisky production has long been the second most important source of income next to agriculture. Stories are still told about the whisky Old Orkney from the distillery formerly at Stromness. Today there are two distilleries in operation in Orkney, and they are both in Kirkwall. Scapa Distillery, which was founded in 1885, is the lesser known of them because most of their production goes to blending. But Highland Park, which goes all the way back to 1798, supplies a well-known quality product, a pure malt whisky which is also called Highland Park.

According to a popular story, Highland Park grew out of the activities of the legendary smuggler and illicit distiller Magnus Eunson. Smuggling was earlier a popular and profitable business, with its headquarters in Kirkwall. Everybody's sympathy was with the smugglers so the excisemen were fighting a hopeless battle. The stories of how Magnus, or Mansie, time and again fooled the excisemen were told so often and for so long that much is now more legend than truth. Mansie took advantage of being a church official and hid most of his illegal spirits in the church. Once, when he learned that the excisemen were going to search the church, he and his helpers moved the liquor over to his house and put it in a coffin. When the excisemen arrived, they were piously kneeling around the coffin.

Close to Mansie's little house there was a spring with the right kind of water for making whisky, and Mansie's homemade product was much in demand. Even today this water helps give the Highland Park whisky a characteristic flavour of its own, for the distillery has been erected over Mansie's spring. Since the barley is malted over a peat fire, the whisky gets a suggestion of peat flavour. Later in the process heather is also used. The Highland Park whisky can be stored for 12 years before it is sent out on the market as a high quality product. The annual production is around 1,000,000 gal (4,545,970 l) of whisky. An equal amount is used for blending at other distilleries in Scotland, and it is part of such well-known brands as Johnny Walker, Cutty Sark and Grouse.

During the last few years the economic recession has also hit the whisky

This 'Old Orkney' poster was daring for its time, c.1900. (Stromness Museum)

producers, who have had serious difficulties. Another reason for this is that successive Chancellors of the Exchequer have looked upon this industry as a natural milch cow for the Government, a view which is also supported by the moral aspect of all alcohol production. Increased government taxes have, therefore, also helped reduce the turnover of the distilleries. The Scapa Distillery in Kirkwall is one of the companies which have had to reduce their production.

Tourism, on the other hand, has been an expanding industry during the last few years, and is one of the most important sectors of the economy. There are close to 70,000 visitors between April and October. More than half of them come during the school holidays in July–August. Many of the visitors choose Orkney as a place to go because it is quiet and peaceful and free of gaudy commercialized facilities aimed at attracting mass-market tourists – free of much of what they want to escape from. It is, therefore, paradoxical that further efforts to promote tourism as an industry might perhaps damage the image of Orkney.

The answer may lie in presenting Orkney as an untouched pastoral idyll, an unspoilt, green contrast to life in the big cities. Orkney cannot in any case attract commercialized mass tourism, as long as a holiday in the southern sun is cheaper and more easily available. Most visitors to Orkney come on their own initiative and not as part of a group. Quite a few come first as young backpackers, who later return year after year, as regularly as migratory birds. Often they are attracted by the friendliness and unfailing hospitality of the local people, and many come back later to visit friends. The majority of the tourists get no further than Stromness and Kirkwall, perhaps because many of them are older people, but the reason may also be that unless one has a car of one's own it is very difficult to get around. Many fine day trips by bus or boat are now offered, but most of them start in Kirkwall.

The objective must be to spread the tourists more in order to promote tourism in the isles. Especially for the North Isles some extra income from tourism would be very welcome and might halt the flight to Mainland. The isles also have much to offer that very few ever get to see. But even for the enterprising tourist it has often been difficult to plan a holiday route in the North Isles and then carry it through. One of the problems is that the transport system is poorly suited to tourism. The boat connections are planned for goods and not for passengers, and the daily plane is overbooked in the tourist season. Therefore planning a holiday in the North Isles can feel like banging one's head against a brick wall. Recently, however, an effort has been made to make everything simpler by providing more facilities for those who want to visit the isles.

The three most popular tourist attractions are Tankerness House Museum, Skara Brae and Maeshowe. Otherwise it is holidays for such special interests as fishing, archaeology and bird watching that attract people to Orkney. Some also come to paint the changing light effects.

Another activity has been added during the last few years – diving – especially in Scapa Flow. Orkney's hidden asset, the German warships – the remains of the Hochseeflotte – makes Scapa Flow the target of diving clubs from all over Britain as well as from abroad. It is true of course that most of the fleet was salvaged for scrap metal between the two world wars. Eight ships from the First World War still remain in Scapa: the British battleship *Vanguard* and the German ships *Dresden, Brummer, Köln, Kronprinz Wilhelm, Markgraf, Karlsruhe* and *König.* Some of these are ships of the Dreadnought class which cannot be seen anywhere else.

The fate of the remaining ships has long been uncertain. Some of the wrecks belong to the Ministry of Defence, whereas others are privately owned. Various companies want to buy the wrecks for scrap. The Orkney Islands Council would prefer the wrecks to remain where they are, because they make Scapa Flow into one of the most interesting and attractive diving areas in the world. Not only is there a unique collection of warships, but they are at a safe diving depth of water in an area which is so sheltered from the wind and tide that diving can be done at any time, regardless of prevailing weather conditions. In addition, under-water visibility is better than further south because the water is clearer.

Craft industries such as knitting, silversmith work and pottery production have been doing well in recent years. These are well-suited industries for remote areas because in many cases they can represent an extra source of income.

Knitting has been a source of income ever since the sixteenth century. Well-known knitting organisations today are Westray Knitters, Isle of Sanday Knitters and Scapa Knitwear. Borne on a wave of folklore interest in knitwear fashions, they have received orders from as far away as Japan. Scapa Knitwear is part of a large organisation, Scapa of Scotland, which produces a collection where the colours and materials are carefully coordinated. The knitted garments of this collection are made in Orkney. The demand has been great, and even a weekly production of 1,000 garments has not covered it: there have just not been enough knitters. Scapa of Scotland was the first British firm to be allowed to exhibit its collection in the Louvre gallery in Paris.

Jeweller Ola Gorie uses traditional Orkney designs, both Pictish and Norse, for her jewellery, which has become very popular. The other jewellery firm is Ortak. Together these two producers, with some 50 employees, cover a large share of the British jewellery market.

The potteries are perhaps harder hit by the high transport costs than the other craft industries. Among those who have been in the market for some time are Orkney Pottery in Rousay and Fursbreck Pottery in Harray. They both excel in form and simple design.

It has become easier for potteries and other craft industries to become established since the oil industry arrived, as the Orkney Islands Council has tried to use the oil revenues to help new enterprises get started. In 1972 the

Ola Gorie, jeweller. She uses traditional Orkney designs, both Pictish and Norse.

British Government awarded six blocks in the North Sea to the recently established oil company The Occidental North Sea Consortium. It consisted of several companies, but the American company Occidental Petroleum were the largest shareholders and gave the name to the new company, whose everyday name is Oxy. The following year the very promising oilfield Piper was discovered, with reserves of recoverable high quality oil estimated as high as 618,000,000 barrels.

The difficult weather conditions in the North Sea were the reason why the company decided against offshore processing of the oil and chose to build a terminal on shore instead, even though this necessitated the laying of a 135 mile (217 km) long pipeline. They considered that even though this required large investments – just the pipe line alone cost £500,000 a mile – having the oil brought ashore was still preferable.

Orkney was selected as the most suitable location for an oil terminal because it was closest to the field. Flotta was at first considered too isolated but was chosen because of its good natural harbour. All planning was done in close co-operation with the county authorities, and there was general agreement on two main objectives: to develop the oil terminal without damaging the environment or the traditional patterns of life, and to provide employment opportunities to the islanders by employing local labour to the greatest possible extent.

The first oil flowed into the terminal in December 1976, and since then the quantity of oil has been increasing all the time. Oil from other fields has been added: Occidental's second field Claymore and Texaco's Tartan, and it is possible that still more will come. Usually the terminal handles approximately 330,000 barrels of oil a day, but there is probably capacity for as much as 500,000 barrels.

The crude oil which enters the terminal goes through a process where residual gas and water are removed before being conveyed to big storage tanks. From these the oil is loaded on to tankers. Two ships can be loaded at the same time in the harbour which has moorings for tankers of up to as much as 200,000 d.w.t. The liquid natural gas, which is rich in ethane, is mostly sold to the petro-chemical plant of the Norwegian company Norsk Hydro at Porsgrunn. There is also some production of propane gas.

To what extent has the oil company succeeded in protecting the environment from any damaging effects of such a large industrial development? The Occidental Group has received several awards for the way the oil terminal has been visually integrated into the natural conditions to make the least impact on Orkney's environment. The storage tanks are painted a brownish-green colour and rise only 52 ft (16 m) above the ground. This has been achieved by lowering the tanks into the ground and then surrounding them with low banks of earth. These are covered with indigenous plant life.

In order to protect the marine environment, the sea-water ballast from the tankers is cleaned in a special plant before it is returned to the sea. Water samples are taken regularly in Scapa Flow, and these are tested for water pollution. Scapa Flow has not suffered from oil pollution to any significant degree since the oil terminal was established.

Although the terminal, even in the planning stage, was secured in all technical ways imaginable, the danger of an oil leakage is always present. Accidents can also happen to the big tankers which come and go in the treacherous Orkney waters. Prevention is better than cure where oil spillage is concerned, for even with the most advanced oil cleaning equipment it is difficult to prevent beaches from being soiled and sea birds killed. It happened in Shetland, and it could happen in Orkney.

Generally we can say, therefore, that ecologically the oil business has functioned satisfactorily, so far at least. The social and economic effects are more difficult to gauge. The oil industry is an expanding industry with a large income, and, when it is first established somewhere, there seems to be a rise in growth, a flourishing. Actually many of the supposed benefits are illusory, and the coming of the oil industry may lead to a thinned out and understimulated social and economic environment because there is little opportunity to develop in a positive direction in other fields. The high wage level in the oil industries affects other industries adversely because their employees also want a piece of the cake. This increases costs for all other industries and ruins their competitiveness. For that reason other industry will often be reduced as the oil industry expands. It also has an inflationary effect, especially on housing and services. It looks as if these conditions work in the same way locally and nationally, so that Orkney shows on a miniature scale what is happening in Britain and Norway.

Part of this flourishing is also that the coming of oil checked the tide of depopulation and there was instead a net immigration. Many Orcadians also returned from overseas to start working in the oil industry. The Occidental Group has recruited as much of the workforce as possible among the local people, so that today 200 out of the 300 employees come from the islands.

19.   Local government

Boreas Domus, Mare Amicus – the North our Home, the Sea our Friend
(Motto of the County of Orkney)

Although local government is a proud and time-honoured tradition in Britain, the tendency during the last few decades has been to concentrate as much of the power as possible in London, in the name of efficiency. Highly developed communications make such a centralized government possible. The need for a national, planned economy and the political pressure for equal social benefits for everybody in all parts of the nation are strong forces working against local government.

It is inevitable that the national government, for the benefit of the majority, must make decisions which will have an adverse, sometimes even disastrous, effect on the small local community. A government decision to reduce the industrial rates paid to local councils in order to make industry more competitive has led to Orkney having its long-term financial planning overthrown because it depends on a stable income from the oil company at Flotta. The recent pressure for uranium mining has also been felt as an abuse of power from outside. In addition, the fact that the fire service for the whole of northern Scotland is now directed from Inverness is a constant source of irritation. The fire service there must be notified of all fires, in spite of their not knowing or understanding Orkney place names. Parliament keeps passing new bills which unload additional burdens on to the local authorities so that it often seems to them as if they are playing a game with an opponent who keeps changing the rules, so that they can never win.

A small island community, with special problems due to isolation and a small scattered population, will be especially vulnerable to many central government decisions. But the isolation also gives a feeling of common identity which makes people feel like spectators in relation to much of what goes on in the rest of the country. This feeling of estrangement, which to some extent is of their own choosing, also gives a certain strength.

In the early 1970's local government in Britain was changed through The Local Government Act. During the preparatory work for the law it was suggested that both Orkney and Shetland should become part of a Highland Region, which would comprise all of northern Scotland and be administered from Inverness. This proposal met with strong opposition, especially in

Shetland, and after a political struggle the plans for centralization were dropped.

Orkney has status as a county and is ruled by an islands council: the Orkney Islands Council (OIC). The Council has 24 members who meet in Kirkwall every six weeks. It elects its own chairman, who is called *convener*. An election is held every four years. OIC has full authority in all public sectors except the police and fire services which come under the Highland Region in Inverness. The OIC and the islands councils for Shetland and Western Isles are unique in Scotland because they are single-tier administrations: they combine the functions which elsewhere are shared between regional and district councils. The Community Council in each parish serves the Islands Council in an advisory capacity.

The new Islands Council took over full executive control in 1975. It has a great number of responsibilities with an annual budget of more than £15,000,000. The council is the largest employer in Orkney with around 1000 employees; it also functions as a landlord, with almost 1400 houses for letting – mostly in Kirkwall. It is also responsible for keeping some 600 miles (970 km) of road in good repair – a task which has turned out to be a constant problem. A large part of the budget, about one third, goes to education. Social care is another expensive sector. The only public services where the Council is not directly involved are the medical services, the power supply and postal and telecommunications. On the other hand, there are those who think that the medical services also ought to become a county responsibility, and that the Islands Council should also play a more active role in solving the transport problems, by taking over the ferry traffic to the Scottish mainland.

Not even in wartime was the county forced to make as great adjustments as those brought on by the discovery of oil in the North Sea, which meant that the first OIC elected after the Local Government Act took effect met enough challenges in their functioning time 1974–78. Again, thanks to Shetland, both island counties got wide powers to cope with the oil business. For Orkney's part those powers were defined in The Orkney County Council Act of 1974. It gave the local authority power to adopt measures which would give the islands maximum financial benefits from the oil business, while also being protected as much as possible from adverse environmental effects. OIC succeeded in confining the oil business to Flotta and Scapa Flow.

One of the most important things done by the OIC was to extend the responsibilities of the harbours department. This department has turned out to be the only profitable activity run by the Council.

The Occidental Group pays all harbour expenses, which make up more than £500,000, but the OIC has retained full control, and levies charges on port users. OIC also gets revenues from all oil and gas coming to Flotta from the Piper, Claymore and Tartan fields – 2p per ton(ne) for oil and 4p for liquid petroleum gas – this being dependent on the retail price index. These

161

oil revenues are paid into a Reserve Fund. The role played by the OIC is so active that in a way it has become almost a business partner for the oil company.

With special powers came new tasks, ranging from archaeology to amateur playgroups, and the OIC has perhaps tried to bite off more than it can chew. The 24 local councillors are not necessarily qualified to deal with all the questions which arise, nor is it fair to expect them to be. They are part-time amateurs in work that is becoming more time-consuming and specialized. For that reason it has been difficult to get people from a cross-section of the population to stand for election. There are few businessmen; farmers make up the largest group. It has also been difficult to get young people. Some go so far as to say that the OIC recruits mainly retired people, but this is not true, even though the average age has often been quite high. It also seems to be difficult to get women elected to the OIC which has never had more than four women members at one time.

It is difficult to create an effective local government in modern society, and one of the important questions is how local elections can best be freed from the issues of national politics and become more relevant to local matters. In Britain local elections tend to become a barometer for the popularity of the government then in power – thus national politics casts a long shadow into local committees and councils.

We should, however, expect more interest in local politics in Orkney where the Orkney County Council Act allows for more responsibility than in most regions, and where the Council members are elected on a non-political basis, purely on their own merits. This has been possible in such a close-knit community where almost everybody knows one another, and knows what a person stands for. Despite this the OIC elections are quiet affairs; in many constituencies there is only one candidate, so the result is already given in advance. An attempt by Labour candidates to run on a party ticket in the spring of 1982 failed, and Labour did not get any of their candidates elected.

That the members of the OIC are not politically elected may make them less biased and less dogmatic in their view of what is best for the islands, as they do not have to toe a party line on every issue. On the other hand, it seems as if such a body is more easily swayed by eloquence and moods, for the OIC has been criticized by many for changing its collective mind rather too often.

Together with Shetland, Orkney returns one representative to the House of Commons. Orkney-Shetland is the northernmost constituency in Britain. Its population of some 40,000 for both island groups also makes it one of the smallest British constituencies. On the other hand, distances make it one of the most difficult to work in, not least because communications are few and uncertain.

For all of 32 years, from 1950 to 1982, Jo Grimond represented Orkney-Shetland and the Liberal party in Parliament. After getting a First in

Lord and Lady Grimond at home. For 32 years Jo Grimond represented Orkney and Shetland on behalf of the Liberal party in the British parliament at Westminster.

political studies at the University of Oxford, he became a lawyer, but he was always more interested in politics. In 1950 his campaigning brought him to the more remote islands, where everybody turned out to listen to him. The questions put to him were sharp and told of political insight. He was happy when he became elected to represent the island people: 'I had long wanted to be an M.P.; for a Liberal that was in itself a remote possibility; now I was not only an M.P. but M.P. for Orkney-Shetland which to me was the most romantic of all constituencies' (*Memoirs*, Heineman 1979).

Jo Grimond originally came from St Andrews in Fife, but in 1951 he bought the old manse just outside Finstown and there he has lived ever since. He is now Lord Grimond. In his time as an M.P. he identified himself strongly with the interests of the two island groups, to the extent that he knew most of his voters personally. In the ten consecutive parliamentary elections that he won, generally with an overall majority, he increased his number of votes almost every time. But the work in such a remote constituency involves a lot of travelling, an average 75,000 miles a year. As Grimond says: 'I have spent too much of my life in airports and aeroplanes'.

Orkney has for a long time been a natural Liberal area. It is a community with few rich and few poor, an almost classless society. The Liberals are traditionally a party which has succeeded because it has paid attention to the needs of the local communities. Their party was also built up locally on the basis of community politics, and has strong roots in many remote constituencies. It has also profited from the failure of both Labour and Tories to halt environmental deterioration caused by modern industrial development.

The Liberal party is also important historically. It was the Liberal politician Gladstone who, in the 1880s, was responsible for passing The Crofters' Act, which changed the life of so many tenant farmers. To vote anything but Liberal felt like sacrilege to many. The story goes that at one of the general elections an old lady in one of the outer islands had promised to vote for the Tory candidate. When the election was over, he asked her whether she had kept her word. She said that she really had meant to vote for him, but as she was leaving her house, she happened to look up at Gladstone's picture on the wall, and then she could not do it after all.

At the 1983 general election, the first since the war without Grimond fighting the seat, there were four contestants, two men and two women, representing the Liberals, the Tories, the Scottish National Party, and Labour. Grimond's hold on the islands had become legendary; it was thought, therefore, that the election would show whether people had been voting for the party or the person. After all, young people are growing up who have barely heard of Gladstone or the Napier Commission.

Among the questions at issue were decentralization and whether the islands could have a measure of discretion on legislation which could prove damaging to their interests. Fishing rights were another controversial issue.

Both the Tory and the Labour candidates were at a disadvantage in these discussions as they were more strongly bound by party policies than the two other contestants, who could run more individual campaigns.

The election was won by the Liberal candidate, a young Edinburgh lawyer, James Wallace, who got 45 per cent of the vote, with a wide margin to the Tory candidate. The SNP and Labour came third and last. Like Grimond before him, Wallace has also settled in Orkney.

Politically both Jo Grimond and the OIC have had to fight some decisive battles during the last few years. The County Council Acts of 1974 for Orkney and Shetland, which gave the islands wide powers respecting oil development, were brought into being after intense lobbying on Grimond's part. Other crucial issues were the status of the islands in the case of Scottish self-government, and the question of uranium mining in Orkney.

In the referendum for greater devolution and an assembly for Scotland in March 1979, only 15 per cent of the Orkney electorate voted for the Scotland Bill. Maybe it is a kind of tribal memory of past misrule which is the cause of the deeply ingrained scepticism of Scottish rule. Maybe the cause is also a general mistrust of more remote control: if the power is to be decentralized, it should be transferred to the islands. As one man put it: 'I can imagine nothing worse than being ruled by Glasgow Trade Unionists and Edinburgh lawyers'. Better the devil they know ...

There was a wide fear in Orkney and Shetland that devolution for Scotland would lead to their losing the special status and special legislation they had won in 1974. Grimond therefore proposed an amendment to the Scotland Bill: if Orkney and Shetland voted 'no' in the referendum they would have the opportunity of being excluded from the terms of the Bill, and a commission would be set up to examine their future government. It was a dramatic moment in the House of Commons, with Scottish Nationalists allegedly trying to hold up proceedings so that Grimond's amendment would not be called. But he made his motion with two minutes to go before time was up. It was carried by a large majority. Thus the political principle of separate status for Orkney and Shetland was confirmed once again.

The question of uranium mining has hung like the sword of Damocles over the island population since deposits were discovered in south-west Mainland. All Orcadians have been firmly against uranium mining, no matter what political views they might otherwise hold. The fight against uranium was begun by the Orkney Heritage Society in 1976, with the well-known Orkney scholar Ernest W. Marwick as its leader. When he died, Marjorie Linklater took over the work after him. Hopefully the fight against uranium mining has now succeeded and the matter has been dropped for good.

Mistrust of government politicians who know no more than that they think Flotta is in Shetland, and worry about the future have led to a growing sense of identity. In 1979 the Orkney Movement was started, again in a

Yesnaby. This beautiful area of southwest Mainland is under threat because of its rich uranium deposits.

Shetland pattern. It now has more than 300 members, and at the 1982 election it got its first member in the OIC. The movement is non-political, but calls itself a watchdog for how government affairs affect Orkney. The threat of uranium mining was the direct cause of the Orkney Movement being formed, and one of their main aims is to gain complete control over mineral rights. They maintain that 'under Udal Law, which still applies in Orkney and Shetland, all mineral rights are vested in the owners of the land contrary to the rest of Scotland'.

The Orkney Movement wants Orkney to secure some measure of autonomy; as models they point to the Faeroes, the Åland islands in the Baltic, or the Isle of Man. They think that Home Rule would solve many of their problems. Reasonable fishing limits to the EEC countries are essential; sea transport must be controlled within the islands, as the high freight charges lead to depopulation of the remote islands. Education also contributes to the depopulation as long as all children over 12 must attend school on Mainland. The Orkney Movement also wants to establish a land bank; as it is now the price of farm land makes it virtually impossible for young people to buy a farm.

Finally the financial powers of the OIC have to be restructured. Instead of the central government allocating money to specific departments, the OIC should have the right to spend it where it is most needed, as the one who is wearing the shoe knows best where it pinches. The OIC should on the whole be given more discretion and also the right to borrow money if it finds it necessary. Further the OIC should be able to pass legislation and also have the right to adapt legislation to suit local conditions.

Jo Grimond has also thundered in the House of Commons that many aspects of local government need to be redefined – and it is especially necessary to define the relationship of the local authorities to the central government. After pressure from Shetland for a change in the relationship between island councils and government, a commission of inquiry was appointed in 1982 to look into the status of Orkney, Shetland and Western Isles and to examine the role played by the island councils. The Inquiry Commission has these terms of reference: because the islands are so remote and especially vulnerable to major industrial development, the Commission is to review the work of the island councils since 1975 and recommend changes.

As a result of these changes many of the worst effects of centralization will be removed. But the Commission's mandate goes beyond the merely formal, and there is a sincere hope in the islands that the final result will be a considerable decentralization of power, so that the local people get more say in the islands' future than they now have.

20. Kirkwall

There is much in Kirkwall reminiscent of the old Norwegian towns, especially Bergen.

P. A. Munch *Reminiscences of Orkney* 1849

The St Magnus Cathedral looms over the houses of Kirkwall. The large church is unexpected and overwhelming so far to the north, so off the beaten track. Still it is not the cathedral that gave the town the name *Kirkjuvágr* – Church Bay – but the St Olaf's church which Earl Rognvald Brusason built to commemorate his foster father King Olaf Haraldsson – St Olaf. There may have been an even earlier church, from Pictish times.

Today Kirkwall is the natural focal point in Orkney, both with regard to administration and commerce, and it is a growing town. The number of inhabitants is just under 5,000, compared to 3,800 in 1920. The growth in population has taken place at the expense of the outer islands.

To the English soldiers stationed in the islands during the two World Wars, the main street of Kirkwall seemed like Bond Street itself. Even today, returning to Kirkwall after a stay in the outer islands can come as a cultural shock.

The town lies on a western slope running down to the original bay, which was the reason why the town was placed as it was. In Norse times this would have been an excellent harbour, sheltered by the sand bank The Ayre. At that time it did not matter so much that it was shallow, as the ships did not draw much water. There is little left of the inner bay, which is now called The Peerie Sea.

The main street runs along the foot of the slope, and narrow lanes branch out from it. Earlier the main street ran close to the sea, but the innermost part of the bay has now been filled in so that it has been possible to expand the town towards the west. We cannot help regret this – the cathedral together with the Bishop's Palace must have been a striking sight from the harbour and have dominated the town even more than today.

Today it is the north end of the town which meets those coming by sea, because the harbour is there. At the beginning of this century an unbroken row of gable-walls faced the sea, as at the German Wharf in Bergen. Unfortunately some of these gables were torn down to give room for the Kirkwall Hotel and other new buildings. Many other parts of the old town have also been threatened by rebuilding and alterations. As in so many other

Albert Street, Kirkwall. The main street runs along the foot of the slope and narrow lanes branch out from it.

places, commercial interests and cultural heritage have been on a collision course. Still Kirkwall has retained its originality and its dignity better than most towns, and it is indeed a strange fact that this town in the North Sea is the best preserved example of a Norwegian mediaeval town!

Kirkwall was one of the important towns of the Norse empire. It is first mentioned in Orkneyinga saga in connection with the death of Earl Rognvald Brusason in 1045, and has had a long changeable history since then. The Orkney earls lived there; King Hakon Hakonsson died there in 1263; and Margrete Eirik's daughter – The Maid of Norway – was buried there for some time in 1290.

The town became a burgh in 1486. Cromwell's soldiers occupied the town during the civil war in the seventeenth century. In the eighteenth century the town carried on a lively trade with the outside world – mainly in potash from the kelp-burning. As agriculture improved and became essential, Kirkwall assumed more and more importance as a port of exportation for farm produce to the rest of Britain. And through two World Wars Kirkwall's streets were filled with all kinds of uniforms.

Through all these centuries the cathedral of St Magnus has dominated the town. In all of Scotland only two large churches have been used continuously since the Middle Ages – St Magnus is one and Glasgow Cathedral the other.

St Magnus Cathedral is a monument to the Norsemen's colonization of the North Sea area and a worthy cultural heritage – along with the Nidaros Cathedral at Trondheim it is the finest Norse church building of the mediaeval period. Stone masons from Durham in England probably built both churches, whose basic structures have many points in common. The cathedral is first of all an Orkney monument. It is built in an uncommonly fine local stone – red sandstone from Head of Holland just outside Kirkwall and yellow stone from Eday – and it was a local effort to honour a local saint.

Earl Rognvald kept the promise he gave when in 1137 he began building a cathedral to the memory of his kinsman. The work was supervised by Rognvald's father, Kol Kalason from Agder, and the original plan was for a cruciform church in the Romanesque style. But only the choir, the transepts and parts of the nave were built in the first round, as there were insufficient means. It took three centuries before the work was completed, and the style reflects the various stages of the building.

Bishop Bjarni Kolbeinsson (1188–1222), known also as a poet and a politician, built on to it in a Gothic transitional style. In the thirteenth century the choir got a Gothic extension, so that the church became longer. But the west facade was not completed until around 1450, under Bishop Thomas Tulloch.

When Kirkwall became a royal burgh in 1486, King James III of Scotland gave the St Magnus Cathedral as a gift to the citizens of Kirkwall, and this civilian status was confirmed in later royal charters as well. Maybe this was the reason why the church came through the Reformation almost unscathed. The situation became more difficult in the seventeenth century. During the conflict with the Stewart earls in 1614 the Earl of Caithness wanted to destroy the church, but he was prevented from carrying out his plan by Bishop Law. When Cromwell occupied Kirkwall he used the church as a stable for his horses, but it did not suffer any serious harm.

Just before the First World War the church got a new copper-covered spire in the neo-Gothic style – a poor exchange for the old four-sided squat roof which would have harmonized better in style. While the interior of the church was being restored in 1919, a box with the skeletal remains of St Magnus was found. Now the skeletons of the sainted earls Rognvald and Magnus are immured in the pillars of the choir, where the high altar used to be. Today the interior of the church is somewhat marred by Victorian bric-a-brac; a more austere style would emphasize its beauty. The graves around the church rather deflect from the simplicity of style, but serve as a reminder that the St Magnus Cathedral is used as a parish church for the Church of Scotland.

After the change in local government in 1974 the Town Council of Kirkwall ceased to function, so that it is now the Orkney Islands Council which owns the cathedral. On the Council also falls the burden of its upkeep and maintenance, and they have planned a long-term systematic restoration. Eight centuries of wind and weather have taken a heavy toll on the soft sandstone walls. Much of the carved stonework of the west front has decayed almost completely. How to save the carved stones and still preserve their detail from further erosion became a highly controversial topic, and the suggested porch to cover the doorways turned out to be a very unpopular idea.

Kirkwall Castle used to lie just west of the church. Today the street name of Castle Street is the only reminder of this stronghold. The castle was probably built at the site where the hall of the Norse earls used to be. It was Henry Sinclair, one of the Scottish earls, who built it around 1380. It was besieged and partly destroyed by the Earl of Caithness in 1614 when Robert Stewart entrenched himself there. The castle ruins were removed by the Town Council in 1865 to improve the access to the harbour.

The masonry of the oldest part of the Bishop's Palace corresponds to the walls in the Romanesque part of the cathedral. It was probably built by William the Old, who was Bishop for 66 years, from 1102 to 1168. He went with Rognvald Kali Kolsson on his crusade as master of one of the ships. It was in 1154, during his time in office, that the bishopric of Orkney became part of the archdiocese of Nidaros at Trondheim, where it remained until 1472, when it was transferred to St Andrews in Scotland.

It was in the old Bishop's Palace that King Hakon Hakonsson lay ill in the autumn of 1263 after the campaign which ended at Largs. He died there on 16 December 1263, and the saga of Hakon Hakonsson tells us that

He was buried in the choir of St Magnus Cathedral on the steps before the shrine of the martyred Earl Magnus.

Earl's Palace, Kirkwall. Erected by Patrick Stewart, Earl of Orkney in the early seventeenth century.

In 1963, when 700 years had passed since he died, a marble tablet was inserted in the floor of the choir in St Magnus Cathedral with an inscription which tells briefly in Latin that King Hakon Hakonsson was buried there in the winter of 1263–64.

The Bishop's Palace was completely rebuilt by Bishop Reid (1541–58), who is also known as the founder of Edinburgh University. The high round tower which Reid built is still standing and is a well-known landmark. Reid lived in troubled times and had the Bishop's Palace fortified almost like a castle.

Around 1600 Earl Patrick Stewart made the Bishop's Palace part of his large fortified palace complex. His regular guard of 50 musketeers were stationed in the Bishop's Palace, and he built his own palace close by it. It was magnificently conceived and built but was never completed. The Earl's Palace is one of the finest Renaissance buildings in Scotland, but it was erected at a cost of grief and suffering, for it was built with slave labour and equipped with stolen goods.

After the downfall of the Stewart earls the whole palace complex became the seat of the bishop, until the Presbyterian Church of Scotland, fearing the power of the king and Catholic practices, abolished episcopacy in 1689.

Afterwards the buildings fell rapidly into decay. Sir Walter Scott set parts of the story in his novel *The Pirate* in the Earl's Palace.

On the whole, the seventeenth century brought great changes to Kirkwall. The old earldom was abolished and so was the bishopric. Kirkwall was no longer of political and ecclesiastical importance: an era was over. Instead the town grew as a centre of commerce, and a prosperous merchant class built elegant houses. The landowners from the outer islands made enough money on potash to be able to build houses in Kirkwall and spend the winter there. The town became known for its lively social life. Tankerness House is one such old town house, beautifully restored and now a museum.

The Scottish incomers carried on much of the trade and therefore left a strong mark on the town. This caused tension between town and country districts. All the same, the farmers used to turn out in large numbers for the Lammas Fair which was held each year in Kirkwall during the first two weeks of August. Originally it was a Mass of thanksgiving held among the farmers who rented Church land, for the first corn they cut, but it developed over the years into a fair with all kinds of entertainment. Till quite recently it was the great annual event. Now it has been succeeded by a cattle show – The County Agricultural Show – which lasts only one day. But every Monday the town is full of farmers from all over the islands. They gather in the auction hall The Mart, which the farmers run on a co-operation basis. There farm equipment and animals are bought and sold.

At times the main street of Kirkwall is so crowded that it seems as if all the islanders have agreed to meet there at the same time. Then it is impossible to understand why it was not banned for cars long ago. It is true that it has mostly one-way traffic but, as there is no pavement, the pedestrian still manages to have quite an exciting life. This is not a new problem, for in a description of Kirkwall from 1868 we can read that 'two wheel-barrows tremble when they meet', because the street is so narrow.

The St Magnus Cathedral traditionally divided the town into two different parts: the Burgh to the north and Laverock to the south of the cathedral. The division was deep. In the Burgh was the market town, where all the trade was carried on and the ordinary townspeople lived. The earl and his men, as well as the clergy belonging to a bishop's seat, lived in Laverock. It is a strange name and nobody knows what it means.

This old town division still comes to the fore in the Ba': a ball-game which takes place on Christmas Day and New Year's Day. In the morning the young boys play and in the afternoon it is the turn of the men – the teams play for the part of the town they come from. Those who play for the northern part of town are called Doonies, the southerners are Uppies. The two parts of town are known as Down-the-Gates and Up-the-Gates.

At the Mercat Cross in Broad Street outside the St Magnus Cathedral the players jostle for position while they wait for the throw-up of the ball. After that it is a free-for-all in one big jumble. Each side can have as many players

The Ba'. This is a ball game, hotly contested by the 'Uppies' and 'Doonies' of Kirkwall each Christmas and New Year's Day.

as it wants, and there are no rules. The aim is to get the ball into the Down-the-Gates harbour or the Up-the-Gates goal at Mackinson's Corner. Lately it has mostly been the Doonies who have won, and the game has ended up in the sea for several of the players. The best and most dedicated player usually gets to keep the ball as a souvenir – a treasured trophy! The game usually takes about four hours. The shopkeepers along the route wisely secure or barricade doors and windows as best they can. The game can also be rough on bystanders who are sometimes badly trampled; they have been known to be pulled unconscious from the pack.

The story goes that a young Scottish policeman, who had recently been stationed in Kirkwall, thought he saw a major fight going on and desperately threw himself in the middle of the melee to try to stop it!

Probably the Ba' has roots back to the Norse ball-game *knattleikr*. This game is described in the saga of Gisli Sursson. It was quite popular in Iceland where it was often played on the ice. It probably originated in Orkney and was brought from there to Iceland. The game was played with a small hard ball between two people or two teams. The purpose of the game was to get the ball first to goal. Everything was permitted, so the game could be quite rough, as it still is in Kirkwall!

21. Stromness

This brief inscription succinctly gives the salient facts of Stromness history. The town owed its existence to and was centred around the sea.

Kirkwall faces the North Isles and is a natural port for the North Sea – in a way turned in on itself, hugging its Norse past. Stromness and its business were bound to the Atlantic and an important part of Orkney's Scottish identity. Still, the Norse name of Stromness was *Hafnarvágr*, meaning 'a bay which makes a good harbour for ships'. Evidently even the Norsemen appreciated its qualities. This name developed into Hamnavoe. At one time the area was also called Cairston, but today the town is known as Stromness, which was originally the name of the surrounding parish. The name means 'the promontory in the sound', or literally 'in the current'.

Stromness is completely sheltered against the Atlantic and the west wind by the 390-ft (119-m) hill of Brinkie's Brae, which forms a striking backdrop for the town. There is still about Stromness the romance of sailing ships and salty sea. For more than 200 years the name of Stromness was associated with the Hudson's Bay Company, and the town developed along with the company's trade.

The Hudson's Bay Company was founded in 1670 and is today the oldest chartered trading company in the world. It was established to trade in fur, especially beaver, with the Indians in North America. It was Prince Rupert, a cousin of King Charles II, who took up the project. The first charter of the Hudson's Bay Company was granted on 2 May 1670 to 'The Governor and Company of Adventurers of England trading into Hudson's Bay'. The territory granted to them was vast – Quebec, Ontario, Manitoba and Saskatchewan. It became known then as Rupert's Land. For 200 years they held a trade monopoly and governed in those parts, until in 1867 the company had to cede their territorial rights to the new Dominion of Canada. The Hudson's Bay Company is still the world's largest fur trading company.

Stromness was the last port of call for ships going on the North Atlantic route to North America or Greenland, the so-called Northabout Route. The bay was probably first used by the sailing ships as a haven and then

THERE WATERED HERE
THE HUDSON BAY COY'S SHIPS
1670 - 1891
CAPT COOK'S VESSELS
RESOLUTION AND DISCOVERY
1780
SIR JOHN FRANKLIN'S SHIPS
EREBUS AND TERROR
ON ARCTIC EXPLORATION
1845

LOGIN'S WELL

Login's Well, Stromness. This historic well was sealed up in 1931 but was opened again recently for a local contracting firm restoring a nearby house. It now has a glass door.

enterprising people set up businesses to cater for them. The oldest house in existence today dates from 1716. The sailing ships stayed in Stromness for two weeks every year in June to take in water and general supplies for their outward voyage and then returned in November. The Company had established a recruiting office in Stromness. The Orcadians were known as hard workers, and at one time as much as 75 per cent of the Hudson's Bay Company's workforce was from Orkney, most of them on five-year contracts. But many Orcadians worked their way up the rungs of power in the company, and ten of them became governors.

In 1717 Kirkwall, as a Royal Burgh, obtained the right to tax all trade in Orkney and Shetland. As Stromness trade increased, this injustice was strongly resented, and matters finally came to a head in 1743 when Stromness refused to pay. The matter was taken to the Supreme court, and in 1754 the judgment was finally made that there was 'no sufficient right in the borough of Kirkwall to assess the village of Stromness; but that the said village should be quit thereof, and free therefrom, in all time coming'. Although Kirkwall appealed against this judgment, it was upheld in the House of Lords, and set a precedent for all similar areas which had been oppressed by the exclusive trading rights of the Royal Burghs of Scotland.

One man was responsible for the Stromness versus Kirkwall case to give the merchants freedom to trade. Alexander Graham poured every penny he had into the campaign for Stromness and he died a ruined man. Graham Place in the centre of the town is named after him.

Stromness also became a favourite stop-over for the whaling ships going to the Greenland Sea or the Davis Straits. The whaling trade was important to Stromness for a whole century. It began about 1760 and declined around 1860. It gave trade and provided employment. The Orkneymen were so popular with the skippers that few left without complementing their crews with men from the islands.

Whaling was dangerous work which took its toll on the whaling crews. Epidemics might break out among the crew while beset in the ice during the winter, with only limited medical facilities on board. The ships might limp into Stromness in the spring with exhausted 'greenlandmen' on board. A small hospital was set up in Stromness to care for the returning whalers.

All this migration of males turned Stromness into a town of women. In 1794 the population had risen to 1,344, and the females outnumbered the males by almost two to one. Still the population grew, especially during the years of the Napoleonic Wars which were golden years for Stromness, as the safety of the northern waters made the Northabout Route very busy. In the census year of 1821 the population reached a peak of 2,236; and for a short time Stromness was larger than Kirkwall. In 1817 Stromness was made a Burgh of Barony, with its own town council with nine councillors and two magistrates or bailies. This town council functioned until it was replaced by the Orkney Islands Council in 1974.

A storm-haven like Stromness, where the ships might lie weather-bound for days, attracted its fair share of adventurers, and the regular seamen could also become quite rowdy. A police force was established to protect the townspeople. Still many seemed at first to have been taken in by the young pirate John Gow when he turned up there in his captured ship the *Revenge*, and he even got himself engaged to a young Miss Gordon of Stromness. Although he was born in Caithness he grew up in Stromness, but his career as a pirate before he was hanged in 1725 was very short. All the many different stories about him have not diminished in the telling, so that it is difficult to sift fact from fiction. Sir Walter Scott used the story of Gow in his novel *The Pirate*. Although he originally meant his Captain Cleveland to suffer the same fate as Gow, he relented and gave him a chance of an honourable death in a war against Spain.

'I learned the history of Gow the pirate from an old sibyl, whose principal subsistence was by a trade in favourable winds, which she told to mariners in Stromness.' This Scott says of Bessie Millie, whom he used as the prototype for the mysterious and prophetic Norna of Fitful-head, one of the main characters of his story, and used as an embodiment of old Norse customs and legends. Bessie Millie was only one of the many women who over the years made a living from selling fair winds. Some, like Bessie Skeabister, went

Graham Place, Stromness. Children taking part in the rag and bone race during Stromness Shopping Week which is held each July.

further and could tell the fishermen whether their boats were in danger or not. So implicitly did they believe in her that 'Giff Bessie say it is weill it is weill' became an island proverb. In the end she was both strangled and burned for allegedly flying to Norway and Shetland on the back of a certain James Sandison. The first Orkney witchcraft prosecution took place in 1594, and Bessie Skeabister was not the first nor the last to go further in the land of fantasy than was acceptable to her times.

Stromness was in 1780 the first British landfall of Captain James Cook's ships, *Resolution* and *Discovery*. They had been on one of the most famous expeditions ever made, which after three years of exploration had ended with the death of their leader in Hawaii. It had been a futile search for a Pacific-Atlantic passage through North America. Cook's ships lay for some time in Stromness, and the crews and officers were hospitably received and entertained by people in the town. One of them was the young master of the *Resolution*, William Bligh.

In 1787 Bligh was sent as master of the *Bounty* on an expedition to bring breadfruit-trees from Tahiti to the West Indies. The young Stromnessian George Stewart was engaged as midshipman on board, and Captain Bligh had this to say about him:

Stewart was a young man of creditable parents, in the Orkneys; at which place, on the return of the Resolution from the South Seas, in 1780, we received so many civilities, that, on that account only, I should gladly have taken him with me; but independent of the recommendation, he was a seaman, and had always borne a good character.

Article in *The Orcadian*

On the way back from Tahiti the famous mutiny occurred. Stewart was arrested by mistake as one of the mutineers and brought back in chains on the *Pandora*, and he died when the ship was wrecked. His beautiful Tahitian wife is said to have died of grief.

The story was used by Lord Byron in his long epic poem 'The Island'. George Stewart there became 'Torquil, the nursling of the northern seas' and 'the blue-eyed northern child' in true romantic style.

Around the turn of the nineteenth century Stromness was a centre of the herring fishing. During the herring season life took on a hectic rhythm, with a fleet of 500 or 600 boats lying in Stromness at times, and girls coming up for the salting.

On the whole the life of sail trading was hard. So many of the vessels, almost one in three, were wrecked. In Stromness they found the shelter they needed while waiting for the right wind. They meant a busy trade for Stromness and much of its importance disappeared with them.

The drive-on, drive-off ferry *St Ola* came in 1975 and brings the majority of Orkney's tourists right into Stromness. Tourism has therefore become quite important. Oil-related business activities have also helped bring new life to the town. Stromness is also a popular place for artists, and today The Pier Arts Centre is housed in an old Hudson's Bay Company building. It has

Miller's Close, Stromness. Mrs Nellie Miller at the door of her house which has been continuously occupied by her family since 1716.

been carefully restored, and besides having an interesting permanent art collection it forms a good background for the works of visiting artists.

Stromness has scenic beauty, and although its look of antiquity is deceptive, much of the town has been designated as a conservation area regarded as 'outstanding', and the district around it is considered as a 'national scenic area'. Stromness has a unique waterfront, with its houses gable-end to sea and with their own private piers jutting into the harbour. The town grew out of necessity to fill the demands made on it, and the result is charming. One long flagstoned street runs the length of Stromness with narrow lanes branching from it up Brinkie's Brae. The problem of two-way traffic in the street increases when the tourists come in the summer, but there are no plans to make it into a pedestrian area.

The Lammas Fair on the first Tuesday of September used to be the great annual event in Stromness, but the Second World War disrupted this tradition and it is no longer observed. Instead since 1949 there has been the Stromness Shopping Week, or Gala Week. It is more of a carnival than a fair, and has become very popular.

One of the distinctive characteristics of life in Stromness has been the number of retired deep-sea sailors living there. They used to gather at the Pierhead, where they would discuss local politics and affairs of the day. Indeed they were known as the Pierhead Parliament. This is perhaps not so common anymore, but still there is about Stromness a sense of close-knit community.

22. Mainland

Although the specific name given to this island was Hrossey – island of horses – even in Norse times it was known as Meginland, meaning Mainland. The density of prehistoric remains and the fact that the Norse earls chose it for their centre of administration and place of residence point to its importance. Orkney's only two towns lie here, and today this tendency towards centralization is more apparent than ever. Both size and central location account for this.

Mainland has unique places of interest that have already been mentioned in other connections as they have played important parts in the history of the islands. It is natural to divide Mainland into two parts, East Mainland and West Mainland, at Kirkwall, as the land between Bay of Kirkwall and Scapa Bay is only 2 miles (3.2 km) wide.

Deerness in the east is connected with Mainland by a very narrow isthmus where a broch was strategically placed. The Thing for East Mainland may also have been held there, judging by the name Dingieshowe – the Thing Mound. It was probably here that Thorkel Amundarson the Fosterer pleaded with Earl Einar to be less harsh with the farmers. It was at his home at Skaill that Thorkel later broke all rules of hospitality by slaying Earl Einar who was a guest at a banquet in his home. Excavations at Skaill have revealed extensive remains of the Norse period as well as the fact that the farm site has been in continuous use since prehistoric times. It is probably identical with the Hlaupandanes mentioned in the Orkneyinga saga.

The east coast of Deerness is rocky, with a long and deep gloup which is very impressive. It is perhaps the most easily accessible of the gloups, and attracts many visitors. The old chapel ruins at the Brough of Deerness are reached by a narrow and dangerous path. The main impression Deerness gives, however, is of being a highly cultivated part of Orkney. The dramatic story behind the Covenanters' Memorial with its echoes of strife and intolerance seems out of place in peaceful and pastoral Deerness.

Just inland from Scarvataing stands a high pillar. It was erected in 1888 close to the spot where the Covenanters were shipwrecked two centuries before, and not far from the valley where most of them are buried.

In Scottish history, the Covenanters were groups of people bound by oath to defend Presbyterianism and their own religious freedom. The Covenant

Covenanters' Memorial, Deerness. This was erected in 1888, close to the spot where the Covenanters were shipwrecked two centuries before.

of 1638 was directed against the attempt by King Charles I to introduce the English Book of Common Prayer, and episcopacy – the government of the Church by bishops – along with it. After the Restoration in 1660, the established Church in Scotland was given episcopal government. The Covenanters were alternately coerced and persuaded to accept episcopacy but stubbornly resisted. The harsh measures taken against them in 1679 led to an uprising which was defeated at Bothwell Bridge.

Of the 1000 Covenanters who were captured, some 250 refused to submit and were subsequently condemned to banishment in the American colonies. The prisoners were stowed into a small ship called the *Crown*, which was poorly equipped and not provisioned for such a long winter voyage. A storm drove the captain to anchor at the entrance to Deer Sound. He ignored the advice of local people to go further into the Sound. The storm rose and drove the ship on to the rocks at Scarvataing. A few of the prisoners escaped, but most of them drowned.

People in Deerness have always believed that this was cold-blooded murder, as the Covenanters were left there to die. The captain's last order is said to have been 'Batten down the hatches and let the dogs die'.

Across Deer Sound lies Hall of Tankerness, which was built in 1630 and was for over three centuries the home of one of the old Orkney families, the Baikies. Like so many of the landowners in Orkney, the Baikies spent the winter in a town house in Kirkwall. Tankerness House in Kirkwall belonged to the Baikies from 1641, and has now been turned into a museum. The estate was, like so many others, broken up after the First World War when there was no longer any profit in owning land. The last of the Baikies sold the Hall and the remaining land before he emigrated just after the Second World War.

Another historic country house in East Mainland is Graemeshall, which used to be the seat of the Graham or Graeme family. It was built at about the same time as Tankerness House by Bishop Graham. The roofless ruins in Breck Ness, near the entrance to Hoy Sound, are of an old mansion also erected by Bishop Graham, in 1633. A later owner of Graemeshall was Alexander Graeme, who served as an admiral in the Napoleonic Wars.

The house as it stands today dates from 1874 and houses the private Norwood collection of antiques – mostly weapons, silver, porcelain and some of the finest lustreware in Scotland. It is the lifework of the collector, Norris Wood. Graemeshall is open to the public.

Graemeshall is part of the parish of Holm. The name is pronounced Ham which may mean haven, but was probably believed by cartographers to refer to Lamb Holm and Glims Holm. P. A. Munch was certain that Ham was derived from *Heimr* – home, and that it meant the western part of the parish. To Paplay, which was the eastern part, belonged the southeastern tip of the island, Hrossanes, which strangely has become Rose Ness.

The parish name also occurs in Holm St Mary, now often called St Mary or 'the Village'. It consists of one long row of houses along the shore. It used to be a busy place during the herring boom. It was from this village that the Marquis of Montrose sailed with his Orkney recruits on his final military expedition, which ended in the Battle of Carbisdale. At the eastern end stands the oldest house in the village – the old storehouse with a pointed roof – this was broken into and looted by French privateers as long ago as 1694. The then owner of Graemeshall fired at them, but missed.

Perhaps the nicest view of Kirkwall is obtained from the top of Wideford Hill. It is a fine walk from Kirkwall; indeed in the old days the annual Lammas Fair celebrations in Kirkwall spread as far as the southern slope of the hill. In *The Pirate* Sir Walter Scott lets one of his main characters, Captain Cleveland, enjoy the sight of the preparations for the Fair while walking up the hill

... to the northward of the ancient Burgh of Saint Magnus. The plain at the foot of the hill was already occupied by numbers of persons who were engaged in making preparations for the Fair of Saint Olla, to be held upon the ensuing day, and which forms a general rendezvous to all the neighbouring islands of Orkney, and is even frequented by many persons from the more distant archipelago of Zetland. It is, in the words of the Proclamation, 'a free Mercat and Fair, holden at the good Burgh of Kirkwall on the third of August, being St Olla's day', and continuing for an indefinite space thereafter, extending from three days to a week, and upwards.

The 3rd August was the day in 1031 when St Olaf's body was taken from the grave – *translatio Sancti Olavi* – and it was celebrated long after the Reformation. Olaf was the saint for corn and other produce in the north Apparently the memory of his connection with the Lammas festivities was still alive at the time Sir Walter Scott was writing.

Another enjoyable view, especially of Hoy and Scapa Flow, is to be had from the Ward Hill in Orphir, at 268 m the highest point on Mainland. It is in Orphir – the Norse *Orfjara*, a place which is dry when the tide is out – that some of the later earls resided. 'There was a great drinking-hall at Orphir, with a door in the south wall over the eastern gable, and in front of the hall, just a few paces down from it, stood a fine church.' This was the scene of the Christmas feast held by Earl Paul Hakonsson where a dramatic murder was committed.

The fine church referred to is the one known as the Round Church of Orphir. Not very much is left of it as, in the eighteenth century, two thirds of the stone were used to build a new church that has later been demolished. It is generally believed that this church was built around 1120 by Earl Hakon Paulsson after his return from a crusade to expiate for the sin of killing Earl Magnus Erlendsson. The church is supposed to have been modelled on the Church of the Holy Sepulchre at Jerusalem. This is the only church of its kind in Scotland, but similar ones are to be found both in England and Norway.

In a description of the church from 1758 it is referred to as 'The Temple of Orphir, or Gerth House'. The latter name is derived from O.N. grið, meaning sanctuary or peace. The foundation of a large building which has been excavated near the church may be the remains of the great drinking-hall – skáli – of the Earl's Bu, as described in the saga.

For the earls to choose Orphir as a place of residence seems logical, as it had a more strategic location than Birsay. It was midway on Mainland, and what is now known as the Bay of Houton would have made an excellent harbour even at low tide for the old type of ship. Not surprisingly it was known in Norse times as Meðallands hǫfn – Midland harbour – and the promontory on the east side of the bay is still known as Midland Ness. Today the Bay of Houton still lives up to its name of Midland Harbour – it is the site of the pier for the South Isles ferry as well as for a pier built by Occidental for the Flotta run.

On his return from Largs in 1263, King Hakon Hakonsson had his ship beached at Midland Harbour:

On the Saturday before Martinmas the King rode out to Midland Harbour, it was towards the evening, and he was very ill. He stayed on board the ship overnight, and in the morning he had a mass sung to him on shore. Then he decided where the ship was to be beached and told them to look after it well. After that he rode to Scapa and from there to Kirkwall.
Saga of Hakon Hakonsson

King Hakon's ship was the *Krist-suðin* – the largest ship made in Norway in mediaeval times. It had a total of 37 rooms, but proved too large for easy manoeuvering. It was built in Bergen during the winter of 1263 for the express purpose of serving as the King's ship on the Scottish campaign. Although it was then in fashion to give the ships Christian names, they were still, as in pagan times, decorated with carved and gilded dragon heads, sometimes, as in the case of *Krist-suðin*, both fore and aft. On the *Krist-suðin* King Hakon's body was brought from Orkney to Norway in the spring of 1264.

The skerry in Scapa Flow called Barrel of Butter is also part of Orphir. Tradition has it that a barrel of butter was the price paid annually for the right to kill seals there. An earlier name was Carling Skerry.

Around the middle of the nineteenth century the village of Finstown in Firth was only a small cluster of houses. According to tradition it got its name from David Phin, an Irishman and a veteran of the Battle of Waterloo. He ran a tavern called The Toddy Hole, which is now Pomona Inn. The village became the commercial centre of the Firth district, and has kept on growing.

The traditional pattern of life in Firth some 150 years ago is described by John Firth in *Reminiscences of an Orkney Parish* which has become a classic. The parish takes its name from the Bay of Firth, which used to be Aurriða-Fjǫrðr – Salmon-trout Firth – or just Fjǫrðr.

Further west, on top of the 492 ft (150 m) high Burgar Hill in Evie, the Orkney wind is being put to good use, as electric power is produced from it. Two aerogenerators – large windmills – were switched on in September 1983, and the electricity they generate goes directly on to the Orkney grid. These two machines produce 300 and 250 kilowatt respectively, but are only the forerunners of a much larger version to be erected in 1985. The third aerogenerator will produce three megawatt, enough power to supply 1,000 homes. It will have a diameter of 197 ft (60 m) and is thus the biggest wind-power generator in Britain.

The design work for the multi-megawatt wind turbine has been carried out by the Wind Energy Group consortium since 1977. The decision was taken by the Department of Energy to construct it on Burgar Hill because it has an exceptionally high annual mean windspeed – indeed it is one of the windiest areas in Britain. Orkney has thus become the centre for some of the largest and most important projects in Europe for the research on renewable energy.

In West Mainland there is still a tradition connected with St Magnus. The Mansie Stanes pilgrimage held in June is about 10 miles (16 km) long and covers the route believed to have been taken by those who carried his body from Aikerness to Christ Church in Birsay, after his death in Egilsay. The stones represent the temporary resting places.

Another story relates that the procession bearing St Magnus' remains from Christ Church to Kirkwall rested on top of Staney Hill in the township

Burgar Hill Windmill, Evie. This is one of two aerogenerators switched on in September 1983, and the electricity they generate goes directly on to the Orkney grid. It also won a design award in the same year.

of Grimeston in Harray. The men of Harray were slow to meet the Birsay procession, whose leader was reputed to have said that the Harray men came crawling out of their huts like crabs out of the ebb. Harray people have been known ever since as Harray crabs.

The inland parish of Harray – from O. N. heraŏ, an administrative district – is otherwise known as the last parish on Mainland where Norn was spoken. In Barry's *History of Orkney* we are told that 'So late as 1756 or 1757 as a respectable native of this County was travelling from Kirkwall to Birsa he, having to spend the night in Harra, was surprised to hear two old men, for an hour or two, converse together in an unknown tongue which, on enquiry, he found was the Norse language'. Harray is also renowned for 'the one hundred Harray lairds'. Most of the holdings in Harray were occupied by the owners themselves. Many of the properties were bought for means earned in whaling or by working for the Hudson's Bay Company.

An old Harray farm that had become quite dilapidated was bought and restored by the Education Committee of the Orkney Islands Council. This was formerly the farmstead of Midhouse in the township of Corrigall. Today the Corrigall Farm Museum is one of Orkney's leading tourist attractions. The museum consists of three main buildings – the house of a type going back to Norse times, with its 'in-by' and 'oot-by', its one-time pig stalls and goose nests – the stable, barn and circular kiln – the byre, with stalls formed of large flagstones set on edge. The buildings date from the mid-eighteenth century, but have been furnished as a typical Orkney farmhouse and steading of the 1860's.

Just south of the village of Dounby is the Click Mill where the Midhouse farmers probably went to have their corn ground. It is a restored example of a type of water-mill that once was common in Orkney. The quern was turned by a horizontal water-wheel system, which is quite old in Orkney even if the Click Mill itself was built fairly recently.

The village of Dounby has grown up as a market centre for a large farming area; it is strategically placed at the junction of two main roads. A notice in the *Orkney Herald* of 4 March 1862 stated that a Cattle Trust was to be held at Dounby. 'This market is established for the disposal of the best fat grazing stock in the district.' Over the years this turned into the West Mainland Cattle Show, and it is now held in August. It is one of the most popular annual events in Orkney.

The West Mainland coast is full of historical relics and also a place of rare beauty, so a walk along it is a rewarding experience. From the 492 ft (150 m) perpendicular red sandstone face of Costa Head to Hoy Sound the coastline is spectacular. The onslaught of the Atlantic has wrought rock stacks like Yesnaby Castle and the Castle of North Gaulton. The coast is studded with caves.

In the summer of 1847 the Scottish naturalist Hugh Miller stayed for some time in the vicinity of Stromness to study fossils, and was overwhelmed by what he found:

Yesnaby Castle. Here an attempt on the stack is being made by a group of local climbers.

Birsay village and brough. The brough is accessible for up to three hours on either side of low water.

The geology of Orkney ... owes its chief interest to the immense development which it exhibits of one formation – the Old Red Sandstone –, and to the extraordinary abundance of its vertebrate remains ... Orkney is emphatically to the geologist ... a 'Land of Fish'; and, were the trade once fairly opened up, could supply with ichthyolites, by the ton and the ship-load, the museums of the world.

Footprints of the Creator or The Asterolepis of Stromness, Edinburgh 1850

Close by the Black Craig is a quarry where Hugh Miller found a bone he described as a 'petrified nail' – one of the most interesting fossils he had ever seen. He believed this bone formed part of a large fish that could become some 20 ft (6 m) long. On the strength of this bone he was able to reconstruct one of the oldest known types of fish called the *asterolepis*, or star-scale fish. Miller wrote a book about it, *Footprints of the Creator, or The Asterolepis of Stromness*, which was published in 1850. Later it turned out that the fossil actually belonged to another species called homosteus, and this particular species has since been called *Homosteus Milleri*. But since Miller's days the stealing of fossils has become quite a problem in Orkney.

The Bay of Skaill, famous for its Skara Brae settlement, is the largest inlet along the coast. Another picturesque spot is Noust of Biggin in Yesnaby; it has been very popular with painters and is impressive even in wintertime. In the summertime lobster fishermen would fish from there. Further north is the 361 ft (110 m) high Vestra Fiold where the stones for the Ring of Brogar are believed to have been quarried. How they could be transported is still an unsolved mystery.

In June and July the Brough of Birsay and much of the cliff edge along the Birsay coast are turfed with thrift. The Brough of Birsay is accessible on foot for up to three hours either side of low water.

Even in Pictish times the Brough of Birsay had religious significance. There are remains of a Celtic community, probably a monastery, and although a later Norse community was built over it, a churchyard can still be seen. Here the famous Birsay stone – a Pictish symbol stone – was found. The original is in an Edinburgh museum, but a replica can be seen at the site. It has the characteristic, enigmatic Pictish symbols: a crescent and v-shaped rod and three warriors with sword, spear and shield.

The Norse remains include the foundations of 13 longhouses dating from the tenth and eleventh centuries, a church and a hall which even had central heating, and a boatslip. It is evident that this must have been a settlement of importance. The excavation work is not finished yet, and the nature of the settlement has not been definitely established. It may have continued as a monastery, but some would have it that the Brough of Birsay is the site of Earl Thorfinn's Christ Church and his small palace, and that he ruled Orkney from there.

However, tradition will also have it that it is Birsay village, also called the P'lace, which was the site of Orkney's first cathedral and the place Earl Thorfinn made into his headquarters in his later years. Tradition also says that the remains of buildings close to the old schoolhouse are of the first Bishop's Palace.

The Earl's Palace in Birsay was probably built in 1574 by Earl Robert Stewart. It formed a large rectangle enclosing a courtyard. It had square towers at all four corners. The main entrance was through an arched gateway in the south wall, and the towers on either side served to defend it. The palace had two stories. Upstairs the whole length of the west wing seems to have been one long gallery with numerous windows giving a panoramic view of the Atlantic. The north wing formed a banqueting hall with a large fireplace in the west wall. The main staircase led directly to this hall.

The north-west tower is different from the other three towers, and seems also to have been constructed in a different way. This may have been part of an older structure. According to tradition it was called Earl Thorfinn's Castle. Although it can hardly have been as old as that, the whole north wing is puzzling. The plan of the palace is said to have been copied from that of the Holyrood Palace in Edinburgh.

Over the gateway was Robert Stewart's coat of arms along with this inscription: *Dominus Robertus Stuartus filius Jacobi Quinti Rex Scotorum hoc opus instruxit.* When his son Patrick stood trial in Edinburgh, one of the charges against him is said to have been that he did not remove this inscription. It may be constructed as treason, as what it says is 'Lord Robert Stewart, King of the Scots, son of James the Fifth, erected this building'. Counsel for the Defence is supposed to have explained this as a grammatical mistake: the nominative *rex* had been written instead of the genitive *regis* which would have changed the meaning of the sentence to 'Lord Robert Stewart, son of James the Fifth, King of the Scots, erected this building.'

Whether the meaning of this inscription was intended or accidental we will never know. Nor will we know why the Palace was built in historic but remote Birsay, perhaps even incorporating older structures. Was it to cement a tradition, a link with the past, to found a new dynasty of earls? Robert Stewart's motto Sic fuit, est, et erit – Thus it was, and is, and ever shall be – does perhaps point in that direction.

23. The South Isles

The islands south of Mainland enclose the large bay of Scapa and make it look like a lake. The four Churchill barriers enhance this impression. The island of Hoy shuts out the view further to the south and makes Orkney into a world apart with only the sea as a neighbour. Its earthen colours are a dramatic, startling contrast to the green of the other islands and make them seem even more fertile.

Graemsay

Graemsay lies like a bulwark against the swells of the Atlantic, but otherwise there is nothing warlike about it. It is a small green island consisting almost entirely of cultivated fields. In the middle of the last century there were no less than 60 families living in Graemsay. Its fertile land must have been appreciated from early times because there are two Celtic sites dedicated to St Bride and St Columba. Earl Robert Stewart gave Graemsay to one of his natural sons, and his descendants settled at the Bu in Sandside, with a view towards Stromness. This is now the only farm on the islands: all the rest of the land is still held as crofts. Graemsay has an excellent pier and a regular boat connection with Stromness.

Hoy

The island of Hoy is divided into two parts – Hoy and Walls – and until the road along the coast came, these two parts of Hoy were as separate as if they were two islands, for almost all connection between them was by sea. At the time of the earldom Hoy and Graemsay were *bordland*, that is they were the personal property of the earls.

In the rocky, mountainous Hoy there were only two places which yielded a living, Rackwick in the west and North Hoy, facing the Burra Sound. Just before the turn of the century Rackwick had 17 crofts which shared 87 acres (35 ha) of arable land between them. Even at that time this was not enough to live on, so they were all forced to find secondary employment of some kind. The women knitted and spun, the men fished. Fishing was a hazardous way of making a living in a place where the only harbour was a beach which lay open and unprotected to the Atlantic. The boats always had to be drawn up on the beach, and then to be launched again between swells. No wonder that the fishermen of Rackwick were known far and wide for their skill at sea!

Rackwick is the most isolated place in Orkney, and the road to it passes

Hoy High lighthouse, Graemsay, with the bay of Sandside and the hills of Hoy in the background.

through an empty valley. The strange Dwarfie Stane is there: a Stone Age grave cut into a boulder. On the hill on the other side of Ward Hill there is also a footpath to Rackwick, which suddenly opens up to the sea. Rackwick is surrounded by mountains on three sides.

Today there are few people living in Rackwick, and most of the land lies derelict. The school was closed as long ago as 1954 and now serves as a youth hostel. But the crofts have been given a new lease of life as country cottages; to spend the summer in Rackwick has now become something of a status symbol. And Rackwick has one new inhabitant at any rate. At Bunertoon, high up in the hillside with a view of both Rackwick and the ocean, the renowned composer Peter Maxwell Davies composes all his music. The journalists of the world press who beat a track to his door wonder why he has to make their work so difficult.

But in the summertime there is not much quiet or concentration to be had here, as right past his house goes the path to the stack which more than anything has become the landmark of Orkney – The Old Man of Hoy – and it is a popular excursion spot. At 450 ft (137 m) it is the tallest and perhaps most impressive needle in Britain. Old pictures show that until 100 years ago or so The Old Man stood firmly on two legs. Then one of them was knocked off by the waves. But there is not supposed to be any risk of the whole of The Old Man disappearing in the foreseeable future, as its base is not of sandstone but of volcanic rock. The Old Man has been climbed many times and by some of the best mountaineers in Britain. It was first conquered in 1966 by Chris Bonington, who went up the east face. The following year another well-known climber, Hamish McInnes, made a free ascent without using pitons. This climb was televised.

The northern townships of Hoy – Orgil, Beneath-the-Hill and Quoyness – have also suffered from a drastic depopulation after the Second World War. At the turn of the century more than 300 people lived here, but around 1970 the number had sunk as low as 30. The place was caught in a vicious circle; as there was no school, shop or church, no young people wanted to settle there.

The whole of Hoy was one estate of 24,000 acres (9,700 ha), consisting mostly of hills and non-arable land. In 1973 the owner, Malcolm Stewart, gave all of this area to a charitable organisation, which was named The Hoy Trust. He considered Hoy to be a place of natural beauty and scientific interest which ought therefore to be preserved for the benefit of the nation and the people of Hoy as a community. Several tasks awaited the trustees. Bird and animal life, as well as vegetation, were to be safeguarded, but perhaps the most important task was to make people want to come back in order to create a vital community. The trustees began their work enthusiastically, but everything soon foundered because of very slender resources.

Then came the Crofting Reform Act which enabled the crofters to buy the land at a price of 15 years' rent. This took considerable parts of the estate out of the ownership of the Trust. Thus the land area of The Hoy Trust diminished, but so did the obligations as well, as the crofters now became responsible for all costs themselves.

It came as a shock, therefore, to many when the trustees decided to sell 8,000 acres (3237 ha) of hill and moorland for £115,000 to the Royal Society for the Protection of Birds. For worst of all, The Old Man of Hoy was part of this area! Selling The Old Man was considered by many to be no better than selling one's birthright – Orkney's famous landmark sold for money. Nobody had ever dreamed that The Old Man would become an issue in such a way. But from the means thus gained it may be possible for The Hoy Trust to realize some of their plans.

The road from Hoy to Walls goes through a lonely hillside. It is not so strange that the minister who in 1627 served both parishes complained that he had to make his way through '6 mylis of wilderness quhairin ar divers great wateris, neither is ther anie hous be the way'. Walls – the bays – is the land around Longhope, which means the long bay. South Walls was formerly a tidal island, connected by a sandbank which could be crossed only at low tide. The road across it has been built up, but still the sea sweeps over it in bad weather.

Lyness was used as a naval base in the two world wars. Both times the base was constructed more or less in a panic, but in spite of that the concrete oil tanks are so solid that it is not possible for the farmers to plough over them as they have sometimes done with defensive structures of the past, such as broch ruins. It is strange that the Ministry of Defence can just pull out of an area to which they have given such a hard-handed treatment. Another such area is the RAF's airfield at Skeabrae in West Mainland where the camouflage-painted hangars become uglier and uglier as time passes.

War relics of earlier times are at the entrance to Longhope which at the time of the sailing ships was an important anchorage where whalers, sealers and Hudson's Bay ships would lie waiting for a fair wind. These two Martello towers were erected during the Napoleonic Wars in the early nineteenth century. They are cannon sites meant to protect the harbour against the Americans, who had declared war on Britain in 1812 and were harassing the British Baltic trade. The towers were in use during the First World War, and when they are restored will become a tourist attraction.

Melsetter House at the head of Longhope Bay is one of the most important historic buildings in Orkney. For more than two centuries it belonged to the Moodie family. Perhaps one of their most distinguished members was Captain James Moodie, the seventh laird. He served in the navy under Queen Anne and was known for his Hanoverian sympathies. Another eighteenth-century Moodie was Commander-in-Chief for the republic of Venice. The Moodie family made Melsetter into one of the largest Orkney estates which included Hoy, Walls, Fara and Rysa Little.

Towards the end of the last century Melsetter was bought by a wealthy English manufacturer of leather who invested both money and effort in the property. He enlarged the house without falling in the Victorian trap of turrets and projections. As architect he engaged one of William Morris' more outstanding disciples who believed in solid craftsmanship and local materials. The furniture was made by craftsmen in Kirkwall from special designs said to have been made by Ford Madox Brown and Dante Gabriel Rossetti, and the result is a simple elegance. Some of the furniture has later been presented to museums in various parts of Britain; a sideboard from the dining-room is now in the Victoria and Albert Museum in London. The work on Melsetter House led to a flowering of design and craftsmanship in Orkney.

When the change came in agriculture in the 1920's, the Melsetter estate was split up and sold. During both world wars the house was requisitioned and used by the admirals.

At Brims, in Aith Hope, the legendary Longhope Lifeboat Station lies like a watchdog for the Pentland Firth. The Longhope lifeboat crew had become known all over Britain for its record of incredible rescues. The coxswain Dan Kirkpatrick had received several medals for gallantry. Their most celebrated rescue was perhaps when they went in under the Hoy cliffs to get the crew off the grounded trawler *Strathcoe*.

Melsetter House, Lyness. This is one of the most important historic buildings in Orkney, once the home of the Moodie family.

The night between 17 and 18 March 1969 will not soon be forgotten by people in Orkney, and especially by the 30 people in the small township of Brims. The lifeboat went out after a Mayday-call from the Liberian cargo ship *Irene* which was in difficulty at Halcro Head on the east side of Orkney. A gale in force nine had been raging from the east for several days and had whipped up huge waves. It is uncertain what happened to the lifeboat, but the next day it was found upturned, and the whole crew of eight were dead. The disaster was all the greater because it hit two families so terribly hard – the coxswain had his two sons along, as did the second coxswain. They were buried in Longhope cemetery.

Pentland Skerries
The Pentland Skerries have always been a death trap, lying as they do right on a main sea lane. At Muckle Skerry there is a chapel dedicated to St Peter, otherwise these skerries are uninhabited. The other islands in the Pentland Firth, Stroma and Swona, were, on the other hand, small thriving communities until quite recently.

Stroma
Today Stroma is part of the county of Caithness. The island is mentioned once in the Orkneyinga saga, because Svein Asleifarson was once forced to spend a night there when a strong gale blew up. In Norse times Stroma was strategically important, and there is a curious old story of how the island came to belong to Caithness instead of to Orkney. There were venomous animals on the island, of an unknown species. When they were sent to Orkney they died, but those that came to Caithness thrived, and this settled the matter.

The story of Stroma is a classical example of how depopulation takes place. In 1914 300 people lived there. In 1955 an expensive new harbour was built to make life easier for the 80 people who were left there. But the money they earned on the building of the harbour made it possible for them to establish themselves on the mainland. Today Stroma is an island of sheep and ghosts. The school, the church and the old crofts are all more or less in ruin and the sheep roam in and out at will.

Swona
Swona had at most nine families who, until the trawlers came, made a living from line-fishing for cod. At the time of the sailing ships they also had an income from pilotage. Farming alone could not support them, so by 1932 there was only one family left.

Flotta
Flotta has three times in a century been invaded by powerful forces out of all proportion to the life as otherwise lived on the island. During the two world wars it was an important base for the navy; the only benefit people were left with afterwards was wider roads and two piers. In addition to this there are

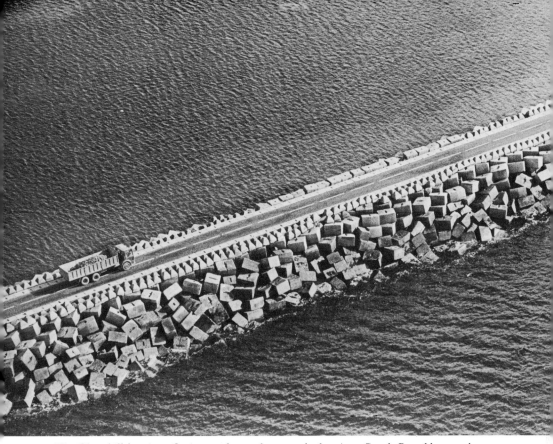

The Churchill barriers. Owing to the road across the barriers, South Ronaldsay and Burray are today an extension of Mainland.

the derelict military installations. At the observation point Stanger Head they are still sufficiently intact to give an idea of what they may have looked like in wartime.

After the last war, Flotta was threatened by depopulation; the number of inhabitants fell as low as 80 and many of them were elderly. The oil business came in the middle of the 1970's when the standard of life for those still living there was seriously threatened. The population has now risen to 170, and many of the newcomers are young families with children. Even now the meeting of the new and the old is more striking in Flotta than anywhere else in Orkney.

South Ronaldsay and Burray

Owing to the road across the Churchill barriers, South Ronaldsay and Burray are today an extension of Mainland. It is not surprising, therefore, that South Ronaldsay is the most populous island after Mainland. The land is fertile, so cultivation here began early. This is probably where the Christian missionaries first landed, and maybe that is why South Ronaldsay more than any other is the church island – every small township seems to have had its own chapel. Altogether there are traces of nine chapels and four churches. Some of them are dedicated to saints from the early Christian

The Bu of Burray. This site, which has been occupied since the early sixteenth century, was for a long time in the possession of the Stewart family.

period such as St Ninian and St Colm, others are to St Olaf and St Margaret. And it is probably from this chapel dedicated to a female saint that the village of St Margaret's Hope has got its name, and not from the little Margrete Eirik's daughter, the Maid of Norway, even if that is the more romantic explanation. Possibly the two names have become one in people's minds. The pious English princess Margaret became Malcolm Canmore's queen after the death of his first wife, Ingibjorg Finn's daughter, widow of Earl Thorfinn the Mighty.

A curious custom which is known only from South Ronaldsay may perhaps be unique in Europe as well. This is the Festival of the Horse, combined with the Boys' Ploughing Match. The young girls in the island dress up as horses in colourful costumes which may have been handed down in their families for a long period of time. The boys are the ploughmen with elaborately made little ploughs. Even these are often heirlooms. After costumes and ploughs have been judged at St Margaret's Hope, the boys bring their ploughs down to the beach at Sands O'Right and compete in getting the straightest and smoothest furrows in the wet sand. The symbolic significance this custom perhaps had once is forgotten long ago. It probably had a certain connection with the farming year, as the festival used to be held at Easter. Today these ties are broken as, out of consideration for the tourists, the event has been moved to the second Wednesday in August.

Not far from the beach where the ploughing competition is held lies Thorfinn's mound at Hoxa. The story used to be that 'the son of a Norse king' was buried there. But the Orkneyinga saga tells us that it was Earl Thorfinn Skull-Splitter who was 'howe-laid' there towards the end of the tenth century. In spite of his name he was one of the few earls who died in his bed. The mound contains a broch; it was not unusual for the Norsemen to use old structures as burial chambers.

Burray is also extremely fertile, and formerly the whole island made up one estate which, as early as the sixteenth century, became the property of the Stewart family. They lived at the Bu by the beautiful white sandy beach on the east side, and they were known for their arrogance and wilfulness. The story goes that one of the owners, Sir James Stewart, in 1725 after a quarrel, shot down and killed Captain Moodie of Melsetter in Walls in broad daylight in the middle of Broad Street in Kirkwall.

It is also said that during the Jacobite Rebellion in 1745, when Prince Charles Edward Stuart raised his standard for the Scottish clans, there might be those who sympathized with his cause in Orkney too, but the only one actually to join him was Sir James Stewart. He managed to escape the English reprisals after the battle of Culloden, and made his way back to Orkney. Through an incredible coincidence he was captured in Burray by the son of Captain Moodie, the man he had killed. Sir James thus ended his days in an English prison.

24. Eynhallow

Eynhallow frank, Eynhallow free,
Eynhallow stands in the middle of the sea;
A roaring roost on every side –
Eynhallow stands in the middle of the tide.
From an old verse

In the sound between Rousay and Mainland lies Eynhallow. It is the Eyin Helga of the saga and the Hildaland of popular imagination – an enchanted island enveloped in myth. It is said that cats, rats and mice shun it, and that when the corn was cut after sunset, blood would flow from the straw.

According to legend it was the home of the sea people, the Fin Folk, a vanishing island only rarely visible to human eyes. It would rise suddenly out of the sea and be gone again as suddenly. To break the spell a man must leap ashore holding steel in his hand. 'There came at last the hour and the man; the vanishing isle was won from the waters and left standing in the middle of the tide.'

It is difficult to get to Eynhallow. There is the roaring roost on two sides, and the Atlantic goes white on the third. Only in the east is it safe for a boat to anchor up.

There are no people living on the island today, and no people go ashore there very often, so the birds and the sheep have Eynhallow mostly to themselves. All kinds of rare sea birds find a sanctuary there, and in May and June there are bird nests all over the islands, even in the ruins of the church and the monastery. Small white discs show the places that ornithologists from the University of Aberdeen have marked as fulmar nests.

There are also rare ocean plants there. But most visitors who come to Eynhallow are drawn by the ruins and a certain air of mystery. Also the name stirs the imagination. Even the name Eyin Helga itself – the holy island – distinguishes it from the other islands. It is the only island name without the ending -ey. And the qualifying word comes last. According to Dr Hugh Marwick, the specialist on Orkney place names, such a use of the adjective is more characteristic of Celtic place names than Norse.

Possibly the Norse settlers gave the island the name of Eyin Helga because in their eyes it was holy; there may have been a church or monastery when they came. It is also possible that the name is translated from a similar Pictish name which the Norsemen made their own. If so, it explains the unusual word order. On the other hand, the sagas use the name Eyin Helga about two other places as well: Iona in the inner Hebrides and the small island today called Helgeöya on Lake Mjösa in Norway.

The only saga reference to Eynhallow is found in Orkneyinga saga, in connection with an incident which took place in 1155. The Viking chieftain Svein Asleifarson from Gairsay had fallen out with Jon Wing who had been on a Viking expedition with him, so he took both Jon's brothers prisoner. Jon did not know what had happened to his brothers, and therefore

he went to Eynhallow and captured Olaf, the son of Svein Asleifarson and foster-son of Kolbein Hruga, taking him to Westray where they ran into Earl Rognvald at Rapness.
'What brings you here, Olaf?' asked the Earl when he saw him.
'Jon Wing had better answer that,' he replied.
The Earl looked at Jon. 'Why did you bring Olaf here?' he asked. 'Svein took my brothers', answered Jon, 'and for all I know he may have killed them'.
'Take him back at once', said the Earl.

Even if Eynhallow is mentioned only once in this text, and this incident reveals very little by itself, it is nevertheless interesting in the light of what is now known. What was Olaf Sveinsson, a chieftain's son, doing on the little island of Eynhallow? Is it not possible to assume that he was being taught by the monks there?

The twelfth century was a time of progress and achievement in Orkney. St Magnus Cathedral was started in 1137; perhaps it caused religious life to flourish. Monasteries were an important part of the social pattern in the Middle Ages, so there must have been some in Orkney as there were in Iceland and Greenland. And there is much to indicate that there were several monasteries in the islands, often built on old Pictish sites. Probable sites are Brough of Birsay, Brough of Deerness, Monk's Green near Stromness, and Eynhallow. There was probably a cloister in connection with the cathedral in Kirkwall, as it was usual for urban communities to have a monastic centre of learning. We must bear in mind that in Norse times Orkney was by no means off the beaten track, but an important part of mediaeval Europe.

Through the times that followed very little is known of Eynhallow, and nothing at all to explain the name. It was a small, green and fertile island which gave a living – barely – to four families who farmed as tenants under changing landowners.

In 1851 a virulent epidemic broke out on the island. It was probably typhoid fever from infected drinking water; at any rate the well was blamed at the time. Several people died, and the landowner decided to move the survivors to Mainland. The thatched roofs were torn off the old buildings where the tenants lived, in an attempt to stamp out the infection. Only then was it discovered that one of the buildings was an old church!

An old church register, *The Booke of Universall Kirk of Scotland* from 1586, mentions a church at Eynhallow. That is the only place where this

Eynhallow Church, Eynhallow. There would appear to have been an important monastic settlement on this site.

church is mentioned, and no one knew that it existed. As the church in Orkney in old times was subject to the Archbishop in Trondheim, it would be natural to look for information there. But there are very few records to be found in Trondheim, as most of them were lost in city fires. In Scotland the Calvinistic reformers were very thorough in their attempts to wipe out every trace of the Catholic Church, so that most records and documents were burnt.

It was the Norwegian scholar Lorentz Dietrichson who, with his friend Meyer, an architect, at the beginning of this century, discovered that the rest of the farm buildings in Eynhallow were in actual fact an old monastery. Professor Dietrichson had started a systematic search for a monastic site in Orkney, and he found Eynhallow a likely place for two reasons: the name and the location. He therefore went to Eynhallow expecting to find a monastery there. 'It was the name of the island which first turned my thoughts in this direction, and I have found this idea confirmed in all its details by what the island itself showed me.' About the location he says that the island has 'a scenery of enchanting beauty, just such as the mediaeval monks were accustomed to choose for the sites of their monasteries' (Lorentz Dietrichson/Johannes Meyer *Monumenta Oradica*, 1910).

To explain why nobody had ever thought of examining the farm buildings around the church, Dietrichson suggests that it is because no one had known what the small Norse monasteries looked like and therefore had not realized what the buildings really were. Dietrichson believed that the ruins in Eynhallow were of a Cistercian monastery from the twelfth century. He based this conclusion to a great extent on the information in an old chronicle that an abbot in Orkney in 1175 had become abbot at the Cistercian monastery at Melrose in Scotland.

Modern historians no longer attach so much importance to this one item of information, but agree that the buildings probably date from the twelfth century. But they claim that it is a Benedictine monastery. The Benedictine order was founded as early as the sixth century. The Cistercian order on the other hand was not founded until 1098, and even though it spread quickly and its golden age was the twelfth century, it is perhaps after all less probable that it would have reached all the way to Orkney so quickly.

The monastery at Eynhallow has points of similarity with the Benedictine monastery on Selje in Nordfjord, and there is the same type of structure in Greenland and Iceland as well. They are different to monasteries of the same order in Scotland. Was there perhaps a separate ecclesiastical tradition in the Norse area?

The twelfth century was a period of transition from the massive Romanesque style to the lofty Gothic style of architecture. Details in the building style of the church at Eynhallow help place it in this period. Whereas the first two doors in the church have rounded Romanesque arches, the choir door has a clumsy, pointed arch, as if in an attempt to ape a new and fashionable style.

The monastery was closed down during the Reformation, or perhaps even before. Since then the buildings have been a good deal changed by the people who used them. For one thing fireplaces were inserted comparatively late. The basic plan of the monastery is mediaeval, but today there is no way of finding out what the various rooms were used for; we can only guess. But according to the customs of the Benedictine order this was basically a work farm – their work was directed at making the monastery self–sufficient and self–contained.

Eynhallow changed owners several times among the old landowning families. When the last owner died, the island was bought by the Orkney Islands Council to secure an important part of the cultural heritage for the future.

25. The North Isles

Far too many of the visitors to Orkney go back without having seen the North Isles. This may be because even if the distances look small on the map, it is difficult to get to most of the islands unless one has plenty of time. It can also be difficult to find a place to stay overnight. But those of an adventurous spirit who are not stopped by such difficulties will not be disappointed. Each island is a small world of its own – a community with a separate identity.

The finest view of the North Isles is from the western Mainland; it is of the cluster of islands Eynhallow, Rousay, Egilsay and Wyre, which together make up the parish of Rousay. The historian J. Storer Clouston says:

> There is no corner of Orkney more steeped in history than this parish with its four islands of Rousay, Egilsay, Eynhallow, and Wyre. Every one of them comes into the Sagas, and on each something more than usually eventful happened.
>
> *The Orkney Parishes*, Mackintosh 1927

Even today Eynhallow has a magic of its own – people in the islands speak of it only as The Isle.

Wyre

Wyre is known as the home of the Norse chieftain Kolbein Hruga. It was Kolbein who in 1142 brought the young pretender Eystein Haraldsson back to Norway from the west to be hailed as king by the people at the Eyrar Assembly in Trondheim. As it happened he did both Norway and Orkney a bad turn, for Eystein became a bad king. And in 1153, while Earl Rognvald was away on his crusade, Eystein made a military expedition to Orkney and forced the young Earl Harald Maddadarson to submit to him. Thus Earl Harald would hardly become Kolbein's friend.

As Kolbein had become entangled in the ongoing struggle for royal power in Norway, it is not so strange that he saw the need for fortifications on Wyre. The stone fort he built there is described in the saga as 'a really solid stronghold'. It was at any rate solid enough to withstand a long siege: in 1231 Snaekoll Gunnason sought refuge there after the killing of Earl Jon. There is still enough left of the fort to make it possible to imagine what it must have looked like. Today it is usually called Cubbie Roo's Castle.

Close by is the ruin of an old Romanesque chapel. It may have been built by Kolbein Hruga or perhaps later by his son, Bjarni Kolbeinsson, who was Bishop of Orkney 1188–1222, and a great poet as well. The old farm The

Bu close by was the seat of the chieftain. It was also at The Bu of Wyre that the poet Edwin Muir grew up towards the end of the last century.

Egilsay

A stone marks the place in Egilsay where Magnus Erlendsson was killed during Easter Week in 1117. The high tower of St Magnus Church dominates the island. After the St Magnus Cathedral it is the most important Norse church in Orkney and it is a pity that it is falling to ruin. It was probably built in 1135–38 in the days of Bishop William the Old on the ruins of the old church where Magnus Erlendsson spent his last night. That Egilsay was a place of pilgrimage must surely be the reason why such a large church was built on the small island.

A small room above the choir was spoken of as the grief house, and it has been a common belief that this room was used to serve as a kind of jail. But it is more likely that *grief* is a distortion of the Norse word *grið*, which meant peace or sanctuary, as given by the church in old times.

Rousay

Rousay is something quite by itself. Both historically and scenically it is one of the most interesting islands. It is mountainous like Hoy; the interior of the island consists of hills and moorland and is uninhabited. The road around the island is beautiful and dramatic, with a constantly changing scenery.

Historically Rousay is the richest of the North Isles, with a time-spectrum ranging from the Stone Age village of Rinyo at Faraclett from about 3,700 B.C. to a Victorian monstrosity such as Trumland House.

The walk along the beach between the farm of Westness and the Midhowe Broch is of great historical interest. In just one mile we walk through thousands of years; for the Viking graves lie side by side with the relics of the Stone Age.

A Norse woman's grave from the middle of the ninth century was discovered while burying a cow at Westness. That was how the magnificent Westness brooch was found. For several summers archaeologists from the University of Bergen have been excavating sites and burial places from Norse times at Westness.

In the saga we are told that Sigurd of Westness was a great chieftain. Today the farm of Westness is the largest in Orkney. A former owner was the notorious General Burroughs who evicted his tenants to make room for sheep. For that reason there are derelict farms as far west as Tofts, which was the first two-storey house in the islands. As Burroughs thought the farmhouse at Westness was not good enough for him, he built Trumland House.

Gairsay

Further east lies Gairsay, which was the winter home of the chieftain Svein Asleifarson. He was a man who lived out his potentialities best while fighting and therefore sought battles. P. A. Munch calls him a genuine Viking. But as long as he lived Svein Asleifarson was also a troublemaker in the relationship between the earls. He early gave his support to Rognvald Kali Kolsson; nevertheless he forced Rognvald to accept the young Harald Maddadarson as joint ruler. At Gairsay he kept a hospitable house and had 80 armed men. Every year when the seed had been sown in the spring, Svein would go on Viking raids; most of the time he harried around the Irish Sea. He died as he lived, attempting to conquer Dublin in 1171.

Around the middle of the seventeenth century the rich merchant Sir William Craigie built a new house on the site of Svein's old hall. Today there is only one family living in Gairsay.

Shapinsay

Shapinsay is the only large island which is never mentioned in the Orkneyinga saga. Still we know from the saga of Hakon Hakonsson that it was in Elwick Bay in Shapinsay that his large Norse armada gathered before the expedition along the west coast of Scotland in 1263.

Shapinsay has indirectly won for itself a place in world literature. Around the middle of the eighteenth century a young man called William Irving grew up at the farm of Quholme. He emigrated quite early to New York, which was then a town of only 23,000 inhabitants. The youngest of his 11 children was christened Washington after USA's first president. Washington Irving has been called the 'father of American literature' and 'inventor of the short story'. In any case he was the first American writer to be read in Europe.

Irving used European folklore material in many of his stories. In his best known story *Rip Van Winkle*, which has become an American classic, there seems to be an obvious parallel with the Orkney story of the fiddler who thought he had been inside the mound only a few hours, but found everything changed when he returned, for he had been gone for many years and there were few who remembered him. Is this an allegorical way of describing the loneliness of being out of step with one's own times? This tale was told again in 'The Two Fiddlers' by George Mackay Brown, and Peter Maxwell Davies set the story to music.

Today Shapinsay is a quite modern farming community. This is mostly thanks to the enlightened rule the Balfour family represented in the last century. They owned all the land in Shapinsay and went in for new cultivation methods, turning the whole island into one big model farm. And they succeeded. Early in this century the farms were sold to the tenants who then became freeholders.

Balfour Castle and the distinctive Balfour village, which may be declared a preservation area, make an interesting period picture, reflecting the social pattern of the Victorian Age. The castle with the farm around it is today owned by the Zawadski family. Tadeusz Zawadski served with the Polish Lancers in England during the Second World War. Then he had, as a Polish officer, first been captured by the Russians, but had managed to escape from the death march to the forest at Katyn.

Balfour Castle, Shapinsay. The castle and the distinctive Balfour village make an interesting period picture, reflecting the social pattern of the Victorian age.

Stronsay

Stronsay is the most fertile of the North Isles, and today the island's economy depends largely on its well-run farms. Nevertheless it is fishing, and especially herring fishing, that we most of all associate with Stronsay. The village of Whitehall sprang up because there was the best harbour for the North Sea fisheries. Thus Whitehall became the most important herring port. In the time of the sailing ships as many as 1,500 women had seasonal work there gutting and salting. The curing sheds were plentiful both in Whitehall and across the sound in Papa Stronsay.

Today the huts of the former fish-curing station in Papa Stronsay are empty and derelict. After having been long used for grazing sheep, Papa Stronsay is once again inhabited – the island where Rognvald Brusason was killed by Earl Thorfinn and Thorkel the Fosterer one dark night in December 1045.

Eday

Eday is centrally located among the North Isles. It is easy to see why the settlers called it Eiðey – isthmus island – as the narrow isthmus makes it look like a sack tied around the middle. Eday has large peat hills which have provided an income through the ages. The peat has gone as fuel to Sanday and North Ronaldsay, but first of all it has been used by whisky distilleries all over Scotland.

Carrick House is north in the Calf Sound. It was built in 1633 by a younger son of the detested Earl Robert Stewart. To the north the entrance to the Sound is guarded by the sandstone cliff Red Head. It is a wild and beautiful place, and perhaps it is not after all so strange a place to choose for a man of the complex Stewart nature. Carrick House is best known for being the place where a later owner, James Fea, managed to capture the pirate John Gow. Gow tried to sail the Calf Sound in a head wind and ran aground on the Calf of Eday. Gow and several of his men were later hanged in London without much of a trial. Both Daniel Defoe and Sir Walter Scott have written about Gow – Defoe published the story of his life as *The Pirate Gow* in 1725, and Scott used his adventures in *The Pirate*.

Westray

Westray is the largest of the North Isles. It was important in Norse times and is often mentioned in the Orkneyinga saga, especially because it had a good harbour for the requirements of the times – the old Hǫfn, near the village of Pierowall.

A few years ago the Orkney archaeologist Dr Raymond Lamb discovered the remains of a large Norse settlement on the east side of Westray, near the old Church of the Cross at Tuquoy. The site has since been excavated by a group of archaeologists from Durham University. The settlement is late Norse, from about the time when Earl Rognvald was building the cathedral in Kirkwall. The walls of a great hall and fortress have been excavated. It may have belonged to Haflidi Thorkelsson, who is mentioned in the Orkneyinga saga, and the hall and the church may have been part of a major settlement.

On the west side of Westray we find the strange and forbidding Noltland Castle. A more correct name would be Notland, as it is derived from Nautland – cattle land – a not very romantic name and not at all in keeping with the castle. In his Orkney description from 1529, Jo Ben mentioned an unfinished castle in Westray. It was possibly built by Bishop Thomas Tulloch (1422–55) at a time when a strong power struggle in the earldom might have made it an opportune stronghold to withdraw to. The similarity to a man-of-war has often been pointed out, and it has also been said that the man who built it must have suffered from a bad conscience. But most of all he must have been deeply afraid, as it looks very much like a place of escape.

Noltland Castle reappears in history in the 1560s, in another troubled period. At that time the castle had somehow become the property of Gilbert Balfour, an adventurer in the circle around Mary, Queen of Scots. He was involved in the murder of Mary's consort Lord Darnley. It was a time of intrigue, and what would happen from one day to the next was uncertain, so Gilbert Balfour may also have felt the need for a place to hide.

But Mary's half-brother, Robert Stewart, seized the castle in Westray and refused to give it up. Gilbert Balfour felt that things were getting too hot for him and went into the service of the Swedish King John III as one of the commanding officers of 3,000 Scottish mercenaries. In Sweden he joined a conspiracy to kill King John and restore the insane Erik XIV Vasa to the throne. For this he was executed in Stockholm in 1576.

Papay (Papa Westray)

People in Papay have fought actively against the threat of depopulation. When the number of inhabitants fell to 90 and the island lost both the only shop and the resident doctor, a co-operative was formed to run a community shop and a hostel of high standard. Hopefully the trend has now been turned.

Papay is a place for nature lovers, but also for the historically inclined. Knap of Howar goes back at least to 3,500 B.C., and is considered the oldest preserved dwelling house in north-western Europe. The house has two rooms, and the stone interior looks homelike even today. It was the dwelling house of a farm where they kept cattle, sheep and pigs, and grew wheat and barley. Sea birds also made up part of the diet, for remains of the now extinct Great Auk were found there.

Knap of Howar, Papa Westray. These are the oldest preserved dwelling houses in northwestern Europe.

This Stone Age community probably buried their dead in the cairns on the Holm of Papay off the east side. The largest of the cairns is 246 ft (75 m) long and divided into 14 chambers. A 20 ft (6 m) long entrance passage leads into it. An unusual feature of this cairn is that it is decorated with an 'eyebrow' motif – perhaps in an attempt to reproduce a human face.

Papay's religious importance is also associated with the legend of Triduana, who was canonized as St Tredwell, but became known among the Norsemen as Trollhöna. She probably came to Pictland early in the eighth century. Nechtan, King of the Picts, wanted her, for she was beautiful. He sent messengers to bring her to him. They told her that it was especially her lovely eyes that drew the King to her. According to the legend she then tore out her eyes, put them on a stick and sent them to King Nechtan. It was a drastic but effective way of securing her personal freedom – she probably realized that she was about to be carried away by force.

Poignant though this story is, it nevertheless presents the conventional picture of the saintly woman: the virgin fleeing a pagan ruler who desires her. The Norse legend of St Sunniva is an exact parallel – she was a Christian Irish princess, and to get away from a brutal pagan suitor she fled with her companions in three ships. They landed at Selje in Nordfjord, where they hid in a cave until a landslide buried them. Sunniva became the saint of West Norway, and a Benedictine monastery was later built at Selje.

According to tradition, Triduana lived alone on a small promontory in the lake that is still named after her. The ruins of the small Norse chapel are probably on top of old Pictish walls. There used to be a spring of running water, and for a long time blind pilgrims would come to Papay to get their sight back in the water from Triduana's spring.

During excavation at the site a woman's skeleton was found – could it be the saint herself? Then again, the site may just have been named after her; according to another tradition she is buried at Restalrig, near Edinburgh.

The Orkneyinga saga tells us that Earl Rognvald Brusason – the best loved earl of them all – was buried in Papay, but there is no trace of his grave.

Sanday

Sanday has a strange shape – like three sprawling peninsulas. Otherwise its most important characteristic is the long white beaches where the sand is sometimes blown into large dunes. The soil here was easy to cultivate for Stone Age man and an unexpected bonus for land-hungry Norsemen.

In Norse times Sanday alone paid one sixth of all tax in Orkney, something which shows that it was highly valued. The big farms of Walls, Tafts and Lopness belonged to the earls from early times. Sanday is also very rich from an archaeological point of view, even if that may not be so evident. Partly the historical monuments have been damaged by all the ploughing and partly the sand has covered them like a carpet. Recently the sea has been eating more and more of the sand dunes. The cause of this coastal erosion is unknown, but it has speeded up the work of saving the most threatened historical monuments. At Pool on the west side, on the edge of the sea, archaeologists are excavating a site which may turn out to be one of the six old administrative huseby farms, according to Asgaut Steinnes' theory (see Chapter 13).

It is characteristic of Sanday and North Ronaldsay that many of the farms have been built on top of old farm mounds. Their presence there even in Norse times is shown by the names of some of the oldest farms: *Garso* in North Ronaldsay from garðshaugr, which means literally farm mound, and *Tafts* in Sanday, meaning a site where a house once stood.

Fishing has until now been an important source of income in Sanday, and in the northernmost part of the parish of Burness the now derelict fishing village of Ortie bears witness to this. Today a small electronics firm operates in Sanday. Another enterprise, Isle of Sanday Knitters Ltd, is run on a co-operative basis and gives work to some 140 home-knitters from Sanday and the neighbouring islands. Their articles have become popular and are sold both to Paris and London.

North Ronaldsay

North Ronaldsay is the most northerly as well as the most easterly of the Orkney islands – so near to Norway that when Bergen was on fire in 1902 a red shimmer could be seen in the east. This is where the Norse settlers came first and where the old Norn language lasted the longest. The dialect of North Ronaldsay still has a distinctive character.

North Ronaldsay is also the most remote of the islands. A difficult harbour makes it impossible for ships to call regularly in all kinds of weather, and in the winter they may cease coming altogether for long periods at a time. For that reason it has happened that food supplies have been low, but it is more serious that the uncertain communications prevent any long-term economic development.

In North Ronaldsay the old communal farming has survived in the sheep rearing. All cultivated land is surrounded by a high stone dyke. The land outside the dyke is called *the ness*, and this is the home of some 4,000 seaweed-eating descendants of the old native breed of sheep. An elected committee of 11, 'The Sheep Court', sees to it that everything is always done according to the old rules.

Perhaps North Ronaldsay has in many ways withstood modern development – for better or worse – for too long. Whereas the rest of the island communities went through great changes in agriculture in the period just after the First World War – changes which broke up the old feudal society and made the farmers freeholders again – time has in a way stood still in North Ronaldsay. The land still belongs to the laird in Holland House.

The new land law of 1976 makes it possible for all tenants to buy the land they farm at a price corresponding to 15 years' rent, and most farmers in North Ronaldsay are availing themselves of this right. For many this means primarily that they will have the right to sell the land, and thus the deed will

North Ronaldsay sheep live on seaweed and are shut out from the pastures by a stone dyke which runs round the whole island.

perhaps be just a one-way ticket away from the island. The population of North Ronaldsay has decreased drastically in the last few years and is now around 100. Besides this there is an ageing population structure, with a very small economically active age group. The young people go away.

In November 1983 North Ronaldsay was connected to the national electric grid – at a price to the public of £14,300 per subscriber. Perhaps electricity will help bring new life to this island which in many ways is the most interesting of all the North Isles.

Many of the economic and social difficulties facing the North Isles are common to sparsely populated and remote areas everywhere. For over 200 years kelp-burning was part of the economy of the North Isles. On summer days the smoke would lie thick along the shores. More working hours were spent on the kelp-burning than on fishing or farming. Coastal fishing was carried on from small boats. The large farms employed both farm workers and servants; and carpenters, masons and dressmakers carried out necessary tasks. Altogether there was work for many, and the population grew accordingly.

Today the kelp-burning is gone, fishing is done with fewer people in larger boats, and the farming is so strongly rationalized that each farm is run by one farmer alone. In many places farms have also been joined together to make larger units. Even if this makes more profitable farms, a new problem arises: the standard of life for those left behind is endangered. It is a paradox that when so much of the toil and the poverty is gone, values like good fellowship and a sense of community are often lost too. The feeling of involvement in the local community with the working together of children and grown-ups, as well as of neighbours, is not the way it used to be.

The depopulation is not only caused by a deteriorating economy: there are obvious difficulties connected with living on a small island. A visit to the dentist must as a rule take place in Kirkwall, and even with today's air and ferry communications it is often necessary to stay overnight. The high freight charges make everything more expensive, and craftsmen must often be called in from Mainland.

Everyday life has been toilsome without connections for water or electricity. A net of submerged electric cables from Scotland now branches out to the North Isles. Temperamental oil-run generators are placed aside as the houses become connected to the electricity network. For the islanders this is a necessary step into the twentieth century, and nostalgic visitors complaining of the islands getting 'spoiled' meet only scorn from those who really know what it is like to live on an old-fashioned farm.

Each island has a modern primary school; but when the children are about 12 years old, they must go to the grammar school in Kirkwall for further education. They must live at the school hostel, and for many of the children this is a great, almost traumatic change. At best they come home for weekends, but mostly once a month. The children are educated away from the islands, and thus everybody's right to an education becomes a double-edged sword for an out-lying district.

An island like Sanday had 2,075 inhabitants at the time of the 1881 census; by 1951 the number had fallen to 866. It went on decreasing during the following years and is now 534. An island like Eday has been even harder hit: from 947 in the last century to 168 in the 1970's.

Of the 534 inhabitants presently in Sanday, 117 are newcomers, mostly from England. Most people are pleased that new and younger people are moving in because it makes it easier to retain the existing services, like air and ferry communications, doctors' services and post offices. All the same the incomers force up the price of land so that it can be difficult for local people to buy a farm. In Westray farms have been sold only to people from that island. In that way they have kept the newcomers out and have an island which still functions socially and culturally. For it turns out that even if people who move to the North Isles give as their main reason that they feel drawn by the way of life there, it is difficult for them to adapt to new conditions, and few succeed in changing their lifestyle completely. The enchanting summer island that they fell in love with turns in the winter into a stormswept outpost in the Atlantic. Even if they move for the express purpose of getting away from the evils of urban life, it turns out that they try

General merchant shop, Rousay. The extra transport costs of many consumer goods make everything more expensive in the islands, but the friendliness of the local shopkeepers well compensates for this.

to recreate the conditions they fled from, and thus they help destroy the cultural heritage and the vulnerable social pattern they wanted to become a part of.

Today half the population of the North Isles is employed in agriculture. The age and sex ratios are rather uneven, as there are many old men and few young women. Among the newcomers the turn-over is often great, for many give up after five or six years. This has especially been the case in Egilsay.

The North Isles are facing a set of difficulties, and to solve them it is necessary to ask the right questions and find a new approach in a number of fields. First of all the harbour conditions must be improved so that communications can become more regular and dependable in all kinds of weather. For the Orkney Islands Council to subsidize greatly, even take over, transport is a possible solution. Many think it is reasonable to consider the ferries as an extended part of the road. Thus conditions could be made more favourable for crafts and cottage industries, fish farming, tourism and other activities that might make for a less uniform employment pattern. In the long run a vital community depends on the young people wanting to stay.

Sources used

Chapter 2
Ronald Miller *Orkney* Batsford 1976
Shearer, Groundwater, Mackay *The New Orkney Book* Nelson 1966
Alexander Fenton *The Northern Isles: Orkney and Shetland* John Donald
   Publishers Ltd 1978

Chapter 3
The Ancient Monuments of Orkney Official Guide, HMSO 1978
John Edwin Moon *Sun, Moon and Standing Stones* Oxford University Press 1980
Colin Renfrew *Investigations in Orkney* The Society of Antiquaries of
   London/Thames and Hudson Ltd 1979
Alexander Thom *Megalithic Sites in Britain* Oxford/Clarendon Press 1972
Euan W. Mackie *Science and Society in Prehistoric Britain* Paul Elek, London 1977

Chapter 4
F. T. Wainwright *The Problem of the Picts* Nelson, Edinburgh 1955
F. T. Wainwright *The Northern Isles* Nelson, Edinburgh 1962
A. W. Brögger *Den norske bosetningen på Shetland – Orknöyene.* Det Norske
   Videnskaps–Akademi i Oslo, i kommisjon hos Jacob Dybwad Oslo 1930
Anna Ritchie *The Kingdom of the Picts* Chambers, Edinburgh 1977
Den eldste Noregs-historia. Umsett frå latin ved Halvdan Koht. Det Norske
   Samlaget. Oslo 1921

Chapter 5
A. W. Brögger *Gamle emigranter* Gyldendal, Oslo 1928
A. W. Brögger *Den norske bosetning på Shetland-Orknöyene* Oslo 1930
Orkneyinga Saga. The History of the Earls of Orkney Hermann Pálsson/Paul
   Edwards. Hogarth Press, London 1978
P. G. Foote/D. M. Wilson *The Viking Achievement* London 1970
Sigrid H. H. Kaland Some Economic Aspects of the Orkneys in the Viking Period
   Norwegian Archaeological Review, Vol. 15, Nos. 1–2, 1982
Dorothy Dunnett *King Hereafter* Michael Joseph, London 1982

Chapter 6
Orkneyinga Saga. The History of the Earls of Orkney Hermann Pálsson/Paul
   Edwards. Hogarth Press, London 1978
John Mooney *St Magnus – Earl of Orkney* W. R. Mackintosh, Kirkwall 1935
Sigrid Undset *Norske helgener* Oslo 1937

Ronald G. Cant *The church in Orkney and Shetland and its relations with Norway and Scotland in the Middle Ages*

Chapter 7
Orkneyinga Saga. The History of the Earls of Orkney Pálsson/Edwards. The Hogarth Press, London 1978
'Ragnvald Kale, Jarl av Orknöyene' Historical thesis for Lars Martin Fosse. Arendal Gymnas, 1969
Sverresoga Omsett av Halvdan Koht. Det Norske Samlaget, Oslo 1967

Chapter 8
P. A. Munch *Det norske folks historie* Chra. 1852–63
Charles Joys *Fra storhetstid til unionstid* Vol. III of *Vårt folks historie* Aschehoug, Oslo 1963
Knut Helle *Norge blir en stat, 1130–1319* Universitetsforlaget, Oslo 1964
Frederik Scheel 'Orknöerne og Hjaltland i Pantsettelsestiden 1468–1667' *Norsk Historisk Tidsskrift* 1912
Delavaud *Les origines norvégiennes des archipels écossais* Annales des sciences politiques. Paris 1910
Barbara E. Crawford *The Earls of Orkney–Caithness and their relations with Norway and Scotland 1158–1470* University of St Andrews 1971
Barbara E. Crawford 'The pawning of Orkney and Shetland' *Scottish Historical Review* 1969, No. 145
J. Storer Clouston (ed.) *Records of the Earldom of Orkney, 1299–1614* Edinbrugh 1914

Chapter 9
J. Storer Clouston *A History of Orkney* W. R. Mackintosh, Kirkwall 1932
J. Storer Clouston (ed.) *Records of the Earldom of Orkney 1299–1614* Edinburgh 1914
Dr Ludvig Daae 'Om beröringer mellem Orknöerne og Hjaltland og moderlandet Norge efter 1468' *Statsökonomisk Tidsskrift* 1895
Eric Linklater *Orkney and Shetland* Robert Hale, London 1965
John Gunn *Orkney – The Magnetic North* Nelson, London 1932

Chapter 10
Malcolm Brown/Patricia Meehan *Scapa Flow* Allen Lane, London 1968
Donald McCormick *The Mystery of Lord Kitchener's Death* Putnam, London 1959
Günther Prien *Mein Weg Nach Scapa Flow* Deutscher Verlag, Berlin 1940
'Loss of HMS Hampshire' Official report. HMSO 1926
Ludwig v. Reuter *Scapa Flow* English ed., Hurst & Blackett Ltd, London 1940
H. J. Weaver *Nightmare at Scapa Flow* Cressrelles Publ. Comp. Ltd 1980
B. H. Liddell Hart *History of the Second World War* Cassel, London 1970

Chapter 11
Ernest W. Marwick 'Creatures of Orkney Legend and their Norse Ancestry' *Norveg* No. 15, 1972, pp177–204
Ernest W. Marwick *The Folklore of Orkney and Shetland* Batsford Ltd, London 1975
Nancy and W. Towrie Cutt *The Hogboon of Hell and other strange Orkney tales* André Deutsch, London 1979

Leslie V. Grinsell *Folklore of Prehistoric Sites in Britain* David & Charles, London 1976

Walter Traill Dennison *Orkney Folklore and Tradition* The Herald Press, Kirkwall 1961

Chapter 12
W. R. Mackintosh *Around the Orkney Peat-fires* The Kirkwall Press, Kirkwall 1938

Walter Traill Dennison *Orkney Folklore and Tradition* The Herald Press, Kirkwall 1961 (New ed.)

Ernest W. Marwick *The Folklore of Orkney and Shetland* Batsford Ltd, London 1975

Peter Andreas Munch 'Erindringer fra Orknöerne (1849)' From *Samlede Afhandlinger* (I–IV), Chra. 1876

John Firth *Reminiscenes of an Orkney Parish* Orkney Natural History Society, Stromness 1974

Chapter 13
Asgaut Steinnes 'The Huseby System in Orkney' *Scottish Historical Review*, Vol. XXXVIII, No. 125, 1959

J. Storer Clouston *A History of Orkney*, Kirkwall 1932

Hugh Marwick *Orkney Farm Names* Kirkwall 1952

F. T. Wainwright *The Northern Isles* Edinburgh 1962

O. Rygh *Norske Gaardnavne*. Kristiania 1898

P. A. Munch *Geographiske Oplysninger om de i Sagaerne forekommende Skotske og Irske Stedsnavne*. Christiania 1852

W. P. L. Thomson 'An Analysis of Orkney Farm Names' (Unpublished)

Chapter 14
Hugh Marwick *The Orkney Norn* London 1930

John Firth *Reminiscences of an Orkney Parish* Stromness 1974

Articles in *The Orcadian* by Gregor Lamb and George Mackay Brown

'Countrywoman's Diary' – articles by signature J.B.G. in *The Orcadian*

Chapter 15
Finnur Jónsson *Den oldnorske og oldislandske litteraturs historie* Copenhagen 1920

Anne Holtsmark 'Bjarne Kolbeinsson og hans forfatterskap' Edda, Oslo 1937

Ernest W. Marwick (ed.) *Orkney Poems* The Kirkwall Press 1949

Robert Rendall *Orkney Variants & Other Poems* The Kirkwall Press 1949

Maurice Lindsay *History of Scottish Literature* Robert Hale, London 1977

Chapter 16
Ronald Miller *Orkney* Batsford, London 1976

A. Douglas Young 'Agriculture (Orkney)' The North of Scotland College of Agriculture 1981

Evan MacGillivray 'The Udal Law Myth' (Unpublished article) Orkney County Library Archives

Chapter 17
Harvest of Silver. The Herring Fishing in Orkney Stromness Museum, 1976

Gordon Thomson *The Other Orkney Book* Northabout Publishing, Edinburgh 1980

Chapter 18
The Flotta Story Educational publication from The Occidental North Sea Group, 1981
Saeter/Smart (ed.) *The Political Implications of North Sea Oil and Gas* Oslo 1975
Gordon Thomson *The Other Orkney Book* Northabout Publishing, Edinburgh 1980

Chapter 19
Jo Grimond *Memoirs* Heineman 1979
David Foulkes *The Local Government Act 1974* Butterworths, London 1974
Marjorie Linklater 'Uranium: A Questionable Commodity' *Orkney Heritage*, Vol. 1, Caithness Books 1981
Roy Grönneberg (ed.) *Island Futures* Thuleprint Ltd, Sandwick, Shetland 1978

Chapter 20
P. A. Munch *Erindringer fra Orknöerne (1849)* Samlede Afhandlinger, Chra. 1876
Meyer/Dietrichson *Monumenta Orcadica* Kristiania 1906
B. H. Hossack *Kirkwall in the Orkneys* Kirkwall 1900
Gourlay & Turner *Historical Kirkwall – the archaeological implications of development* Scottish Burgh Survey 1977

Chapter 21
Gordon Thomson *The Other Orkney Book* Edinburgh 1980
R. M. Fergusson *Rambles in the Far North* London 1884
J. R. Tudor *The Orkneys and Shetland* London 1883
Eric Linklater *Orkney and Shetland* London 1965

Chapter 22
As for Chapter 21
Firth, Bichan, Spence *Harray, Orkney's Inland Parish* Stromness 1975

Chapter 23
As for Chapter 21
Ronald Miller/Susan Luther-Davies *Eday and Hoy – A Development Survey* University of Glasgow 1969

Chapter 24
Meyer/Dietrichson *Monumenta Orcadica* Kristiania 1906
John Mooney *Eynhallow: The holy island of the Orkneys* Kirkwall 1923
Information given by Dr Raymond Lamb, Resident Archaeologist for Orkney

Chapter 25
Thomas Rendall 'Island of Sanday: The Changing Population' Open University thesis in sociology, 1982
Eric Linklater *Orkney and Shetland* Robert Hale, London 1965
Gordon Thomson *The Other Orkney Book* Northabout Publishing, Edinburgh 1980
Gordon Wright *A Guide to the Orkney Islands* Gordon Wright Publishing, Edinburgh 1983

Index